Gray Matter

Gray Matter

Aviation Mechanics Most Frequently Asked Questions

Denny Pollard

The grey area of aviation is an area where no clear guidelines or precdent exists, or where the CFRs has not been applied in a long time thus making it unclear if it is applicable at all. However, there isn't any such thing in aircraft maintenance as gray, no matter what you have heard.

Useful Skills and Step-by-Step Instructions including:
IA Test Instructions, Airworthiness Chart, Definitions, Forms, Publications, IA Functions, Tort Action, Continued Airworthiness, Implied warranty, Contracts, Liability, Aircraft Records, Approved Data, Equivalent Tooling, Part Replacement, Deferred Maintenance, Field Approvals, Questions & Answers.

Order this book online at www.trafford.com
or email orders@trafford.com

Most Trafford titles are also available at major online book retailers.

Printed in the United States of America.

ISBN: 978-1-4669-1929-7 (sc)
ISBN: 978-1-4669-1928-0 (e)

Trafford rev. 03/15/2012

 www.trafford.com

North America & international
toll-free: 1 888 232 4444 (USA & Canada)
phone: 250 383 6864 ♦ fax: 812 355 4082

Lab Tessed

"Senator Wyden, I strongly take exception to her comments.
When we say an airline is safe to fly, it is safe to fly. There is no gray area."
*David R. Hinson, Federal Aviation Administrator, under oath to
the Senate Commerce Committee, May14, 1996.*

Gray Matter
Aviation Mechanics Most
FQA

NOTICE AND DISCLAIMER

The information provided in this book is not intended to supercede or supplement the FAA approved engine, airframe, propellers, or appliance maintenance and/or operator's manuals. Those FAA accepted air or approved manuals must be utilized when performing maintenance and/or operating Type Certificated products. The opinions appearing in this book as well as the advice you are about to receive herein, while based on 35 years of experience are solely the opinions of the author. The author makes no warranty, express or implied, or assumes any legal liability or responsibility for the accuracy, completeness, or usefulness of any information, apparatus, product, or process disclosed, or represents that its use would not infringe privately owned rights. Reference herein to any specific commercial product, process, or services by trade name, mark, manufacturer, or otherwise, does not necessarily constitute or imply its endorsement, or recommendation. The views and opinions of the author expressed herein do not necessarily state or reflect those of the United States Government. All information contained herein is believed to be correct at time of going to press. Reference to any product, service or other offering of any third party by name, trademark, company name or otherwise does not necessarily constitute or imply the endorsement or recommendation. This book was not designed to take the place of any study material, but rather was intended to be used in conjunction with that material. It is not kept current, and therefore, cannot and should not be used as a substitute for current published service or manufacturing documents, service bulletins, and airworthiness. The author disclaims any liability for the technical data contained herein. Regulations, procedures, address, and phone numbers change frequently. Information contained in this book was believed to be correct at the time of publication. Neither the author nor the publisher can be responsible for any loss or damage from the use or misuse of information contained in this book. The following hints and tips are culled from my personal experience, and that of others over the past several of years. They are not presented as magic cures for drinking situations. I make no warranty as to their effectiveness for your particular case. I take no responsibility for any damage resulting from application of these hints and tips. I wish I didn't have to say all this, but I'm afraid not to.

Prepared by Denny Pollard
Airframe and Powerplant Mechanic
http://www.stacheair.com

About the Author

Denny Pollard was born in Jerome, Idaho in 1954. He grew up and went to school in Hansen, Idaho. He currently lives in Eastern Japan after retiring from the Federal Aviation Administration as a maintenance field inspector in Oakland, CA.

His aviation career started in the summer of 1964 as he watched the crash of an agriculture airplane in Hansen, Idaho. He heard the sounds, smelled the burning flesh, and watched the pilot burn to death; the thoughts and smell have never left him.

Denny is currently an Airframe and Powerplant (A&P) mechanic, holds an Inspection Authorization (IA) and a parachute Senior Rigger certificate. He has cut his knuckles and smashed his fingers bucking rivets and fitting sheet metal on aircraft. He has owned and operated an aviation repair business restoring damaged aircraft to serviceable condition. He has taught for a Part 147 aviation school training mechanics to become technicians on aircraft. He has written and published an aviation newsletter "The Aviator" for several years and his first book Handbook of Aeronautical Inspections and Pre-Purchases in 2005, available at www.Trafford.com and other on-line book stores.

Denny has received an Associate Science Degree in Aeronautic. He spent 36 years working in aviation, and was the recipient of the Federal Aviation Administration Maintenance Field Inspector of the year in 2004. Currently, he provides aviation workshops and teaches an FAA approved Inspection Authorization course for renewal.

Introduction

To be completely frank about it, I'm increasingly aware that there are as many gray areas in aviation as there are black and white ones and I'm beginning to feel as if I know less and less about what I do. I'm a trained and reasonably experienced A&P mechanic and I'm supposed to know this airplane stuff, but my experiences are often contradictory to that I know are theoretical facts. It's frustrating and sometimes I think I knew more back when I knew less. Or at least I thought I did.

To keep aircraft in peak operating condition, aircraft mechanics and service technicians perform scheduled maintenance make repairs, and complete inspections required by the Federal Aviation Administration (FAA).

Many aircraft mechanics specialize in preventive maintenance. They inspect engines, landing gear, instruments, pressurized sections, accessories-brakes, valves, pumps, and air-conditioning systems, for example-and other parts of the aircraft and do the necessary maintenance and replacement of parts. Inspections take place following a schedule based on the number of hours the aircraft has flown, calendar days, cycles of operation, or a combination of these factors. To examine an engine, aircraft mechanics work through specially designed openings while standing on ladders or scaffolds, or use hoists or lifts to remove the entire engine from the craft. After taking an engine apart, mechanics use precision instruments to measure parts for wear and use x-ray and magnetic inspection equipment to check for invisible cracks. Worn or defective parts are repaired or replaced. They may also repair sheet metal or composite surfaces, measure the tension of control cables, and check for corrosion, distortion, and cracks in the fuselage, wings, and tail. After completing all repairs, mechanics must test the equipment to ensure that it works properly.

Mechanics specializing in repair work rely on the pilot's description of a problem to find and fix faulty equipment. For example, during a preflight check, a pilot may discover that the aircraft's fuel gauge does not work. To solve the problem, mechanics may troubleshoot the electrical system, using electrical test equipment to make sure no wires are broken or shorted out and replace any defective electrical or electronic components. Mechanics work as fast as safety permits, so the aircraft can be put back into service quickly.

Large, sophisticated planes are equipped with aircraft monitoring systems, consisting of electronic boxes and consoles that monitor the aircraft's basic operations and provide valuable diagnostic information to the mechanic.

Some mechanics work on one or many different types of aircraft, such as jets, propeller-driven airplanes, and helicopters. Others specialize in one section of a particular type of aircraft, such as the engine, hydraulics, or electrical system. Some are authorized to work on engines and do limited work on propellers. Others are authorized to work on any part of the aircraft except the instruments, powerplants, and propellers. A&P mechanics-work on all parts of the plane, except instruments and majors repairs to propellers. The majority of mechanics working on civilian aircraft today is A&P mechanics. In small, independent repair shops, mechanics usually inspect and repair many different types of aircraft. Most of these mechanics hold the Powerplant and Airframe combination airframe-and-powerplant or better know as A&P.

Avionics systems are now an integral part of aircraft design and have vastly increased aircraft capability. A&P's repair and maintain components used for aircraft navigation and radio communications, weather radar systems, and other instruments and computers that control flight, engine, and other primary functions. These duties may require additional licenses, such as an FCC radiotelephone license. Because of technological advances, an increasing amount of time is spent repairing electronic systems, such as computerized controls. Technicians may also be required to analyze and develop solutions to complex electronic problems.

Technicians Working Conditions

Mechanics usually work in hangars or in other indoor areas, although they can work outdoors-sometimes in unpleasant weather when hangars are full or when repairs must be made quickly. Mechanics often work under time pressure to maintain flight schedules or, in general aviation, to keep from inconveniencing customers. At the same time, mechanics have a tremendous responsibility to maintain safety standards, and this can cause the job to be stressful.

The Federal Aviation Administration (FAA) initiated the issuance of the inspection authorization (IA) more than 35 years ago. This system of allowing qualified mechanics the privilege of performing certain inspections has served well in the maintenance of the U.S. civil fleet. The attainment of an IA and performance of the duties of that certificate greatly enhance the privileges and responsibilities of the aircraft mechanic. The IA permits the airframe and powerplant (A&P) mechanic to perform a greater variety of maintenance and alterations than any other single maintenance entity.

The determination of airworthiness during an inspection is a serious responsibility. For many general aviation aircraft, the annual inspection could be the only in-depth inspection it receives throughout the year. In view of the wide ranging authority conveyed with the authorization, the test examines a broader field of knowledge than required for the A&P certificate and reflects the emphasis that is placed on the holder of the certificate in perpetuating air safety.

As a FAA maintenance inspector, I was asked many questions and decided to write them down and provide answers. This is how this book started answering mechanic and pilot question as a Federal Maintenance Inspector.

The information in this book is provided to increase you knowledge to obtain the necessary information for passing the inspection authorization knowledge test and keep you out of the Gray Area.

This book is dedicated to my devoted yellow Labrador "Tess" who stayed with me for hours on end and my wife Ritsuko who has supported in all my adventures. A man could ask for nothing more than a devoted supporting wife and a faithful dog. To both I am deeply grateful.

Table of Contents

Chapter 3. MECHANIC LIABILITIES

Chapter 4. FREQUENTLY ASKED QUESTIONS AND ANSWERS

Chapter 5. MECHANIC GENERAL KNOWLEDGE

Chapter 1
MECHANIC GENERAL INFORMATION
Airworthiness Chart

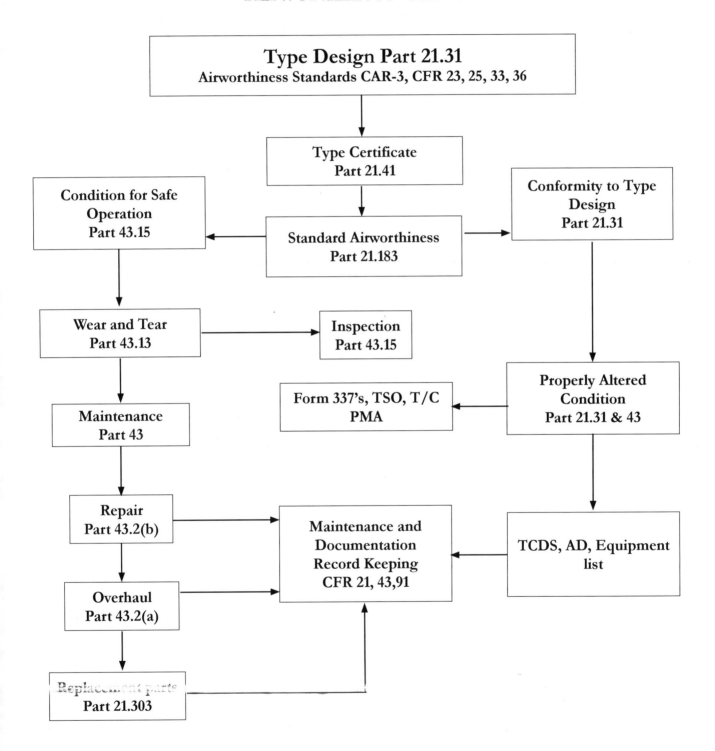

Just when I think I know something, it becomes clear I don't. Usually, it's something I thought I totally understood but obviously didn't.

Flow Chart Hot To Obtain A&P

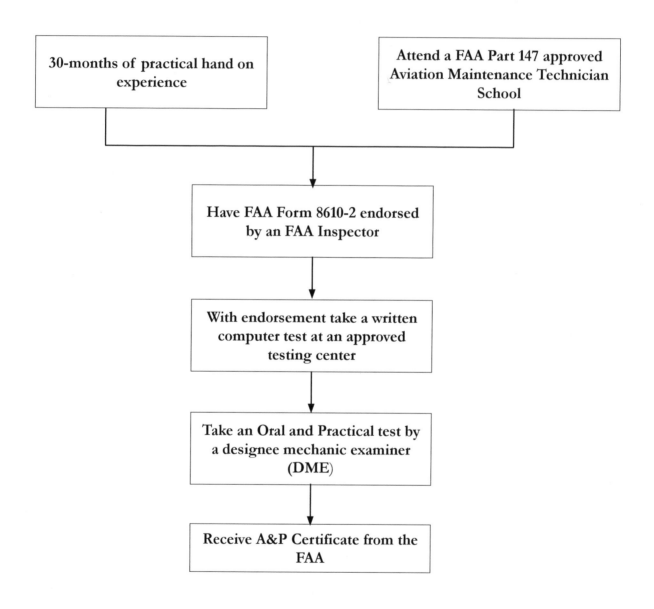

30-months of practical hand on experience

Attend a FAA Part 147 approved Aviation Maintenance Technician School

Have FAA Form 8610-2 endorsed by an FAA Inspector

With endorsement take a written computer test at an approved testing center

Take an Oral and Practical test by a designee mechanic examiner (DME)

Receive A&P Certificate from the FAA

Flow Chart Obtain Your Inspection Authorization

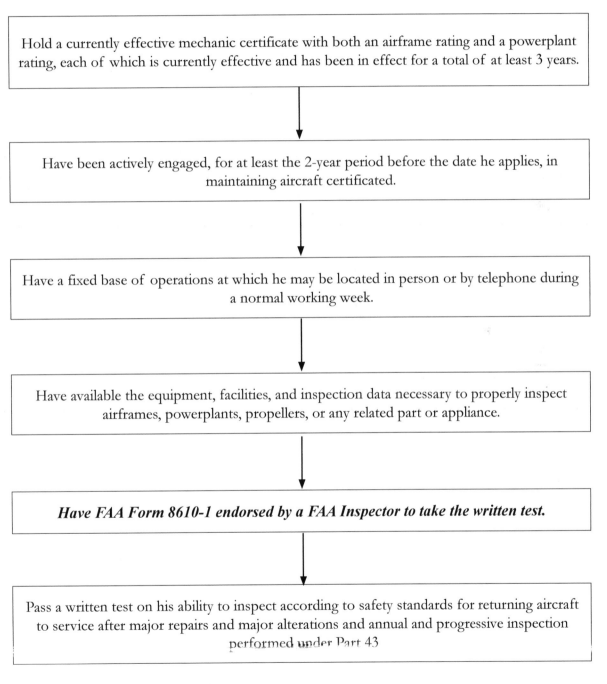

Hold a currently effective mechanic certificate with both an airframe rating and a powerplant rating, each of which is currently effective and has been in effect for a total of at least 3 years.

Have been actively engaged, for at least the 2-year period before the date he applies, in maintaining aircraft certificated.

Have a fixed base of operations at which he may be located in person or by telephone during a normal working week.

Have available the equipment, facilities, and inspection data necessary to properly inspect airframes, powerplants, propellers, or any related part or appliance.

Have FAA Form 8610-1 endorsed by a FAA Inspector to take the written test.

Pass a written test on his ability to inspect according to safety standards for returning aircraft to service after major repairs and major alterations and annual and progressive inspection performed under Part 43

NOTE: 14 CFR Section 65.91 for complete rule

New Rule for Duration and Currency of IA Certificates

Issuance

Beginning in March 2007, ASIs will issue new IAs for a maximum of 2 years, with an expiration date of March 31 of an odd-numbered year (i.e., 2009, 2011, etc . . .).

NOTE: There are no changes concerning experience and testing requirements to issue an IA (see 14 CFR, § 65.91).

Renewal

1. Beginning in March 2007, Aviation Safety Inspector (ASIs) will issue IA renewals for 2 years expiring on March 31 of an odd-numbered year. (All IAs renewed in 2007 and 2008 will expire on March 31, 2009.)

2. If an ASI issues an IA fewer than 90 days before March 31 of an odd-numbered year, the IA still has to be renewed, but the applicant does not have to meet activity requirements listed in § 65.93(a)(1) through (5) to be eligible for renewal for that 90-day period.

3. If an ASI issues an IA fewer than 90 days before March 31 of an even-numbered year, the applicant does not have to meet activity requirements for that 90-day period in order to renew the IA.

4. Beginning in March 2009, for an ASI to renew an IA, the applicant must show the activity requirements listed in § 65.93(a)(1) through (5) for each year the IA was active.

5. If an applicant for an IA does not meet the activity requirements at the end of an even-numbered year, he or she may not exercise the privileges of the IA certificate in the odd-numbered year without taking and passing an oral test with the local Flight Standards District Office (FSDO) or International Field Office (IFO).

NOTE: ASI—Aviation Safety Inspector
Reference: Order 8900.1 Vol. 5 Chapter 5

General Definitions

AIRWORTHINESS

Definition: Section 603I of the FAA Act of 1958 and CFR 21.183 (a), (b), (d), and (e), both set two conditions necessary for issuance of an airworthiness certificate: ❶ the aircraft must conform to the type design (certificate); and ❷ it is in a condition for safe operation. The above conditions also appear on the front of the standard airworthiness certificate, FAA Form 8100-2.

Discussion: Regarding condition ❶, conformity to type design is considered attained when the required and proper components are installed and they are consistent with the drawings, specifications and other data that are a part of the type certificates and approved alterations. (Cf. CFR 21.31)

Condition ❷ refers to the condition of the aircraft with relation to wear and deterioration conditions such as skin corrosion, window delamination or crazing, fluid leaks, tire wear, etc.

Conclusion: An aircraft can be considered airworthy when the Administrator finds it conforms to the specifications of its type certificate, and it is in a condition for safe operation. If one or both of these conditions are not met, the aircraft would not be considered airworthy.

CFR 1 Section. 1.1 General definitions

Administrator means the Federal Aviation Administrator (FAA) or any person to whom he has delegated his authority in the matter concerned.

ACO means Aircraft Certification Office.

Aircraft means a device that is used or intended to be used for flight in the air.

Aircraft engine means an engine that is used or intended to be used for propelling aircraft. It includes turbo superchargers, appurtenances, and accessories necessary for it's functioning, but does not include propellers.

Airframe means the fuselage, booms, nacelles, cowlings, fairings, airfoil surfaces (including rotors but excluding propellers and rotating airfoils of engines), and landing gear of an aircraft and their accessories and controls.

Appliance means any instrument, mechanism, equipment, part, apparatus, appurtenance, or accessory, including communications equipment, that is used or intended to be used in operating or controlling an aircraft in flight, is installed in or attached to the aircraft, and is not part of an airframe, engine, or propeller.

Approved, unless used with reference to another person, means approved by the Administrator

CFR means Code of Federal Regulations means same as CFR.

Civil aircraft means aircraft other than public aircraft.

Current status: for a life-limited part that might require an audit trail back to the origin of the life-limited part.

DER means Designated Engineer Representative

CFR means Federal Aviation Regulation means same as CFR.

Fireproof—
(1) With respect to materials and parts used to confine fire in a designated fire zone, means the capacity to withstand at least as well as steel in dimensions appropriate for the purpose for which they are used, the heat produced when there is a severe fire of extended duration in that zone; and
(2) With respect to other materials and parts, means the capacity to withstand the heat associated with fire at least as well as steel in dimensions appropriate for the purpose for which they are used.

Fire resistant—
(1) With respect to sheet or structural members means the capacity to withstand the heat associated with fire at least as well as aluminum alloy in dimensions appropriate for the purpose for which they are used; and
(2) With respect to fluid-carrying lines, fluid system parts, wiring, air ducts, fittings, and powerplant controls, means the capacity to perform the intended functions under the heat and other conditions likely to occur when there is a fire at the place concerned.

Flame resistant means not susceptible to combustion to the point of propagating a flame, beyond safe limits, after the ignition source is removed.

Flight time means, Pilot time that commences when an aircraft moves under its own power for the purpose of flight and ends when the aircraft comes to rest after landing.

Instrument means a device using an internal mechanism to show visually or aurally the attitude, altitude, or operation of an aircraft or aircraft part. It includes electronic devices for automatically controlling an aircraft in flight.

Landing gear operating speed means the maximum speed at which the landing gear can be safely extended or retracted.

Large aircraft means aircraft of **more than 12,500 pounds**, maximum certificated takeoff weight.

Light-sport aircraft means an aircraft, other than a helicopter or powered-lift that, since its original certification, has continued to meet the following:
1. A maximum takeoff weight of not more than—
    (i) **660 pounds** (300 kilograms) for lighter-than-air aircraft;
    (ii) **1,320 pounds** (600 kilograms) for aircraft not intended for operation on water; or
    (iii) **1,430 pounds** (650 kilograms) for an aircraft intended for operation on water.
2. A maximum airspeed in level flight with maximum continuous power (VH) of not more than **120 knots** CAS under standard atmospheric conditions at sea level.

3. A maximum never-exceed speed (VNE) of not more than **120 knots** CAS for a glider.
4. A maximum stalling speed or minimum steady flight speed without the use of lift-enhancing devices (VS1) of not more than **45 knots** CAS at the aircraft's maximum certificated takeoff weight and most critical center of gravity.
5. A maximum seating capacity of no more than two persons, including the pilot.
6. A single, reciprocating engine, if powered.
7. A fixed or ground-adjustable propeller if a powered aircraft other than a powered glider.
8. A fixed or auto feathering propeller system if a powered glider.
9. A fixed-pitch, semi-rigid, teetering, two-blade rotor system, if a gyroplane.
10. A nonpressurized cabin, if equipped with a cabin.
11. Fixed landing gear, except for an aircraft intended for operation on water or a glider.
12. Fixed or repositionable landing gear, or a hull, for an aircraft intended for operation on water.
13. Fixed or retractable landing gear for a glider.

Maintenance means inspection, overhaul, repair, preservation, and the replacement of parts, but excludes preventive maintenance.

Major alteration means an alteration not listed in the aircraft, aircraft engine, or propeller specifications—
   (1) That might appreciably affect weight, balance, structural strength, performance, powerplant operation, flight characteristics, or other qualities affecting airworthiness; or
   (2) That is not done according to accepted practices or cannot be done by elementary operations.

Major repair means a repair:
   (1) That, if improperly done, might appreciably affect weight, balance, structural strength, performance, powerplant operation, flight characteristics, or other qualities affecting airworthiness; or
   (2) That is not done according to accepted practices or cannot be done by elementary operations.

Manifold pressure means absolute pressure as measured at the appropriate point in the induction system and usually expressed in inches of mercury.

Minor alteration means an alteration other than a major alteration.

Minor repair means a repair other than a major repair.

Operate means to use, cause to use or authorize for the purpose of air navigation, including piloting.

Person means an individual, firm, partnership, corporation, company, association, joint-stock association, or governmental entity. It includes a trustee, receiver, assignee, or similar representative of any of them.

Preventive maintenance means simple or minor preservation operations and the replacement of small standard parts not involving complex assembly operations.

Preventive maintenance means simple or minor preservation operations and the replacement of small standard parts not involving complex assembly operations.

Privilege means; the word privilege on the certificate means what is commonly ascribed to the term. The privilege is one, which can be given by the FAA and can be terminated if there is a showing that the holder no longer meets the qualifications, which the FAA has been authorized to prescribe. The certificate, once granted, can be revoked by a showing, among other factors, that the certificate holder has failed to maintain the required skill, knowledge or physical condition.

A certificate holder does not waive any constitutional rights. If the FAA proposes to revoke the certificate, it must usually provide a notice and opportunity for hearing in accordance with Section 609 of the Federal Aviation Act of 1958.

Section 609 provides, in pertinent part, that the Administrator may reexamine any civil airman and amend, suspend, or revoke any airman certificate if safety and the public interest require such an action. If one of the latter action's is taken, the certificate holder must be advised of the charges and, except in an emergency, be given an opportunity to answer the charges and appeal the order to the National Transportation Safety Board before amendment, suspension, or revocation. The Board may, after hearing, amend, modify or reverse the Administrator's order. Finally, a certificate holder may obtain judicial review of the Board's order.

Public aircraft means any of the following aircraft when not being used for a commercial purpose or to carry an individual other than a crewmember or qualified non-crewmember. An aircraft used only for the United States Government.

Rating means a statement that, as a part of a certificate, sets forth special conditions, privileges, or limitations.

Time in service, with respect to maintenance time records, means the time from the moment an aircraft leaves the surface of the earth until it touches it at the next point of landing.

Legal Interpretations

Actively engaged means: maintaining aircraft requires that a person be participating, occupied, or employed in inspecting, overhauling, repairing, preserving, or replacing parts on aircraft. Actively engaged may include supervising others, including students. Section 65.91I(2).

The term "check" is understood to mean work in the nature of a simple inspection.

Departure to means: the time the aircraft leaves the takeoff surface.

Hands on experience means: maintaining real aircraft and parts, which they return to service.

Measurable means: that which can be measured by physical means pertaining to installed fasteners.

Qualified Inspector means: a person employed by the station, who has shown by experience as a journeyman that he understands the inspection methods, techniques, and equipment used in determining the airworthiness of the articles concerned. He must also be proficient in using various types of mechanical and visual inspection aids appropriate for the article being inspected. The qualified inspector need not be the holder of an FAA inspection authorization issued under CFR Section 65.91.

Take-off means: has been defined as "the act of beginning flight in which an aircraft is accelerated from a state of rest to that of flight."

Rules Of Construction

Throughout the regulations the following word usage applies:

1. **Shall** indicates a mandatory requirement.
2. The words **"no person may . . ."** or **"a person may not"** mean that no person is required, authorized, or permitted to do an act described in a regulation.
3. **May** indicates that discretion can be used when performing an act described in a regulation.
4. **Will** indicates an action incumbent upon the Authority.
5. **Includes** means "includes but is not limited to.
6. **Approved** means the Authority has reviewed the method, procedure, or policy in question and issued a formal written approval.
7. **Acceptable** means the Authority has reviewed the method, procedure, or policy and has neither objected to nor approved its proposed use or implementation.
8. **Prescribed** means the Authority has issued written policy or methodology, which imposes either a mandatory requirement, if the written policy or methodology states **"shall",** or a discretionary requirement if the written policy or methodology states **"may"**.

Job Requirements

AIRCRAFT MECHANICS have the important responsibility of keeping planes operating safely and efficiently. They service, repair, overhaul, and test aircraft. This guide covers two mechanical specialties: Airframe and Power Plant (A&P) Mechanics and Inspection Holders (IA).

Airframe and Power Plant (A&P) Mechanics work on various parts of the aircraft. The airframe includes the wings, fuselage, brakes, tail assembly, and the oil and fuel tanks. The power plant is the engine and propellers (if used) on the aircraft. Some of the important tasks they may perform include the following:

- Adjust, align, and calibrate aircraft systems using hand tools, gauges, and test equipment.
- Examine and inspect engines or other components for cracks, breaks, or leaks.
- Test engine and system operations using test equipment.
- Listen to engines to detect and diagnose malfunctions.
- Use tools such as ignition analyzers, compression checkers, distributor timers, and ammeters.
- Take apart and inspect parts for wear, warping, or other defects.
- Maintain aircraft systems by flushing crankcases, cleaning screens, greasing moving parts, and checking brakes.
- Assemble and install electrical, plumbing, mechanical, hydraulic, structural, parts, and accessories.
- Use hand tools and power tools.
- Remove or install engine using hoist or forklift truck.
- Read, understand, and work from aircraft maintenance manuals and specifications.
- Modify air or spacecraft systems, or components.
- Ride aircraft and make necessary in-flight adjustments and corrections.

Aircraft Mechanics who work on private planes or for charter airlines usually perform a variety of duties and have more responsibility than mechanics employed by scheduled airlines. The latter most often have specialized work assignments, which tend to be more routine.

Mechanics who have become inspectors are included in the occupation. They inspect aircraft and systems repairs, making sure that work is done according to standards. They also certify aircraft airworthiness.

WHAT SKILLS ARE IMPORTANT?

Important skills, knowledge, and abilities for Aircraft Mechanics include:

- **Installation**—Correctly installing equipment, machines, wiring, or programs.

- **Equipment Selection**—Determining the kind of tools and equipment needed to do a job.

- **Repairing**—Repairing machines or systems using the needed tools.

- **Problem Identification**—Identifying the nature of problems.

- **Troubleshooting**—Determining what is causing an operating error and deciding what to do about it.

- **Equipment Maintenance**—Performing routine maintenance and determining when and what kind of maintenance is needed.

- **Product Inspection**—Inspecting and evaluating the quality of products.

- **Testing**—Conducting tests to decide whether equipment, software, or procedures are working as expected.

- **Mathematics**—Using math to solve problems.

- **Manual Dexterity**—The ability to quickly make coordinated movements of one hand, a hand together with its arm, or two hands to grasp, move, or assemble objects.

- **Arm-Hand Steadiness**—The ability to keep the hand and arm steady while making an arm movement or while holding the arm and hand in one position.

Chapter 2
INSPECTION AUTHORIZATION

Inspection Authorization History (DAMI)

CAA Part 418 SUBPART C—Types of Designations and Privileges, Section 418.23 Designated aircraft maintenance inspectors (DAMI).

•**§ 418.23 Designated aircraft maintenance inspectors (DAMI).**A person authorized to act as a DAMI may approve maintenance on civil aircraft used by U.S. military flying clubs in foreign countries.
•**[F.R. Doc. 60-12072; Filed, Dec. 28, 1960; 8:47 a.m.] (25 Fed. Reg. 13877)**

Part 183, Subpart C—Kinds of Designations: Privileges
•**Sec. 183.27 Designated aircraft maintenance inspectors**.
A designated aircraft maintenance inspector (DAMI) may approve maintenance on civil aircraft used by United States military flying clubs in foreign countries.

The birth of the Inspection Authorization (IA), as we know it today, took place in **1939**. The Civil Aviation Authority (CAA) in the U.K. was having trouble keeping up with the repairs and maintenance from the increased activity in the civilian pilot training programs. Certifications were taking up to a year on major repairs on general aviation aircraft. This was unacceptable, so the CAA started **Designating Aviation Maintenance Inspectors**, DAMI for short. These designations were hard to come by, and were not taken lightly by the CAA or the inspectors.

By 1948, there were just 1,700 inspectors that were designated by the Civil Aviation Authority. DAMIs were used up until the **mid-1950s** when they started to find themselves entangled with **legal problems**. Like today with the Designated Airworthiness Inspectors (DAR), the CAA was held liable for their designated personnel and they were being sued. Just like today's Federal Aviation Administration (FAA), they do not want to assume responsibility for anything, so the CAA had to can the whole DAMI program. **In June of 1956, the Inspection Authorization was born**. The (FAA) issues Inspection Authorization (IAs) on a daily basis now, and anyone that has met their minimum requirements is eligible to take the test and gain the IA endorsement.

Eligibility Requirements Inspection Authorization

Eligibility is established at the local FAA Flight Standards District Office (FSDO) prior to taking the inspection authorization knowledge test.

You are eligible for the inspection authorization knowledge test if you meet the requirements of **Title 14 of the Code of Federal Regulations (14 CFR) Part 65, section 65.91I.**

Section 65.91 Inspection Authorization.

(1) Hold a currently effective mechanic certificate with both an airframe rating and a powerplant rating, each of which is currently effective and has been in effect for a total of at least 3 years;

(2) Have been actively engaged, for at least the 2-year period before the date he applies, in maintaining aircraft certificated and maintained in accordance with this chapter;

(3) Have a fixed base of operations at which he may be located in person or by telephone during a normal working week, but it need not be the place where he will exercise his inspection authority;

(4) Have available to him the equipment, facilities, and inspection data necessary to properly inspect airframes, powerplants, propellers, or any related part or appliance; and

(5) Pass a written test on his ability to inspect according to safety standards for returning aircraft to service after major repairs and major alterations and annual and progressive inspection performed under Part 43 of this chapter . . ."

*** NOTE ***

Actively engaged requires that a person be participating, occupied, or employed in inspecting, overhauling, repairing, preserving, or employed in inspecting, overhauling, repairing, preserving, or replacing parts on certificated aircraft. Teaching methods or techniques would not by itself meet the requirements of the regulation.

August 18th, 2011 IA Renewal received news from the FAAST Team concerning the issue of Actively Engaged. This softened stance is helpful to those who do not work full time in aviation. Below is the quote . . .

FAA Clarifies "Actively Engaged" for IAs In a notice of policy dated Aug. 04, 2011, the FAA has clarified the term "actively engaged" with regards to those applying for and renewing an inspection authorization (IA). Current regulations state (among other requirements) that an IA must be actively engaged in maintaining aircraft for a two-year period before obtaining or renewing an IA. The new policy notice addresses the confusion caused by the term "actively engaged" and has broadened its application to cover IAs providing maintenance in rural areas, and those offering specialized expertise with rare or vintage aircraft. The definition also recognizes part-time employment and occasional activity, which does not require employment and may occur on an infrequent basis, valuing the substantive nature of experience rather than a strict quantity formula.

However, for someone who only participated in maintenance activities on a part-time or occasional basis, regardless of employment status, the FAA proposed that an aviation safety inspector (ASI) "would use documentation or other evidence provided by the applicant detailing the maintenance activity to determine whether the type of maintenance activity performed, considering any special expertise required, and the quantity of maintenance activity demonstrated the applicant was actively engaged."

In order to renew an IA under CFR 65.93(a), an applicant will need to present evidence to the ASI to demonstrate that he or she still meets the four requirements of CFR 65.91(c), and **according to the FAA, refresher training alone does not satisfy those requirements**. Thus, applicant's will need to demonstrate that they are **"actively engaged"** in some way other than by simply attending refresher training.

Reference Federal Register / Vol. 76, No. 150 / Thursday, August 4, 2011 / Rules and Regulations

IA Test Description

The Inspection Authorizations test is a computer test and is taken at a computer test site. Your local FSDO can provide you a list of test centers in your area.

All test questions are the objective, multiple-choice type. The test contains 50 questions, numbered 1 through 50. Each question can be answered by the selection of a single response. Each test question is independent of other questions; therefore, a correct response to one does not depend upon, or influence the correct response to another.

The maximum time allowed for the test is **3 hours**. The allotted time is based on previous experience and educational statistics. This amount of time is considered more than adequate if you have prepared properly.

The inspection authorization knowledge test has been considered by some as an **open book test** because of the use of reference material during the test. To view the test in this manner is a misconception. There has always been a core knowledge requirement for which no reference material was provided. Therefore, it should be noted that, during the tests, there are subject areas for which reference material is not included in the test supplement. These areas will draw on skills acquired as an airframe and powerplant mechanic and which are necessary to properly inspect work performed by others.

The IA test supplement provides appropriate segments of Title 14 of the Code of Federal Regulations, all necessary charts, graphs, and technical data necessary to solve problems contained in the test. Prior to taking the test, you should take a few minutes to look through the supplement to determine what is included.

You should carefully read the information and instructions given with the tests, as well as the statements in each test item.

When taking a test, you should keep the following points in mind:

• Answer each question in accordance with the latest regulations and procedures.

• Read each question carefully before looking at the possible answers. You should clearly understand the problem before attempting to solve it.

• After formulating an answer, determine which of the alternatives most nearly corresponds with that answer. The answer chosen should completely resolve the problem.

• From the answers given, it may appear that there is more than one possible answer; however, there is only one answer that is correct and complete. The other answers are either incomplete or are derived from popular misconceptions.

• If a certain question is difficult for you, it is best to mark it for review and proceed to the other questions. After you answer the less difficult questions, return to those, which you marked for review and answer them. The review marking procedure will be explained to you prior to starting the test. When you have finished taking the test, make sure an answer has been recorded for each question. However, the computer will alert you to all unanswered questions. This procedure will enable you to use the available time to the maximum advantage.

The FAA computer written consists of the following:

Test Code	FAA Test Name	Questions	Age	Allotted Time	Passing Score
IAR	Inspection Authorization*	50	21	3.0	70

*Available ONLY at testing centers authorized to administer the IAR knowledge test.

Acceptable Forms of Authorization:
- Federal Aviation Administration (FAA) Form 8610-1, "Mechanic's Application for Inspection Authorization".

  - *NOTE 1: Item 12 on the form, "REMARKS" block, must state, "Expires 30 days from date of inspector's signature."*

  - *NOTE 2: Item 14 must be completed, including inspector signature, endorsement block checked, and office identification provided. (Refer to Order 8080.6D, Appendix 1)*

  - *NOTE 3: After reviewing Form 8610-1 for proper completion and endorsement, proctors must retain the form.* **The original 8610-1 must be destroyed by the test proctor once the applicant has been issued an official test report.** *The proctor must make a copy of the form and attach it to the applicable daily log. (Refer to Order 8080.6, par. 6-1.c.)*

- Failed, passing or expired Airman Knowledge Test Report, provided the applicant still has the ORIGINAL test report in his/her possession. (See RETESTING explanation(s) below.)

- "Expired test/credit" letter issued by the Airmen Certification Branch (in lieu of a duplicate Airman Knowledge Test Report).

Retesting:

- Requires a 90-day waiting period for retesting.

- Applicants taking retests AFTER FAILURE are required to submit the applicable score report indicating failure to the testing center prior to retesting. The original failed test report must be retained by the proctor and attached to the applicable sign-in/out log. The latest test taken will reflect the official score.

Applicants retesting IN AN ATTEMPT TO ACHIEVE A HIGHER PASSING SCORE may retake the same test for a better grade after 30 days. The latest test taken will reflect the official score. Applicants are required to submit the ORIGINAL applicable score report indicating previous passing score to the testing center prior to testing. Testing center personnel must collect and destroy this report prior to issuing the new test report.

What Forms Are Required And Where To Obtain Them

The first step in taking the inspection authorization knowledge test is to contact your local Flight Standards District Office (FSDO) to make an appointment to interview with an Aviation Safety Inspector (ASI) (Airworthiness) to determine eligibility before registering for the knowledge test. At the interview, the inspector will ask you to complete an **FAA Form 8610-1 (Two copies)**; Mechanic's Application for Inspection Authorization and provides positive proof of identification. An acceptable identification document includes your current photograph, signature, and actual residential address, if different from the mailing address. This information may be presented in more than one form of identification.

The application forms are only good for 30-days from the date the ASI signs them, so make sure you are ready to take the test when you apply.

The applicant must pass the IA knowledge test, testing the ability to inspect according to safety standards for approval constituting return to service an aircraft, related part, or appliance after major repairs, major alterations, annual, and progressive inspections performed under 14 CFR Part 43. There is **no practical test required** for an IA. Reference CFR 65, Section 65.91.

The knowledge test establishes the applicant's ability to read, understand, interpret, and apply the regulations, policies, and procedures set forth in Federal Aviation Administration (FAA) publications. The ASI should discuss the test procedures with the applicant, ensuring the applicant understands the test procedures.

The following documents will be required at the test site:

1. An ID with current photo, signature, and applicant's residential address.

2. A completed FAA Form 8610-1, Mechanic's Application For Inspection Authorization, with signature of approving inspector.

There is a three-hour time limit that is controlled by the computer.

The test has 50 questions and one section.

When the applicant enters the actual testing area, he/she is only permitted to take scratch paper furnished by the test administrator and an authorized calculator, approved for use in accordance with FAA Order 8080.6, Conduct of Airman Knowledge Testing Via the Computer Medium, and AC 60-11, Aids Authorized for Use by Airman Written Test Applicants. All reference material will be provided by the test center, the applicant need not take IA reference materials to the test.

The applicant will be instructed by the test administrator on the operation of the computer for the test, and will be given an opportunity to do a practice test prior to taking the actual test.

The applicant is responsible for making arrangements with the Computer Test Center for his/her knowledge test.

Retesting Procedures

The minimum passing score is 70, and if the test is failed, there will be a **90-day** waiting period before retesting is allowed. An attempt to retest prior to the waiting period is contrary to part 65, and could result in **revocation of any** airman certificates held. The original Form 8610-1 is still good for the retest so you do not have to reapply at the FSDO.

When the applicant returns with a test report the ASI should review it, noting the number of the test takes and date. If the applicant has taken the test more than once the ASI should determine the reason. It may be that the applicant has used the option of retaking a **passed** test after 30 days in hopes of obtaining a better score or has fraudulently retaken a **failed** test in less than the 90-day waiting period. If the ASI cannot determine this to his/her satisfaction locally, the ASI will contact AFS-630, Operations Standards Support Branch. (405) 954-6677, for a complete review of the applicant's testing activity.

Publications and Technical Data

Aircraft Type Certificate Data Sheets and Specifications are separated into six volumes. Only five of the six volumes are required for the inspection authorization. The volume numbers, titles, and contents of the following volumes are required:

(1) Volume 1 (Single-Engine Airplanes) contains material for all single-engine, fixed-wing airplanes regardless of maximum certificated takeoff weight.

(2) Volume II (Small Multiengine Airplanes) contains material for multiengine, fixed-wing airplanes of 12,500 pounds or less maximum certificated takeoff weight.

(3) Volume IV (Rotorcraft, Gliders, Balloons, and Airships) contains material for all rotorcraft, gliders, manned balloons, and airships.

(4) Volume V (Aircraft Engines and Propellers) contains material for engines and propellers of all types and models.

(5) Volume VI (Aircraft Listing and Aircraft Engine and Propeller Listing) contains information pertaining to older aircraft, engines, and propellers, which is not subject to frequent revision.

Volumes I through V are sold by the FAA on a subscription-basis in both paper and microfiche editions.

(1) Subscription service includes the paper copy edition, the basic volume and monthly supplements for a 2-year period.

(2) Paper copies of Volume VI are sold on a single-sale basis, and are included in the microfiche edition. There are infrequent changes to this material.

(3) Microfiche edition is sold by subscription only. All six volumes are consolidated into one file that is prepared in January of each year. Subscription service includes the basic volumes and monthly supplements for 1 year from January through December.

(4) To determine the current cost of Type Certificate Data Sheets and Specifications and for additional information on ordering, refer to AC 21-15, (or most current revision) Announcement of Availability: Aircraft, Aircraft Engines, and Propeller Type Certificate Data Sheets and Specifications.

All the AD listing and Type Certificated Data Sheets can be found on the FAA web site:
http://www.airweb.faa.gov/Regulatory_and_Guidance_Library/rgAD.nsf/
MainFrame?OpenFrameSet

Another good FAA site is:

http://www.faa.gov/aircraft/

Under this section you can click on the following topics:

1. FAA Aircraft Registration by N-number
2. FAA Forms
3. SARS Interim Guidance
4. FAA Inspectors Handbooks
5. Federal Aviation Regulations (CFR's)
6. Airworthiness Directives (Ads)
7. Type Certificate Data Sheets
8. Supplemental Type Certificates (STCs)
9. Technical Standard Orders (TSOs)
10. Special Airworthiness Information Bulletins
11. Master Minimum Equipment Lists (MMEL)
12. Maintenance Alerts
13. Operations Specifications (OpSpecs.com)
14. Fractional Aircraft Ownership
15. Sport Pilot and Light Sport Proposal

Service Bulletins and Service Letters for Part 91

Service Bulletins and Service Letters are **_NOT_** manufactory if you are working on a part 91 General Aviation aircraft.

- Manufacturer's maintenance instructions is required when:

  a. Made **_mandatory by an AD_** or other specific rule within the CFR (CFR).

  b. Made **_mandatory by a type certificate data sheet_**, only maintenance people are subject to this requirement since they have been advised to comply through CFR 43; however, caution must be exercised since an equivalent procedure could be found to be acceptable at an enforcement hearing.

Note
Reference FAA Order 8620-2 dated 11/2/1978

Manufacturers' **service documents communicate are useful recommendations** and information on available alterations, suggested repairs, inspections, etc., to operators. It is the operators' (not the manufacturers') ultimate responsibility to ensure that FAA approval has been obtained if FAA approval is required before implanting manufacturers' advice, recommendations, alterations, repairs, etc., prescribed in service documents. The CFR requires manufacturers to provide descriptive data covering required design changes to operators of their products. **When FAA approval is required, it is necessary for operators and FAA field inspectors to know which recommendation or information has been reviewed and approved by the FAA upon issuance of the service document.** For this reason it is desirable and expedient to assist the operator by indicating in an appropriate fashion in the body of service documents specifically which recommendation or information has been reviewed and approved by the FAA.

It has also been common practice in the past for manufacturers to mark entire service documents, such as service bulletins and all-operators' letters, as **_"FAA-Approved," "FAA/DER Approved," or "DER Approved."_** This practice implies that the service document has been reviewed, evaluated, and approved in toto by the FAA. **_However, since there is no regulatory basis for FAA approval of certain information in service documents, only the type certification data should be indicated as FAA Approved._** A single statement to this effect should be included on the appropriate page of this document.

If determined the service bulletin should become mandatory by law then it would have to be tied to one of the following documents.

(1) AD Note
(2) Revision to the TCDS

---

(3) Revision to the aircraft flight manual

(4) Operations Specifications

(5) Manufacturer's Inspection Program

Reference: AC 20-114

The FAA clearly states in this regard that, "***mandatory service bulletins (SB's) issued by manufacturers are to be considered advisory only.*** Small airplane design approval holders cannot unilaterally impose mandatory compliance with manufacturer's SB's. FAA policy does not permit this approval to be delegated to organizations or individuals."

Reference: Michael Gallagher, Manager Small Airplane Directorate, April 25, 2001.

Service Instructions

Beech Aircraft Corporation issues service information for the benefit of owners and fixed base operators in the form of three classes of Service Instructions. CLASS I (Red Border) are changes, inspections and modifications that could affect safety. ***The factory considers compliance is mandatory.*** These are mailed to:

- Owners of record on the FAA Registration list;
- Those having a publications subscription:
- Beechcraft Parts and Service Outlets

Those owners previously requesting notification by card will receive a card on Class II Service Instructions and I. CLASS II (Green Border) covers changes, modifications, improvements or inspections ***the factory feels*** will benefit the owner and ***although highly recommended, they are not considered mandatory compliance***, unless specified at the time of issuance CLASS III (No Border) covers changes which are optional, maintenance aids, product improvement kits and miscellaneous service information. ***Compliance is at the owner or operator's prerogative***. Copies of Class II and III are distributed per b and c above information on Owner Notification Service or Subscriptions can be obtained through any BEECHCRAFT Aero or Aviation Center. International Distributor and Dealer, or the Factory. As Service Instructions are issued, temporary notation in the index should be made until the index is revised Warranty will be allowed only when specifically defined in the Service Instructions and in accordance with Beech Warranty Policy.

Reference: AC 43-204 Visual Inspection for Aircraft.

Required CFR's

Title 14 of the Code of Federal Regulations (CFR's)

CFR Part Number	Title
Part 1	Definitions and Abbreviations
Part 21	Certification Procedures for Products and Parts
Part 23	Airworthiness Standards: Normal, Utility, Acrobatic, and Commuter Category Airplanes
Part 27	Airworthiness Standards: Normal Category Rotorcraft
Part 33	Airworthiness Standards: Aircraft Engines
Part 35	Airworthiness Standards: Propellers
Part 39	Airworthiness Directives
Part 43	Maintenance, Preventive Maintenance, Rebuilding, and Alterations
Part 45	Identification and Registration Markings
Part 47	Aircraft Registration
Part 65	Certification: Airmen Other Than Flight Crewmembers
Part 91	General Operating and Flight Rules
Part 120	Drug and Alcohol
Part 135	Air Taxi Operators and Commercial Operators
Part 183	Representatives of the Administrator

Overhaul and Rebuilt

CFR 43 Section 43.2 Records of overhaul and rebuilding.

(a) No person may describe in any required maintenance entry or form an aircraft, airframe, aircraft engine, propeller, appliance, or component part as being ***OVERHAULED*** unless—

(1) Using methods, techniques, and practices acceptable to the Administrator, it has been disassembled, cleaned, inspected, repaired as necessary, and reassembled; and

(2) It has been tested in accordance with approved standards and technical data, or in accordance with current standards and technical data acceptable to the Administrator, which have been developed and documented by the holder of the type certificate, supplemental type certificate, or a material, part, process, or appliance approval under §21.305 of this chapter.

(b) No person may describe in any required maintenance entry or form an aircraft, airframe, aircraft engine, propeller, appliance, or component part as being ***REBUILT*** unless it has been disassembled, cleaned, inspected, repaired as necessary, reassembled, and tested to the same tolerances and limits as a new item, using either new parts or used parts that either ***conform to new part tolerances and limits*** or to approved oversized or undersized dimensions.

Remember when you return an aircraft or part to service to use the correct word for the maintenance you performed. ***And only sign off for the work performed.*** As an example when you replace O-rings in a nose strut you have overhauled it. It would be considered an overhaul because you "**disassembled, cleaned, inspected, repaired as necessary, and reassembled**".

Remember overhaul and rebuilt are legal terms and care should be taken to use the correct term for the work performed.

Current Manuals and Tools

CFR 43 Section 43.13 Performance rules (general).

a. Each person performing maintenance, alteration, or preventive maintenance on an aircraft, engine, propeller, or appliance shall use the methods, techniques, and practices prescribed in the **current manufacturer's maintenance manual or Instructions for Continued Airworthiness** prepared by its manufacturer, or other methods, techniques, and practices acceptable to the Administrator, except as noted in 43.16. He **shall use** the tools, equipment, and test apparatus necessary to assure completion of the work in accordance with accepted industry practices. If special equipment or test apparatus is recommended by the manufacturer involved, he **must use** that equipment or apparatus or its equivalent acceptable to the Administrator.

b. Each person maintaining or altering, or performing preventive maintenance, **shall do** that work in such a manner and use materials of such a quality, that the condition of the aircraft, airframe, aircraft engine, propeller, or appliance worked on **will be at least equal to its original or properly altered condition** (with regard to aerodynamic function, structural strength, resistance to vibration and deterioration, and other qualities affecting airworthiness).

This is the one rule that is almost always cited during any maintenance enforcement case or violation written against mechanics. Why because it states "shall and must", means you have to have the correct data and tooling and have it available during maintenance.

As a recommendation I would suggest you cite the data and revision number in the return to service statement and it will take care the liability about not having the current data. This also applies to the special tooling; cite the calibration date and serial number of the tooling used.

Type Certificate Data Sheets CFR 21.31

Type Certificate Data Sheets (TCDS): The official specifications issued by the FAA for an aircraft, engine, or propeller. This is considered the mother of all data.

Aircraft Specifications: Documentation containing the pertinent specifications for aircraft certificated under the Civil Air Regulations (CARs).

The type certificate data sheet describes the type design and sets forth the limitations prescribed by the applicable Federal Aviation Regulations. It also includes any other limitations and information found necessary for type certification of a particular model aircraft.

You should be familiar with aircraft type certificate data sheets and specifications. This should include the differences and history of these documents. Applicant should know how revisions are noted.

Unlike the specifications, type certificate data sheets do not contain a list of equipment approved for a particular aircraft. The list of required and optional equipment can be found in the **equipment list** furnished by the manufacturer of the aircraft. Sometimes a later issue of the list is needed to cover recently approved items. Serial number eligibility should always be considered.

Aircraft Type Certificate Data Sheets and Specifications are separated into six volumes. Only five of the six volumes are required for the inspection authorization. The volume numbers, titles, and contents of the following volumes are required:

1. Volume 1 (Single-Engine Airplanes) contains material for all single-engine, fixed-wing airplanes regardless of maximum certificated takeoff weight.
2. Volume II (Small Multiengine Airplanes) contains material for multiengine, fixed-wing airplanes of 12,500 pounds or less maximum certificated takeoff weight.
3. Volume IV (Rotorcraft, Gliders, Balloons, and Airships) contains material for all rotorcraft, gliders, manned balloons, and airships.
4. Volume V (Aircraft Engines and Propellers) contains material for engines and propellers of all types and models.
5. Volume VI (Aircraft Listing and Aircraft Engine and Propeller Listing) contains information pertaining to older aircraft, engines, and propellers, which is not subject to frequent revision.

Type Certificate Data Sheet (TCDS). The TCDS is the controlling document for an airplane, its model number and serial number. The TCDS can be found online at **http://www.airweb.faa.gov/Regulatory_ and_Guidance_Library/rgMakeModel.nsf/MainFrame?OpenFrameSet**

CFR section 21.41 states that each type certificate includes the type design, the operating limitations, the type certificate data sheet, and the applicable regulations, conditions, and limitations. CFR section 21.31

states that the type design consists of drawings and specifications, information on dimensions, materials and processes, airworthiness limitations, and data necessary to produce later copies of the product.

The holder of the type certificate is the repository of all basic information on the safety aspects of that aircraft; he accedes to the privileges of producing aircraft to that approved design; he also has the corresponding responsibility for the continued airworthiness of the certificated product's type design imposed by the CFR.

The continuity of regulatory responsibilities under a type certificate accrues to the current holder for the practical reason that the holder possesses all the type design data on which to base changes necessary for safety. This is reflected in CFR section 21.99, which imposes on the type certificate holder the duty to provide design changes to correct an unsafe condition noted in an airworthiness directive. This duty devolves on the current holder, notwithstanding that the aircraft or other product in question may have been manufactured by a prior holder of that type certificate. A current holder, who purchased or otherwise acquired the type certificate, succeeds to all the rights, as well as the responsibilities, of the type certificate and stands in the shoes of all prior holders.

CFR section 21.3 requires the holder of a type certificate to report specific failures, malfunctions, and defects in any product manufactured by it. While the literal wording of the regulation could be read to limit its applicability to products manufactured by the current holder, the FAA and the holders themselves, as a practical matter, have interpreted the requirement to include any product manufactured under that type certificate. Under the section 21.3 requirement to report on an aircraft "manufactured by it," the "it" refers to the type certificate holder. However, the reporting requirement is on the holder of the type certificate at the time a reportable event occurs. It is the purpose of the section 21.3 reporting requirement, supplemented by the type certificate transferability and duration rules, to provide the FAA with the earliest possible notification of failures, malfunctions, or defects in order that the FAA may take appropriate mandatory action such as the issuance of an airworthiness directive.

Advisory Circulars (ACs)
Not Mandatory

The purpose of advisory circulars (ACs) is to provide guidance that is acceptable, but not exclusive, means of complying with the law. The flying public will benefit from voluntary adherence to the enhanced safety standards set out in the regulations. The FAA will continue to provide assistance to public agencies, which seek to voluntarily comply with the regulatory requirements.

A list of the most used AC's is provided below:

AC 20-33B Technical Information Regarding Civil Aeronautics Manuals 1, 3, 4A, 4B, 5, 6, 7, 8, 9, 13, and 14.

AC 20-37D Aircraft metal propeller maintenance.

AC 20-62D Eligibility, quality, and identification of aeronautical replacement parts.

AC 20-77 Use of manufacturer's maintenance manuals.

AC 20-94 Digital clock installation in aircraft.

AC 20-106 Aircraft inspection for the general aviation aircraft owner.

AC 21-25A Approval of modified seating systems initially approved under a technical standard order.

AC 21-34 Shoulder harness—safety belt installations.

AC 23-2 Flammability tests.

AC 39-7C Airworthiness Directives.

AC 43.9-1E Instructions for completion of FAA form 337 (OMB No. 2120-0020) major repair and alteration (airframe, powerplant, propeller, or appliance).

AC 43-9C Maintenance records.

AC 43-12A Preventive maintenance.

AC 43.13-1B Acceptable Methods, Techniques, And Practices\Aircraft Inspection And Repair.

AC 43.13-2A Acceptable Methods, Techniques, And Practices—Aircraft Alterations.

AC 43-16A Alerts (Aviation Maintenance Alerts).

AC 43-210 Standardized procedures for requesting field approval of major alterations, and repairs.

AC 45-2B Identification and registration marking.

AC 45-3 Installation, removal, or change of identification data and identification plates on aircraft engines.

FAA-G-8082-11 Inspection authorization knowledge test guide.

Inspection Authorizations and Liabilities References

FAA Order 8900.1 Volume 5, Chapter 5 Evaluate Inspection Authorization
FAA-G-8082-11 Inspection Authorization Knowledge Test Guide
AC 65-13 FAA Inspection Authorization Directory replaced by 65-13W (8/02; AF-640)

Required Inspections

Federal Aviation Regulations (CFR) provide for the inspection of all civil aircraft at specific intervals, depending generally upon the type of operations in which they are engaged, for the purpose of determining their overall condition. Some aircraft must be inspected at least once each 12-calendar months, while inspection is required for others after each 100 hours of flight. In other instances, an aircraft may be inspected in accordance with an inspection system set up to provide for total inspection of the aircraft over a calendar or flight-time period.

In order to determine the specific inspection requirements and rules for the performance of inspections, reference should be made to the Federal Aviation Regulations, which prescribe the requirements for the inspection and maintenance of aircraft in various types of operations in Part 91 Section 91.409.

Annual Inspection

A reciprocating-powered single-engine aircraft flown for pleasure is required to be inspected at least annually by a certificated airframe and powerplant mechanic holding an Inspection Authorization, or by a certificated repair station that is appropriately rated, or by the manufacturer of the aircraft. The aircraft may not be operated unless the annual inspection has been performed within the preceding 12 calendar months. **A period of 12 calendar months extends from any day of any month to the last day of the same month the following year.** However, an aircraft with the annual inspection overdue may be operated under a special flight permit for the purpose of flying the aircraft to a location where the annual inspection can be performed.

100-Hour Inspection

A reciprocating-powered single-engine aircraft used to carry passengers or for flight instruction for hire must be inspected within each 100 hours of time in service by a certificated airframe and powerplant mechanic, a certificated repair station that is appropriately rated, or the aircraft manufacturer. An annual inspection is acceptable as a 100-hour inspection, but the reverse is not true.

Other Inspection Programs

The annual and 100-hour inspection requirements do not apply to large airplanes, turbojet or turbo-propeller-powered multiengine airplanes, or to airplanes for which the owner or operator complies with the progressive inspection requirements. Details of these requirements may be determined by reference to 14 CFR Parts 43 and 91 and by inquiry at a local FSDO.

Special Flight Permits

A special flight permit is an authorization to operate an aircraft that may not currently meet applicable airworthiness requirements, but is safe for a specific flight. Before the permit is issued, an FAA inspector may personally inspect the aircraft or require it to be inspected by a certificated airframe and powerplant mechanic or repair station to determine its safety for the intended flight. The inspection must be recorded in the aircraft records.

The special flight permit is issued to allow the aircraft to be flown to a base where repairs, alterations, or maintenance can be performed; for delivering or exporting the aircraft; or for evacuating an aircraft from an area of impending danger. A special flight permit may be issued to allow the operation of an overweight aircraft for flight beyond its normal range over water or land areas where adequate landing facilities or fuel is not available.

If a special flight permit is needed, assistance and the necessary forms may be obtained from the local FSDO or Designated Airworthiness Representative (DAR).

Publications

Aeronautical publications are the sources of information for guiding aviation mechanics in the operation and maintenance of aircraft and related equipment. The proper use of these publications will greatly aid in the efficient operation and maintenance of all aircraft. These include manufacturers' service bulletins, manuals, and catalogs, as well as FAA regulations, airworthiness directives, advisory circulars, and aircraft, engine and propeller specifications.

Maintenance Manual

The aircraft maintenance manual provided by the manufacturer contains complete instructions for maintenance of all systems and components installed in the aircraft. It contains information for the mechanic who normally works on units, assemblies, and systems, while they are installed in the aircraft, and not for the overhaul mechanic. They are required in accordance with Part 43.13.

The FAA recognizes that maintenance practices and requirements are not static and may change as information is developed during the service life of an aircraft. Manufacturers may provide a systematic manual revision system to implement changes to their maintenance instructions. Owner and operators should make allowances for such changes.

Structural Repair Manual

This manual contains information and specific instructions from the manufacturer for repairing primary and secondary structure. Typical skin, frame, rib, and stringer repairs are covered in this manual. Also included are material and fastener substitutions and special repair techniques. The SID manual may be mandatory if you are under § 91.409(f) inspection program.

Illustrated Parts Catalog

This catalog presents component breakdowns of structure and equipment in disassembly sequence. Also included are exploded views or cutaway illustrations for all parts and equipment manufactured by the aircraft manufacturer.

Federal Aviation Regulations (FAR's) Code of Federal Regulations (CFR's)

Federal Aviation Regulations were established by law to provide for the safe and orderly conduct of flight operations and to prescribe airmen privileges and limitations. Knowledge of the CFRs is necessary during the performance of maintenance, since all work done on aircraft must comply with CFR provision. The Code of Federal Regulations (CFR's) the same regulation as the CFR's just a different name.

Basic Privileges and Limitations of an A&P

The basic functions of the holder of an Airframe and Powerplant mechanic (A&P) are set forth in **14 CFR Part 65, section 65.81**. If you read and understand the privileges and limitations of your certificate, and stay within those bounds, you will avoid the "wrath" of the FAA. Since the regulations are written with legal expertise, they are sometimes difficult to thoroughly understand. You are encouraged to contact your local FAA Flight Standards District Office for clarification of any point that is not fully understood.

Basic Functions of an A&P

To do good work and provide the owner with an airworthy aircraft. Mechanics determine the maintenance classification (major repair, minor repair, preventive maintenance) of the replacement of aircraft components with new, rebuilt, or repaired components of similar design.

Basic Functions of an IA

The basic functions of the holder of an inspection authorization (IA) are set forth in **14 CFR Part 65, section 65.95**. With the exception of aircraft maintained in accordance with a Continuous Airworthiness Program under 14 CFR parts 121 or 127, an IA may inspect and approve for return to service any aircraft or related part or appliance after a major repair or major alteration. Also, the holder of an IA may perform an annual inspection and he or she may supervise or perform a progressive inspection.

There are additional requirements for annual and progressive inspections listed in **14 CFR Part 43, section 43.15**. The scope and detail of 100-hour and annual inspections are the same. **Record entries are very important, as they are the only evidence an aircraft owner has to show compliance with the inspection requirements of 14 CFR Part 91, section 91.409.**

The owner should be made aware that the annual or progressive inspection does not include correction of discrepancies or unairworthy items and that such maintenance will be additional to the inspection. A person authorized to perform maintenance if agreed on by the owner and holder of the IA may accomplish maintenance and repairs simultaneously with the inspection.

The regulatory scheme recognizes that the mechanic with inspection authorization is required to posses a higher degree of skill and experience than in the person who may only repair and maintain aircraft, without the ability to conduct the required inspection.

The A&P/IA in the course of certifying an aircraft to be airworthy, may be laying their certificates on the line for work of unknown quality, done at unknown times, and in some cases by unknown persons, and at times that may not be known.

Privileges of an IA

When exercising the privileges of an IA, the holder may:

1. Inspect and approve for return to service major repairs and major alterations, if the work was done according to technical data approved by the Administrator.
2. Perform an annual inspection.

3. Perform or supervise a progressive inspection.
4. Perform inspections on Aircraft Approved Inspection Program (AAIP) 9 or less Part 135.

An IA holder **shall not** approve, for return to service, major repairs, major alterations, or inspection on an aircraft maintained in accordance with a **continuous airworthiness maintenance program** (CAMP) under 14 CFR Part 121.

Required Data

1. A current and appropriate set of Airworthiness Directives (AD's).
2. A current and appropriate set of type certificate data sheets.
3. Current and appropriate Federal Aviation Regulations.
4. Manufacturers' maintenance instructions, as required by **CFR Part 43. Section 43.13**.
5. Other data as needed. Recommended data may include maintenance alerts, service difficulty reports, etc.

IA Required Functions

The holder of an IA **MUST** personally perform the inspection. The Code of Federal Regulations (CFR's) do not provide for delegation of this responsibility.

Approving major repairs and major alterations is a serious responsibility. The approval action should consist of a detailed investigation to establish, at least that:

1. All replacement parts installed conform to approved design and/or have traceability to the original equipment manufacturer (OEM).
2. As installed, the installation conforms to approved data that is applicable to the installation.
3. Workmanship meets the requirements of **14 CFR Part 43, section 43.13** (the aircraft or product is equal to its original or properly altered condition).
4. The data used is appropriate to the aircraft certification rule (e.g. CAR 3, 14 CFR Part 23).
5. Work is complete and compatible with other structures or systems.

Design Data by the FAA

Reports necessary to define and substantiate the product. This includes information on configuration, materials, and processes. Data submitted for approval by an applicant should be complete and in a logical format for review by the FAA. The FAA may reduce its own participation in a project to the minimum necessary to substantiate compliance with the airworthiness requirements. For example, instead of making a complete evaluation, the FAA may make spot-check comparisons of the later applicant's data with the first applicant's data. **The FAA is only responsible for the review of the data submitted by the applicant, not for the development of methods or calculations.**

Type Design CFR 21.31

The type design consists of: The drawings and specifications and a listing of those drawing and specifications, necessary to define the configuration and the design features of the product shown to comply with the requirements of that part of this subchapter applicable to the product. Information on dimensions, materials, and processes necessary to define the structural strength of the product.

Continued Airworthiness CFR 21.41

The Airworthiness Limitations section of the Instructions for Continued Airworthiness (ICA) are required for type certification because it is part of the type design defined in CFR 21 Section 21.31 and also part of the Type Certificate (TC) as defined in CFR Section 21.41.

Equipment Function and Installation CFR 23.1301

Each item of installed equipment must—
- (a) Be of a kind and design appropriate to its intended function.
- (b) Be labeled as to its identification, function, or operating limitations, or any applicable combination of these factors;
- (c) Be installed according to limitations specified for that equipment; and
- (d) Function properly when installed

Chapter 3
MECHANIC LIABILITIES

Inspection Authorization Liabilities

*** NOTE ***

When the holder of an IA approves an aircraft for return to service, he or she will be held responsible for the condition of the aircraft AS OF THE TIME OF APPROVAL.

Could have known and should have known.

"Need not and should not". Note this early precedent of the precedent **"could have known and should have known",** ruled in the case of **Lashley v. Koerber, California, 1945.** In this 1945 case, the appellant court held a physician liable because he **could have known and should have known.** It was summarized that a physician could be expected to exercise a " . . . reasonable degree of skill and learning and care ordinarily exercised by other doctors of good standing in the community." Considered was the doctrine of ***res ipsa loquitur*** (the thing speaks for itself), where the plaintiff does not cause the problem, and the defendant is assumed guilty if defendant knowingly allowed or caused the harm to happen, or was negligent in preventing that harm when defendant **should have and could have** prevented it.

Forest Glen Durland insists that this precedent implies and applies to all people licensed by the public to be trusted by that public to perform in a capacity demanded of their profession. This precedent, then, reaches out to all professionals licensed by the public. Furthermore, those licenses are for the protection of that public. Forest Glen Durland insists that all professional people, bankers, real estate agents, car salesmen and certainly all government workers (politicians, Congress Persons), especially those elected to offices of trust and power, are affected by that court ruling, which **must be considered a precedent of the land.**

The above is an abstract of Lincoln's monetary policy from Mayor McGeer's *Conquest of Poverty* and **has been certified as correct** by the Legislative Reference Service of the Library of Congress at the instance of Hon. Kent Keller, Member of the House of Representatives. See 76th Congress, 1st Session, Jan 3-Aug 5, 1939, Senate Documents #10304, Vol 3, Senate Document 23, "National Economy and the Banking System of the United States" by Robert L. Owen, presented by Mr. Logan on January 24, 1939, page 91.

Tort Action

If I am sued what must the plaintiff prove?

The essential elements to prove in a tort action are:
1. A duty owed the plaintiff by the defendant.
2. A breach of this duty.
3. Injury occasioned by such breach

A plaintiff must show and prove the existence of all these elements if he is to recover.

Standard of Care

We assume that there is a duty to use care and how much care should be exercised?

Judicially, that degree of care, which a **reasonably prudent person** would have exercised under the same or similar circumstances. The law requires those engaging in activities requiring unique knowledge and ability to give a performance commensurate with the undertaking. You would only be liable for negligence.

Negligence of Employee

If an airplane is damaged in your shop while you are working on it how much can you be held responsible?

If the airplane is damaged, while in the custody of the bailee, the bailor must show that it was the bailee's actionable ordinary negligence in failing to exercise ordinary care in the protection of the bailor's property. The negligence of an employee of the bailee is likewise actionable if within the scope of his employment. Contact an aviation lawyer in a matter such as this. The concept of negligence involves primarily four elements:
1. One's duty to others.
2. Whether that duty was breached.
3. Whether that breach of a legally recognizable duty was the legal cause of the harm of which the injured party complains.
4. Whether any legally recognizable damages resulted from the breach of the duty owed to someone else.

Implied Warranty

If I repair an aircraft and it breaks again after leaving my shop am I responsible?

Maybe. In addition to liability for negligence or express warranty one may be held liable for breach of an implied warranty. Implied warranties arise from the general rule that articles placed in the stream of commerce should be reasonably fit for the purpose for which they are sold. To recover under implied warranty you would have to prove:

1. There was a defect, which existed at the time the product left the hands of the manufacture/operator/owner/repair station/FBO.
2. Prove that the defect was of such nature that he would not be expected to know of is presence and that it made the product unreasonably dangerous.
3. The defect was the proximate cause of his injury.

Contracts

Should an A&P/IA have a written contract with the owner before performing any inspections or repairs?

NO. Title 49 U.S. Code **does not** require it. However, it is a very good idea so you and the owner will know how and what standard you are going to use for their inspection.

Yes, you should have Authorization. A contract should have an authorizations statement as follows: The owner authorizes Contractor and its subcontractors to perform repair work described on the reverse side (work order). In the event the party signing this Agreement is not the owner of the aircraft, that party and/or aircraft shall be responsible for payment to the Contractor in the event the owner fails to or otherwise refused to pay said bill or any portion thereof within ten (10) days after the completion of the repairs, including payment of court costs, attorney's fees and the maximum interest rate allowable by law on any unpaid portion of the Work Order from the date of completion of repairs.

If repairs are going to be included during the 100-hour or annual inspection it needs to be spelled out in the contract. And how will the owner be notified if additional repairs are required verbal or in writing it needs to be in the contract. Will cost be a factor in the repair costs? Remember inspections do not require repairs.

In the absence of such contract or prior relationship, it would seem that a authorization by the customer to perform an inspection would not necessary carry with it the authorization to make repairs. The person performing the inspection needs specific authorization to make the repairs shown to be necessary. Are you going to use the manufacture checklist or one of your own in accordance with CFR 43 Appendix D?

Shop Liability

When a maintenance shop does business, does it exposes itself to liability?

Yes, in three basic areas:

1. It can be liable for the **improper conduct** of repair and overhaul services that it makes. Including a vicarious liability for the negligence of subcontractors to whom it might send certain systems or assemblies for inspection or repair outside of the particular shop's own facility.
2. May be liable **for parts** that he supplies and incorporates into the repairs or overhaul services that he provides.
3. Be liable for **negligence maintenance** inspection function. A problem cannot be repaired, properly or negligently, if it is not discovered during inspection.

Aircraft parts are the biggest area where mechanics have liability. You as the installer are held responsible for knowing the certification basic for the parts you install. All parts have to be traceable. This is accomplished by having and FAA Form 8130-3 from the manufacture (OEM), PMA, TSO or some other documentation showing the certification. Having the owner provide parts is one thing, but as the installer you have to know the certification and if it is an approved part. This requires documentation.

The Defense Disposal Manual DOD 4160-21-M, Chapter VII, and all DOD notices announcing the sale of surplus aircraft state that the DOD does not assume any liability or in any way represent the aircraft as meeting, or being capable of meeting the Federal Aviation Administration (FAA) Standard Airworthiness Certification Requirements. This will also cover **any parts** obtained from these aircraft.

Before a Standard Certificate of Airworthiness can be obtained for any surplus military aircraft or aircraft assembled (manufactured) from spare and surplus parts, the applicant must (1) obtain an FAA Type Certificate or Part 21.27 and be able to show that the aircraft conforms to that Type Certificate or, (2) show that the aircraft conforms to an existing Type Certificate or a Supplemental under Federal Aviation Regulations, Part 21.21 Type Certificate of a civilian model. In addition, he must (in either case) prove that it is in condition for safe operation.

Aircraft Records

There are two types of aircraft records **temporary** and **permanent**, which the regulations require the owner to keep for the three major components of every aircraft. These include airframe, each engine, and propeller or rotor.

Temporary Records

1. These consist of a record of all minor maintenance and minor alterations performed on the aircraft by mechanics in accordance with **CFR 91 Sub Part E.**

2. A record of the required inspection performed on the aircraft; whether it is a 100-hour, annual, a progressive inspection, or any other required or approved inspection.

Minor maintenance and alterations records may be discarded when the work is repeated or superseded by other work. The record of routine inspections my also be discarded when the next inspection is completed. However it is good to retain the records indefinite as it shows continuity in the maintenance program.

Permanent Record

Permanent records will include the following:

1. Total time in service of the airframe, engine, and propeller.
2. The current status of the life limited parts of each airframe, engine, propeller, rotor, and appliance.
3. Time since last the overhaul of item on the aircraft, which are required to be overhauled on a scheduled time basic.
4. The current inspection status of the aircraft.
5. The current status of applicable Airworthiness Directives (AD's) and method of compliance.
6. A list of the current major alterations to each airframe, engine, propeller, or rotor.
7. Current operating limitations, including revisions to the aircraft weight and center of gravity, caused by the installation or removal of equipment or alterations.

Maintenance Record Responsibility

CFR 91 Section 91.405 clearly places the burden upon the aircraft owner/operator for making sure that the aircraft is kept in an airworthy condition, including compliance with Airworthiness Directives. In addition the owner/operator is required to make sure that the appropriate entries are made in the aircraft permanent maintenance records.

The aircraft permanent maintenance records (logbooks) are deemed to be the primary evidence as to whether the airplane has received the required maintenance and inspection. It is therefore incumbent upon the owner/operator to see that the maintenance records are complete.

The FAA has taken the position that record keeping is fully as important as the physical maintenance of an aircraft. The NTSB on cases appealed to it has upheld this contention. The NTSB has written; "A policy of leniency toward record keeping inevitably encourages carelessness in the timely performance of required maintenance, to the derogation of safety in air transportation." (See NTSB Order EA 3832)

When an A&P mechanic returns an aircraft to service he/she is both the mechanic and the inspector. Accordingly, when they sign the logbooks certifying that the aircraft is airworthy, it must be so in all respects.

The same reasoning applies to circumstances in which the mechanic fills out a Major Repair and Alteration (Form 337) before the work is completed. The FAA interprets the completion and signing of a Form 337 to be equivalent to returning the airplane to service in block #6. Even though the aircraft might need to be inspected by an Inspector Authorization (IA) and signed in block #7 or the FAA in block #3, the airplane must be completely airworthy when the mechanic signs this form. If discrepancies are found, the mechanic may be subject to sanctions of his/her violation.

Acceptable Maintenance Return to Service Words

(1) Overhauled
(2) Rebuilt
(3) Repaired
(4) Inspected
(5) Serviceable
(6) Approved
(7) Altered
(8) Modified
(9) Replaced
(10) Installed

Un-acceptable Maintenance Return to Service Words

(1) Okay
(2) Fixed
(3) Should be fine
(4) Deferred (Part 91 without an MEL)
(5) Check next inspection
(6) Not guaranteed
(7) Better than the original
(8) Checked OK!!!
(9) Good to Go!!!

General Requirements

The person performing the work must make CFR 43.9 Record entries.

CFR 91.417(a), (b) Registered owner or operator shall keep the records described in ❶ until the work is repeated, superseded, or for one year:

❶ *Records of:*
  ❑ Maintenance
  ❑ Alterations
  ❑ Inspections
    For each:
      ✈ Aircraft
      ✈ Engine
      ✈ Propeller
      ✈ Rotor
      ✈ Appliance
To include:
  • Description of the work
  • Date of the work
  • Signature and certificate number of person approving the work for return to service

Record Entries

43.9(a) The person who does the work **shall** make an entry in the maintenance records containing:
- ✓ A description of the work performed
- ✓ Date of completion of the work
- ✓ The name of the person performing the work
- ✓ Certificate number
- ✓ Kind of certificate (Airframe & Powerplant A&P, Private Pilot PP, Repair station, etc)

CFR 43.11 Specifies the content and form of record entry for inspections conducted under CFR 91.409, 125.243(a)(4), 135.411, and 135.419.

The person approving or disapproving for return to service makes an entry in the maintenance record, including:
- ✓ Type of inspection (e.g. Annual, Progressive, owner's approved, manufacturer's recommended)
- ✓ The date and aircraft time in service
- ✓ The signature, kind of certificate, and number of certificate held by the person approving or disapproving the work
- ✓ Statement certifying airworthiness, if approved
- ✓ Statement certifying airworthiness if not approved. (If not approved, owner must be given a list of discrepancies.)

Sample Entries

Airworthiness Directive Logbook Entry: *One-Time Compliance*

> January 03, 2011. Total time 435 hours. Complied with AD 92-01-03 by installing new rubber float and new bowl cover screws. Inspected solder on float valve bracket and found satisfactory as of this date. Stamped 64 on nameplate.
>
> John I. Be Good IA 00000000

Airworthiness Directive Logbook Entry: *Recurring Inspection*

> January 03, 2011. Total time 350 hours. Complied with AD 86-08-11R paragraphs a (1) and a (2) by tapping and magnifying glass. No cracks found. Void on top of blade number 2. B2.248.53A. S/N 123. Is 2" long and extends from 25" to 27" outboard of blade butt rib. Next inspection due at 377 hours
>
> John I. Be Good IA 00000000

Annual Inspection Logbook Entry: *Aircraft Found "Airworthy"*

> January 03, 2011. Total aircraft time 853.00 Hours. Tach time 420.80. Replaced right main wheel bearing, p/n 19844 upper bushing in R & l landing gear frames, both brake hoses, p/n 34052 and bled brakes. I certify that this aircraft has been inspected in accordance with part 43 Appendix D an annual inspection and was determined to be in airworthy condition.
>
> J. I. Be Good IA 00000000

Note: The date, aircraft total time, and tach or recorder reading are included. The tach or recorder reading should not be confused with the total time, and should only be shown in addition to the total time entry. The mechanic has indicated he holds an inspection authorization by prefixing his certificate number with letters, "IA".

Annual Inspection Logbook Entry: *Aircraft Found "Unairworthy"*

January 03, 2011. Total aircraft time 853.0 Hours. Tach time 420.80. I certify that this aircraft has been inspected in accordance with part 43 Appendix D an annual inspection and a list of discrepancies and unairworthy items dated (insert date) has been provided for the aircraft owner or lessee.

Leonard I. Be Good, IA 00000000

Note: The date, total time, and tach reading are included.

Logbook Entry: Pilot Owner/Operator Accomplished Preventive Maintenance

---

January 03, 2010. Total aircraft time 1000.00 Hours. Tach reading 500.00. Changed oil and filter and cleaned spark plugs in accordance with the current (make Cessna, Beech, Piper, Etc.) maintenance manual.

J. I. Be Good, ATP 000000000

Note: Entries are to be made in each appropriate airframe, powerplant and propeller maintenance record.

Airworthiness Directive Record Entry:
One-Time Compliance

MAKE: **Cessna**   MODEL: **172**   SERIAL NUMBER: **123232324**   N- **1234P**

AD NORMAL AND AMENDMENT NUMBERS	SUBJECT	DATE AND HOURS OF COMPLIANCE	METHOD OF COMPLIANCE	ONE TIME	RECUR	NEXT COMP DUE DATE/HOURS	AUTHORIZED SIGNATURE, CERTIFICATE TYPE AND NUMBER
92-01-03	Carburetor	02-09-92 435 Hours	New Float New Bowl Cover	X		One-Time	John. D. Nunenber IA 130968470

Airworthiness Directive Record Entry: *Recurring Inspection*

MAKE: **Hughes**   MODEL: **500C**   SERIAL NUMBER: **541932H**   N- **7431X**

AD NORMAL AND AMENDMENT NUMBERS	SUBJECT	DATE AND HOURS OF COMPLIANCE	METHOD OF COMPLIANCE	ONE TIME	RECUR	NEXT COMP DUE DATE/HOURS	AUTHORIZED SIGNATURE, CERTIFICATE TYPE AND NUMBER
_02 _10	M. Rotor	01-10-92 350 Hours	Inspect by tapping and magnifying glass		x	377 hours	Hon. A. Donald IA 364 1901

Return To Service

"Return to service" is any action by any person to put an aircraft or article into an operational status after it has been maintained or altered.

The **signed record entry** of a person accomplishing preventive maintenance does constitute return to service.

CFR 91.407(a) No person may return to service an aircraft or article that has undergone maintenance unless:
- ✓ It has been approved for return to service
- ✓ Maintenance record entries have been made. (Including preventive maintenance)
- ✓ The major repair or alteration has been executed. (FAA Form 337)
- ✓ Any change in operating limitations or performance determined by the test flight prescribed in 91.407(b) is properly recorded

Operation

CFR 91.407(a) No person may operate any aircraft that has undergone maintenance, preventive maintenance, rebuilding, or alteration unless:

- ○ It has been *approved for return to service* by a person authorized under sec. 43.7 of this chapter; and
- ○ The maintenance *record entry* required by sec. 43.9 or sec. 43.11, as applicable, of this chapter has been made

Test Flights

CFR 91.407(b) No person may carry any person (other than crewmembers) in an aircraft that has been maintained, rebuilt, or altered in a manner that may have *appreciably changed its flight characteristics* or *substantially affected its operation in flight* until:

- ➤ An appropriately rated pilot flies the aircraft and makes an operational check of the maintenance performed or alteration made; and
- ➤ Logs the flight in the aircraft records.

Conditional Airworthiness Release

The rule is crafted to ensure that a conditional release **cannot** be used as a way of avoiding thorough maintenance and verification of the work performed. There can be no conditions attached to the airworthiness release statement to the effect that the airplane **will be** airworthy at some later time.

The NTSB has stated emphatically "He (the A&P) may certify that an aircraft is airworthy and make such an entry in the logbook only if it is in fact airworthy.

Weight and Balance

The largest weight changes that occur during the lifetime of an aircraft are those caused by alterations and repairs. It is the responsibility of the A&P/IA doing the work to accurately document the weight change and record it in both the maintenance records and the POH/AFM. This means the weight and balance sheet must be signed, certificate number, and dated.

Weight and balance is of such vital importance that each mechanic maintaining an aircraft must be fully aware of his or her responsibility to provide the pilot with current and accurate information for the actual weight of the aircraft and the location of the center of gravity. The pilot in command has the responsibility to know the weight of the load, CG, maximum allowable gross weight, and CG limits of the aircraft.

The weight and balance report must include an equipment list showing weights and moment arms of all required and optional items of equipment included in the certificated empty weight.

When an aircraft has undergone extensive repair or major alteration, it should be reweighed and a new weight and balance record started.

Any major alteration or repair requires the work to be done by an appropriately rated A&P/IA or facility. The work must be checked for conformity to FAA-approved data and signed off by an A&P holding an Inspection Authorization, or by an authorized agent of an appropriately rated FAA-approved repair station. A repair station record or an FAA Form 337, Major Repair and Alteration, must be completed which describes the work. A dated and signed revision to the weight and balance record is made and kept with the maintenance records, and the airplane's new empty weight and empty weight arm or moment index are entered in the POH/AFM. Reference FAA-H-8083-1 Aircraft Weight and Balance Handbook.

Equipment List

An equipment list is furnished with the aircraft, which specifies all the required equipment, and all equipment approved for installation in the aircraft. The weight and arm of each item is included on the list, and all equipment installed when the aircraft left the factory is checked. All of the required equipment **must be** properly installed, and there should be no equipment installed that is not included in the equipment list.

When a mechanic adds or removes any item on the equipment list, he or she **must** change the weight and balance record to indicate the new empty weight and EWCG, and the equipment list is revised to show which equipment is actually installed. The POH for each individual aircraft includes an aircraft specific equipment list of the items from this master list. When any item is added to or removed from the aircraft, its weight and arm are determined in the equipment list and used to update the weight and balance record.

Addition or removal of equipment included on the equipment list is considered by the FAA to be a minor alteration. The weights and arms are included with the items in the equipment list, and these minor alterations can be done and the aircraft approved for return to service by an appropriately rated A&P/IA. The only documentation required is an entry in the aircraft maintenance records and the appropriate change to the weight and balance record in the POH/AFM.

Data Acceptable to the Administrator

A ll work on an aircraft having a U.S. airworthiness certificate including those used in U.S. air carrier or air taxi service must use methods, techniques, and practices acceptable to the Administrator (FAA). The recorded description of these methods, techniques, and practices is known as data acceptable to the Administrator. This acceptable data can become approved when made a part of an installation and specifically approved. Data may come from many sources and may take a number of different forms. The most common forms are described in the following paragraphs.

Acceptable versus Approved Data. If the data is approved by the Administrator, it is also data acceptable to the Administrator. **However, acceptable data is not necessarily approved data**. Under **CFR 21.97**, all major alterations must be accomplished using data approved by the Administrator. Under CFR 21.95, minor alterations may be accomplished with data acceptable to the Administrator.

Advisory Circular. The FAA publishes and distributes Advisory Circulars (AC's) to the aviation public as a means of communicating necessary and helpful information regarding safety and compliance with the regulations. AC's dealing with regulatory compliance usually present an acceptable means of compliance although it may not be the only means. All data presented in AC's except AC 43.13-lB and 43.13-2A under certain restrictions is data acceptable to the Administrator.

Manufacturer's Information. Manufacturer's maintenance and overhaul manuals and non-FAA approved service documents generally provide methods, techniques, and practices that are acceptable to the Administrator. This information is primarily of a service and maintenance/overhaul nature and if followed does not result in a change to the type design of the product. Some maintenance manuals include airworthiness limitations sections, which are approved data.

Other. Other methods, techniques, and practices that are accepted as aviation industry practice may be acceptable to the Administrator even though not specified in a given document. If any person desires to use these practices and is not sure if they are acceptable to the Administrator, contact the nearest Flight Standards District Office or Aircraft Certification Office for help.

Approved Data
Reference FAA Order 8900.1 Vol. 4, Chapter 9

S ubstantiating and descriptive technical data, used to make a major repair or alteration that is approved by the Administrator. The following list, although not all-inclusive, contains sources of approved data:

(a) Type Certificate Data Sheets (TCDS).

(b) Supplemental Type Certificate (STC) data, provided it specifically applies to the item being repaired/ altered. Such data may be used in whole or part as included within the design data associated with the STC.

(c) Appliance manufacturer's manuals or instructions, unless specifically not approved by the Administrator, are approved for major repairs.

(d) Airworthiness Directives (AD).

(e) FAA Form 337, which has been used to approve multiple identical aircraft, by the original modifier.

NOTE

Aviation Safety Inspectors (ASI) no longer approves data for use on multiple aircraft.

(f) U.S. Civil Airworthiness Authority (CAA) Form 337, dated before 10/1/55.

(g) FAA-approved portions of Structural Repair Manual (SRM).

(h) Designated Engineering Representative (DER)-approved data, only when approval is authorized under his/her specific delegation.

(i) Designated Alteration Station (DAS) FAA-approved data, when the major alteration is performed specific to the authorization granted.

(j) Data in the form of Appliance Type Approval issued by the Minister of Transport Canada for those parts or appliances for which there is no current Technical Standard Order (TSO) available. The installation manual provided with the appliance includes the Transport Canada Civil Aviation (TCCA) certificate as well as the date of issuance and an environmental qualification statement (see paragraph 13).

(k) Repair data issued under Special Federal Aviation Regulations (SCFR) 36.

(l) Foreign bulletins, for use on U.S.-certificated foreign aircraft, when approved by the foreign authority.

(m) Data describing an article or appliance used in an alteration, which is FAA-approved under a TSO. As such, the conditions and tests required for TSO approval of an article are minimum performance standards. The article may be installed only if further evaluation by the operator (applicant) documents an acceptable installation, which may be approved by the Administrator.

(n) Data describing a part or appliance used in an alteration, which is FAA-approved under a Parts Manufacturer Approval (PMA). (An STC may be required to obtain a PMA as a means of assessing airworthiness and/or performance of the part.).

NOTE

Installation eligibility for subsequent installation or reinstallation of such part or appliance in a Type Certificated (TC) aircraft, other than the aircraft for which airworthiness was originally demonstrated, is acceptable, provided the part or appliance meets its performance requirements and is environmentally and operationally compatible for installation. The operator/applicant must provide evidence of previously approved installation by TC, STC, or field approval on FAA Form 337 that will serve as a basis for "follow-on" field approval.

(o) Any FAA-approved Service Bulletins (SB) and letters or similar documents, including DER approvals.

(p) Foreign bulletins as applied to use on a U.S.-certificated product made by a foreign manufacturer located within a country with whom a Bilateral Agreement (BA) is in place and by letter of specific authorization issued by the foreign civil air authority.

(q) Other data approved by the Administrator.

(r) AC 43.13, as revised, for FAA-approved major repairs on non-pressurized areas of aircraft only when the user determines that it is:
1. Appropriate to the product being repaired.
2. Directly applicable to the repair being made.
3. Not contrary to the airframe, engine, propeller, product, or appliance manufacturer's data.

Data Not Approved or Acceptable To The Administrator

There is much information available to the aviation public, which has had no evaluation of acceptability or approval. This information is not FAA approved, and it usually has not been put to the test of practical experience. Some alterations, which have been installed, may appear to have undergone practical experience. But in reality, the aircraft involved have never approached the edge of the aircraft safe operating envelope, and the effects of the alteration evaluated. Information of this nature is found in sales catalogs or brochures, newsletters, magazines, etc. Additionally, manufacturer's parts lists, illustrated parts catalogs, and similar documents, while useful, are not approved and do not provide data acceptable to the Administrator unless they are an integral part of a maintenance manual and are not just listed as a reference.

When in doubt about the status of data or a prospective methodology, contact the nearest Flight Standards District Office or Aircraft Certification Office. An Airworthiness Inspector, Aerospace Engineer, or Flight Test Pilot, or Manufacturing Inspector will be available to provide guidance in their appropriate discipline, or make certain that the answer is forthcoming. However, these FAA personnel cannot approve or otherwise change the status of data over the telephone.

Information contained in manufacturer and/ or FAA-approved/acceptable data always takes precedence over advisory or textbook referenced data.

What cannot be Approved Without Engineering Approval?

Some repairs and alterations are so complex they are actually design changes and require an STC. The following alterations are examples of alterations that cannot be Field Approved without FAA engineering assistance:

1. Increase in gross weight and/or changes in center of gravity range
2. Installation, changes, or relocation of equipment and systems that may adversely affect the structural integrity, flight, or ground handling characteristics of the aircraft.
3. Any change (alteration) of movable control surfaces that may adversely disturb the dynamic and static balance, alter the contour, or make any difference (plus or minus) in the weight distribution.
4. Change in control surface travel outside approved limits, control system mechanical advantage, location of control system component parts, or direction of motion of controls.
5. Changes in basic dimensions or external configuration of the aircraft, such as wing and tail platform or incidence angles, canopy, cowlings, contour or radii, or location of wing and tail fairings.
6. Changes to landing gear, such as internal parts of shock struts, length, geometry of members, or brakes and brake systems.
7. Any change to manifolding, engine cowling, and/or baffling that may adversely affect the flow of cooling air.
8. Changes to primary structure that may adversely affect strength or flutter and vibration characteristics or damage the tolerance design philosophy.
9. Changes to systems that may adversely affect aircraft airworthiness, such as:
   a. Relocation of exterior fuel vents
   b. Use of new type or different hydraulic components
   c. Tube material and fittings not previously approved
10. Changes to oil and fuel lines or systems that may adversely affect their operation, such as:
    a. New types of hose and/or hose fittings
    b. Changes in fuel dump valves
    c. New fuel cell sealant's
    d. New fuel or oil line materials
    e. New fuel or oil system components
11. Any change to the basic engine or propeller design controls, operating limitations, and/or unapproved changes to engine adjustments and settings having an affect on power output.
12. Changes in a fixed fire extinguisher or detector system that may adversely affect the system effectiveness or reliability, such as:
    a. Relocation of discharge nozzle or detector units
    b. Use of new or different detector components in new circuit arrangements
    c. Decreasing amount or different type of extinguishing agent
13. Changes that do not meet the minimum standards established in a Technical Standard Order (TSO) under which a particular aircraft component or appliance is manufactured.
14. Modifications to approved type (TSO) radio communications and navigational equipment that may adversely affect reliability or airworthiness, such as:
    a. Changes that deviate from the vacuum tube or semiconductor manufacturer's operating limitations
    b. Any changes to IF frequency
    c. Extension of receiver frequency range above or below the manufacturer's extreme design limits
    d. Major changes to the basic design of low approach aids
    e. Changes that deviate from the design environmental performance
15. Changes to aircraft structure or cabin interior of aircraft that may adversely affect evacuation of occupants in any manner.

Incorporation by Reference

The legal effect of incorporation by reference is that the material is treated as if it were published in full in the federal register.

- Some information is referred to in the rule, but not specifically written in the rule.
- Information incorporated by reference, like any other properly issued regulation, has the force of law.
- **Remember:** **The material is only made mandatory by the language of the regulation.**

Publications that may be incorporated by Reference

- Aircraft Specifications and TCDS
- STC's
- TSO's
- Flight Manuals
- Service Bulletins
- Advisory Circulars
- Airport Operations Manuals
- Airport Security Programs
- Air Carrier Security Programs
- Any Required Training Manuals

Record a Lien

You must send the original claim of lien with $5 (U.S. funds) to the Aircraft Registration Branch.

The lien must comply with the form and the requirements for recording claims of lien in the State having jurisdiction over the claim. Not all States record claims of liens. FAA may only record liens if the applicable State law provides for recording claims of liens.

The claim of lien must include, at minimum, the following:
- The amount of the claim
- A description of the aircraft by N-Number, manufacturer name, model designation, and serial number
- Dates on which labor, materials, or services were last furnished
- The ink signature of the claimant showing signer's title as appropriate
- A recording fee of $5 (U.S. funds) for each aircraft affected by the claim with a check or money order made payable to the Federal Aviation Administration

NOTE: You must mail the FAA aircraft registry your Claim of Lien

The FAA Will Do
Once we record the lien, we will return to you AC Form 8050-41, Conveyance Recordation Notice. This notice describes the aircraft, lists the parties and the date of the claim document, and shows the FAA recording number and date of recordation. You may use this form as a release if the claimant signs it and returns it to the Aircraft Registration Branch.

Another acceptable release of lien is a letter executed by the claimant, containing the same information, and a statement releasing all the claimant's rights and interest in the aircraft.

Reference the following web site:
http://www.faa.gov/licenses_certificates/aircraft_certification/aircraft_registry/record_aircraft_lien/

Phone Number: (405) 954-3116
Mailing Address:
FAA
Aircraft Registration Branch, AFS-750
PO Box 25504
Oklahoma City, OK 73125

Equivalent Tools

Repair stations, air carriers and mechanics **must** make a determination of acceptability for equivalency of special equipment and/or tools used in maintaining aircraft and their associated components. Part 43.13(b) states "Each person maintaining or altering, or performing preventive maintenance, shall do that work in such a manner and use materials of such a quality, that the condition of the aircraft, airframe, aircraft engine, propeller, or appliance worked on **will be at least equal to its original or properly altered condition** (with regard to aerodynamic function, structural strength, resistance to vibration and deterioration, and other qualities affecting airworthiness).

The term equivalency means recommended equivalent to that recommended by the Original Equipment Manufacture (OEM) for the purpose of performing specifics tests or making required measurements to determine the airworthiness of an article. To determine equivalency, you should compare the required test operations or specifications and the technical data of the special equipment or test apparatus may look different, be made of different materials, be a different color, etc. However, as long as the tool is functionally equivalent for the specific test application the tool may be used in most cases.

A finding of equivalency can only be made based on an evaluation of a technical data file. Additionally, demonstrating functionality of special equipment or test apparatus may sometimes be required. This file should also describe any special manufacturing processes that are used in the controlling processes, including gauges and recording equipment.

Some tools have been manufactured by a method known as reverse engineering. Reverse engineering alone without data; drawings, testing, or reports may not adequately produce a tool or fixture functionally equivalent to an OEM's requirements.

Most of the test apparatus used for making airworthiness decisions are generic in nature and designed to make measurements that are not unique to a specific manufacturer's product or process. Equipment that is not "special" in nature only needs to be designed and calibrated to make measurements with the specific manufacturer's tolerances to be considered equivalent for those tests or measurements.

With recent technological advances, highly specialized test equipment or test apparatus is frequently required. Use of such equipment supports the continued airworthiness of aircraft systems and components to the manufacturer's specifications and tolerances.

Determining the equivalency of equipment and/or apparatus is the primary responsibility of the repair station, air carrier, mechanic, and not the FAA. The basis of equivalency for equipment or apparatus for products being maintained must meet the manufacturer's standards and specifications for tolerances and accuracy.

An Aircraft Engineering Division AIR-100 memorandum dated December 21. 1999, states, "Designated Engineering Representatives (DER) <u>may not</u> approve or determine equivalency of tooling and test equipment." The FAA and DER may only make an Acceptance of functional equivalency for special equipment of functional equivalency for special equipment or test apparatus. It is important to emphasize that the burden of demonstrating equivalence is borne by the repair station, air carrier or mechanic and not the FAA.

Standard industry practice would dictate that any special equipment or test apparatus that is used to make a critical airworthiness decisions or that requires calibration or inspection be given a unique part number and serial number to identify it with the repair station, air carrier or mechanic inventory system.

Tools of the Trade

An A&P mechanic working in General Aviation should have at least the following basic special tools to work and inspect General Aviation aircraft.

	Tool of the Trade General Aviation	Required	Recommended
1	Torque wrenches with calibration certification		
2	Cable tension meter gage with calibration certification		
3	Multi meter, with calibration certification		
4	Magneto time box		
5	High tension ignition harness tester		
6	Wire crimpier tools and sets with calibration certification		
7	Propeller protractor		
8	Differential Pressure compression tester with master orifice and with calibration certification		
9	Spark plug gap tool		
10	Jacks aircraft		

Record Retention Requirement for CFR 91 Section 91.417(b)

Record Retention Requirements of CFR 91.417(b)

TYPE OF RECORD	LEGAL RETENTION	LOGICAL RETENTION
Routine servicing	Until repeated	30 days
Scheduled Inspections / routine maintenance	Until repeated or superseded / 1-year	3 to 5 years
Non-routine maintenance / pilot reported defects	1-year	3 to 5 years
Altimeter and transponder tests	2-years / repeated	2 years / repeated
Modifications & Alterations Form 337	Permanent	Permanent
Life-Limited parts	Until scrapped	Permanent
Airworthiness Directives	Permanent	Permanent
Total time in service of airframe, engines, rotor, and propellers	Permanent	Permanent
Total time in service of all components having specified overhaul period	Permanent	Permanent
Current inspection status and time since inspection	Current	1-year history
List of open or deferred defects	Until repaired	Until repaired

Data Plates

The data plate is permanently affixed to the aircraft fuselage by the manufacturer. However there are several other data plates many of which are on life limited or critical parts.

Removal of Data Plates. Section 45.13 permits persons performing maintenance operations under 14 CFR part 43, Maintenance, Preventive Maintenance, Rebuilding, and Alteration, to remove an aircraft data plate. The removal must be done in accordance with the methods, techniques, and practices acceptable to the Administrator. The ID plate removed may be reinstalled only on the product from which it was removed.

Replacement Data Plates. When FAA personnel receive inquiries regarding replacement, removal, or destruction of identification (ID) plates, the FAA will send a letter on the procedures to follow.

When a new ID plate is required, the owner or the owner's authorized representative contacts the appropriate certification office. The FAA determines whether the request is valid and provides a letter to the applicant with the FAA's finding. If the FAA determines that the request is valid, the applicant includes the FAA letter with his or her request for the replacement data plate from the appropriate manufacturer. Upon notification by the applicant, which must include the FAA's letter, the product manufacturer may then issue the replacement ID plate. The old ID plate, when available, must be voluntarily surrendered by the owner with a written statement to the FAA office that authorized the replacement. The FAA office must make a copy of the plate and then physically destroy it. The FAA office must then submit a letter to AFS-750 stating that the surrendered plate has been destroyed. AFS-750 will include the letter in the permanent aircraft records file.

New Data Plates. The appropriate FAA office (for example, FSDO, MIDO, or MISO) may authorize a builder of an aircraft authorized to be assembled from spare and/or surplus parts in accordance with Advisory Circular (AC) 21.13, Standard Airworthiness Certification of Surplus Military Aircraft and Aircraft Built From Spare Parts, to make a new data plate for that aircraft upon a satisfactory showing that the aircraft conforms to its type design and is in a condition for safe operation. The data plate will be made in accordance with part 45 and affixed to the aircraft prior to the issuance of any airworthiness certificate.

Aviation Safety Inspectors from both Flight Standards Service (AFS) and Aircraft Certification Service (AIR) are receiving requests to issue original or replacement standard airworthiness certificates for type-certificated rotorcraft. The Federal Aviation Administration (FAA) has recently identified several instances in which persons had installed data plates on rotorcraft that did not meet FAA type design. Although applications submitted to the FAA by these persons indicated that such rotorcraft met FAA type design, investigations conducted by the FAA and other government agencies have established that, in fact, they were military surplus aircraft sold to the public. These particular aircraft are potentially eligible for special, restricted category certification only.

Permanently marking or stamping aircraft parts, subparts, and material as "NOT SERVICEABLE." (Ink stamping is not an acceptable method).

Because of the harsh environments that wheels and brakes experience, decals or adhesive backed are not considered permanent forms of marking. Metal stamping, etching or permanently affixing a data plate with rivets or drive screws in a non-critical area is satisfactory. Laser marking is also acceptable if it can be read under 2X magnification. Ink stamping is allowed only if more permanent means are not possible.

Where the part is found by the FAA to be too small (or to have other characteristics that make it impractical) to mark all (or any) of the information on the part, the information not marked on the part should be put on the tag that is attached to the part or marked on the container for the part. If the number of certificated products or TSOA articles on which the part is eligible for installation is too long to be practicable to include with the part, the tag or container may refer to a readily available manual or catalog made available by the PMA holder for part eligibility information.

Manufacturers producing approved aircraft parts should maintain records of serial numbers for "retired" life-limited or other critical parts. In such cases, the owner who mutilates applicable parts is encouraged to provide the original manufacturer with the data plate and/or serial number and final disposition of the part.

References:
FAA Order 8130.2 as amended
FAA-H-8083-19 Plane Sense General Aviation Information
AC 23-17 Systems and Equipment Guide or Certification of Part 23 Airplanes
AC 21-38 Disposition of Unsalvageable Aircraft Parts and Materials

General Shop Practices

The purpose of this section to provide personnel engaged in the maintenance and repair of aerospace equipment information to aid in the selection and correct use of aerospace fasteners and parts and their installation. Because of the small size of most hardware items, their importance is often overlooked; however, the safe and efficient operation of any aerospace vehicles greatly dependent upon correct selection and use of aerospace hardware.

*** NOTE ***
If there is a conflict this handbook and the manuals for a particular aerospace vehicle subsequent manufacturers manuals will govern in all cases.

Many fasteners on aerospace vehicles are used either for a special purpose or were developed specifically the make and model and have no substitute. These parts may include quick release type fasteners, spring pins, stress panel fasteners, press nuts, and special latches. No substitutes may be listed for these fasteners. Fasteners selection and installation is potentially the most serious problem in design of aircraft structure if not done correctly. To preserve the integrity of the airframe, a complete inspection of the area where fasteners are added or replace is recommended. Look for nicks, scratches, and possible cracks, inspect the holes for radial and longitudinal flaws. Longitudinal flaws should be removed by polishing or reaming surfaces flaws should be polished smooth.

Predictable Fastener Problems

Many problems surface during the fasteners installation process, from preparing the hole to torquing the fastener. The following is a list of areas in which problems commonly occur:

a. **Fastener Installation:**
   - Automatic Mechanical Tools
   - With Hand-held Tools
   - By Untrained Mechanics

b. **Identification:**
   - For Strength Verification
   - For Approved Source of Supply

c. **Hole Preparation:**
   - Hand Held Portable Tool Alignment
   - Drivematics —Mechanical Tools for Feed and Speed Rates
   - By Untrained Mechanics

d. **Clamp-Up**
   - Torque Control
   - Grip Selection
   - Thread Protrusion

e. **Joint Reparation:**
   - Drilling an dreaming
   - Deburring, Cleaning, and Corrosion

f. **Wrenching:**
   - Elements and Size
   - Protection and Clearance

g. **Material:**
   - Corrosion Protection
   - Joint Material Compatibility

Cutting off Bolts and Re-Treading For Grip Change

Reworking bolts or screws by cutting off the end and re-threading in order to change the grip length is not acceptable. Adding thread to the cut-off bolt by had, either rolled or cut, cannot be done to a comparable quality or precision as was done by the manufacturer. Cracks commonly occur in the thread root due to stress concentration in sharp radii and as a result of cutting flaws, leading to failure in the fastener.

Over-heating the bolt during thread forming can cause loss of strength. Any bolt modification will void liability on the part of the manufacturer in case of failure.

Taper Shank Bolts

Taper shank bolts are part of a very special fastener system. They are used with a self-aligning washer and nut that protects the surface of the structure when the nut is tightened. When installed correctly this fastener system makes a very structurally sound joint. The fasteners are installed with controlled interference fit, and since the fastener shank and holes are tapered, this creates a preload in the material which will enhance the fatigue properties of the joint and also provide a very efficient means of transferring shear leads. Another favorable feature is that this system is fuel tight around the fasteners shanks when installed at fuel boundaries.

Installation of these fasteners demands special care and strict attention to the applicable installation specifications. Hole quality is paramount to a good installation. Each fastener must be check for correct fit before installation. Because of the care and control involved in the installation, these fasteners have been used only when necessary.

Removal of Installed Hi-Loc Pin Fasteners

In non-interference fit holes, Hi-Loks can be removed with common hand tools in a manner similar to removing a nut from a bolt. Use an Allen hex wrench to prevent the pin from rotating while the collar is being unscrewed with pliers. If not damaged curing collar removal, the Hi-Lok pin can be reused.

To more easily remove Hi-Lox collars from pins installed in interference fit holes and in limited access areas, the HLH128 series of hand tools are available in individual sizes or in sets as in HLK10 Hi-Lok/ Hi-Tigue Collar Removal Tool Kit. The Hi-Lok pin can be reused.

Light Drive Fit

A light-drive fie is defined as an interference fit of 0.0006 inch for 5/8-inch diameter bolts, or a proportionate amount of interference for other sized bolts. When drilling for a light-drive fit. Particular care must be taken to avoid elliptical, eccentric, or otherwise untrue holes. Although such untrue holes may permit the bolt to be driven according to interference requirements, they will not provide the necessary hole contact along the entire bolt grip length. A light-drive fit can be obtained in this manner:

1. Measure several bolts of the correct nominal size with micrometer. Segregate them into large, medium, and small groups according to the micrometer readings.
2. Drill the initial holes in the material approximately 1/32-inch undersized, then re-drill to 1/64-inch undersize.

Note
For holes ¾-inch or lager, the initial holes may be drilled 1/8-inch undersized instead of 1/32-inch

3. Select a reamer that is known to cut a hole that will give proper interference when using bolts in the small group. Ream one or two holes and try the fit of the small bolts in the reamed holes.

---

4. If the hole is too small it can be made lager by using a reamer of the same nominal size, yet one that is known to cut a hole very slightly larger.
5. If either of these first tow holes is too large for light-driven fits with the small bolts, use the medium or large group of boles to obtain light-driven fits.

Blind Fasteners

Blind fasteners are used when access to one side of the work is impractical. The type of blind fastener selected depends on location, material, and strength requirement. Any substitution of hardware requires approved data in accordance with CFR 21.303.

*** NOTE ***
Before you substitute any hardware contact you local Flight Standard District Office to obtain written approval before proceeding.

Keep in mind blind fasteners **SHALL NOT** be used for primary tension applications. Blind fasteners **SHALL NOT** be in any of the following:
a. Areas requiring a fluid tight seam.
b. Control systems, operating devices, or mechanism.
c. Primary structure fittings.
d. Any item or assembly that must be periodically removed.

If you have to replace a Hi-shear rivet with a Hi-shear blind bolt in most cases it can be, however contact a Designated Engineer Representative (DER) for assistance and approved data on FAA Form 8110-3.

Fasteners Identification Codes

A standard code number can identify each rivet. This code number represents style, material, diameter, and maximum grip length of each rivet.

* Military Standard—MS
* National Aerospace Standard—NAS
* Cherry Rivet—CR
* Olympic Rivet—RV
* Taper Loks—TL (TL Trade mark)

Sleeves for Oversized Holes

Fastener sleeves are to be used with standard size fasteners as an alternative method in the repair of oversize fastener holes. When an oversized fastener is not available and the original fastener can be used in an application (i.e., for interchangeable panels), the fastener sleeves may be used.

MIL-STD-85069, the Procurement Specification for fastener sleeves, is approved for use by all agencies of the Defense Department. The sleeves are made of thin-walled stainless steel construction and have that types that adapt to the various fasteners head styles. They are made in one-inch lengths and may be stacked to fill a hole longer than one inch; however, no segment shall be less than ¼-inch long. The sleeve is made with angular grooves every 1/16-inch along its length and also made straight with no groves. The more popular is the grooved sleeve, which can be broken off by the use of a simple tool to the desired grip length. The ungrooved sleeve must be sheared off with a special shearing tool. There are documented M-slash sheet for the different over sizes thicknesses and head styles. The basic part numbers are: NAS646-, NAS675-, NAS1436H and etc.

Remember these are approved for all Defense Department aerospace vehicles and may require a FAA Form 337 or FAA Form 8110-3 form a DER before installing. Contact your local FSDO for assistance.

Solid Rivets

Solid rivets are made to two standards AN and MS take note that MS20426 and MS20470 rivets of like dash numbers are interchangeable with AN426 and AN470 rivets respectively.

Cable Ties

Ty-Raps aid in the binding of harnesses, bundles, or groups of wires in a secure manner. Attach to ribs on the inside surface the TY-Rap in a tight position. They will not vibrate loose and can be applied anywhere.

Ty-Raps may be used in two ways:
1. As a cable tie-to-tie, lace, wrap, bundle, or harness groups of wires together.
2. As a cable strap to strap, clamp, or fasten wire harnesses to a supporting member or structure.

When used on the front of the firewall ty-raps become brittle and may break because of excessive hear. These may need to be changed at the 100-hour or annual inspection.

Safety Wire and Safety Wire Twisting

Safety wire is common in aircraft as an extra precaution to keep vital fastenters from loosening and parts falling off. Safety wire comes in several types depending on material used. In aviation different types of wire is used for different applications and is available in copper, brass, stainless steel, and galvanized or tinned steel. Safety wire also comes in diameters from 0.020 to 0.051 inches. Always follow the manufactures instructions for size and material to use. Be sure that the number of twists is tight and even, and the twisted wire between hardware is taut, but not over tight. The industry recommendation for twists per inch depends upon the diameter of the wire used as follows:

Wire diameter	Twists per inch
0.020-0.025	8-14
0.032-0.041	6-11
0.051-0.060	4-9

The safety wire should be as short as practicable and must be installed in such a manner that the pull on the wire is in the direction, which tightens.

A pigtail of 1/4 to 1/2 inch (three to six twists) should be made at the end of the wiring. This pigtail must be bent back or under to prevent it from becoming a snag.

The safety wire should always be installed and twisted so that the loop around the head stays down and does not tend to come up over the bolt head, causing a slack loop.

The standard part number for safety wire is MS20995.

List of Reference Materials and Subject Matter Knowledge Codes

The subject matter knowledge codes establish the specific reference for the knowledge standard. When reviewing results of your knowledge test, you should compare the subject matter knowledge code(s) on your Airman Test Report to the ones found below.

Title 14 of the Code of Federal Regulations

(14 CFR) Part 1-Definitions and Abbreviations

A01

General Definitions

A02

Abbreviations and Symbols

14 CFR Part 21-Certification Procedures for Products and Parts

A100

General

A102

Type Certificates

A104

Supplemental Type Certificates

A108

Airworthiness Certificates

A110

Approval of Materials, Parts, Processes, and Appliances

A112

Export Airworthiness Approvals

A117

Technical Standard Order Authorizations.

14 CFR Part 23-Airworthiness Standards: Normal, Utility, and Acrobatic Category Aircraft

A150

General

A151

Flight

A152

Structure

A153

Design and Construction

A154

Powerplant

A155

Equipment

A157

Operating Limitations and Information

14 CFR Part 27-Airworthiness Standards: Normal Category Rotorcraft

A250

General

A253

Flight

A255

Strength Requirements

A257

Design and Construction

A259

Powerplant

A261

Equipment

A263

Operating Limitations and Information

14 CFR Part 39-Airworthiness Directives

A13

General

A14

Airworthiness Directives

K12

AC 20-32, Carbon Monoxide (CO) Contamination
in Aircraft-Detection and Prevention

K13

AC 20-43, Aircraft Fuel Control

K20

AC 20-103, Aircraft Engine Crankshaft Failure

K45

AC 39-7, Airworthiness Directives

K46

AC 43-9, Maintenance Records

K47

AC 43.9-1, Instructions for Completion of FAA
Form 337

K48

AC 43-11, Reciprocating Engine Overhaul
Terminology and Standards

K49

AC 43.13-1, Acceptable Methods, Techniques, and
Practices-Aircraft Inspection and Repair

K50

AC 43.13-2, Acceptable Methods, Techniques, and
Practices-Aircraft Alterations

L25

FAA-G-8082-11, Inspection Authorization
Knowledge Test Guide

L70

AC 91-67, Minimum Equipment Requirements for
General Aviation Operations Under CFR Part 91

M02

AC 120-27, Aircraft Weight and Balance Control

M52

AC 00-2, Advisory Circular Checklist

Type Certificate Data Sheets and Specifications

Y300

**Type Certificate Data Sheets and
Specifications Alphabetical Index and Users
Guide**

Y301

Type Certificate Data Sheet No. 2A13 Piper

Y302

Type Certificate Data Sheet No. 3A19 Cessna

Y303

Type Certificate Data Sheet No. E-295 Lycoming

Y304

Type Certificate Data Sheet No. A7CE Cessna

Y305

Type Certificate Data Sheet No. 3A13 Cessna

Y306

Type Certificate Data Sheet No. A7S0 Piper

Y307

Type Certificate Data Sheet No. A11EA
Gulfstream American

Y308

Type Certificate Data Sheet No. E-273
Continental

Y309

Aircraft Specification No. 1A6 Piper

Y310

Type Certificate Data Sheet No. P57GL McCauley

Y311

Type Certificate Data Sheet No. P920 Hartzell

Y312

Type Certificate Data Sheet No. 2A4 Twin
Commander

Y313

Chapter 4
Frequently Asked Questions and Answers

Questions and Answers
General A&P/IA

<u>Definition</u> of <u>the</u> <u>Term</u> <u>"Airworthy"</u>

1) The aircraft must conform to its type certificate. **Part 21.41.**
   a. When aircraft configuration and the components installed are consistent with drawings, specifications, and other data that are part of the type certificate (T/C), and include any supplemental T/C and field approval alterations incorporated into the aircraft.
2) The aircraft must be in condition for safe operation. **Part 43.15.**
   a. Aircraft relative to wear and deterioration i.e., corrosion, fluid leaks, tire wear, window delimitation/crazing.

*** NOTE ***
If one or both of these conditions are not met, the aircraft would be considered unairworthy. **Order 8130.2**

---

1. What is the definition of maintenance?

Maintenance means the preservation, inspection, overhaul, and repair of aircraft, including the replacement of parts. A PROPERLY MAINTAINED AIRCRAFT IS A SAFE AIRCRAFT. The purpose of maintenance is to ensure that the aircraft remains airworthy throughout its operational life. After a mechanic performs maintenance a properly certificated maintenance person must approve the aircraft for return to service. **Reference CFR 1.1.**

2. What is Preventive Maintenance?

The term preventive maintenance refers to simple or minor preservation operations and/or the replacement of small standard parts not involving complex assembly. CFR Part 43, Appendix A(c), contains a list of preventive maintenance items. Qualified mechanics or certificated pilots may accomplish preventive maintenance and approve the aircraft for return to service. **Reference CFR 1.1**.

3. Can I use my A&P/IA outside of the district I am based?

Yes. However when operating away from the district office having geographic responsibility, the IA holder **should** notify the district office in the area where the work will be performed, before exercising

---

the authorization. The IA holder **should** submit FAA Form 337 to the local office where the work was performed. **Reference CFR 65.95.**

4. **Can an A&P/IA have more than one fixed base of operation?**

No. An IA holder who changes the fixed base of operation may not exercise the privilege of the authorization before notifying the district office or international field office for the area where the new base is located. This notification **must be** in writing. **Part 65.91(c).**

5. **How long is the Inspection Authorization (IA) good for?**

An IA expires March 31, of every other year and ceases to be effective whenever either of the following occur:

   a. The authorization is surrendered, suspended, or revoked. When this occurs, the inspector shall request the holder to return the authorization, FAA Form 8310-5.
   b. A holder fails to meet the renewal requirements of **Part 65. Sec 65.91**.

On January 30, 2007 the FAA placed an amendment to Title 14 of the Code of Federal Regulations (14 CFR) part 65, §§ 65.92 and 65.93, in the Federal Register, Volume 72, No. 19. The amendment becomes effective on March 1, 2007. This amendment changes the duration of the IA from 1 year to 2 years and places the IA renewal on March 31 of an odd-numbered year (i.e., 2009, 2011, etc . . .). It also changes the renewal and currency requirements to keep the IA in effect during the even-numbered years.

6. **I missed the dead line of March 31 to renew do I have to retest?**

Yes. Sorry, you will have to start the process all over again and retake the IA certification written test. **CFR65, Section 65.93**.

7. **If my A&P is suspended during the year and I hold an IA certificate can I renew my IA in March?**

NO you cannot. If your A&P certificate was suspended you no longer meet the requirements of **Part 65, Section 65.91** and will have to wait for three years to be eligible to apply again to test.

8. **If an IA changed their base of operation do they have to notify anyone?**

Yes. When the base of operation changes for an IA holder, the Flight Standards District Office (FSDO) for the area of the new base must be notified **in writing** before the holder can again exercise the privileges of the authorization.

9. **If I receive my original IA in February do I have to reapply by March 31 to retain the certification?**

No. An IA issued less than 90 days before the expiration date need not comply with **Section 65.93(a)(1) through (5)** for that quarter for the first year. If an ASI issues an IA fewer than 90 days before March 31 of an even-numbered year, the applicant does not have to meet activity requirements for that 90-day period in order to renew the IA.

10. If I work at a repair station can I count those aircraft I work on toward my IA renewal?

Yes and No. When the applicant is employed by a repair station, credit for renewal activity can be claimed only for those aircraft that the authorization holder **personally inspected**. Evidence supporting the activity should be presented in addition to the signed application.

11. Does an aircraft have to be in a certain configuration during an inspection?

Yes. The aircraft should conform to the aircraft specification or type certificate data sheet, any changes by supplemental type certificates and/or it's properly altered condition. When the aircraft does not conform, use the procedures for "unairworthy" items listed in **14 CFR Part 43, section 43.11 (a)(5).**

12. Alterations to the product may have changed some of the operating limitations. Unrecorded alterations or repairs may have been made in the past and warrant one of the following:

1. Contact owner for pertinent information.
2. If approved data is available, conduct inspection and personally approve for return to service by completing FAA Form 337 info.
3. Contact local ASI for assistance.

13. The aircraft specification or type certificate data sheet indicates when a flight manual is required. It also identifies limitations, which must be displayed in the form of markings and placards.

Unlike the specifications, type certificate data sheets do not contain a list of equipment approved for a particular aircraft. The list of required and optional equipment can be found in the equipment list furnished by the manufacturer of the aircraft. Sometimes a later issue of the list is needed to cover recently approved items. Serial number eligibility should always be considered.

14. Does an A&P/IA have to use a condition checklist?

Yes. The holder of an IA may use the checklist in 14 CFR Part43 (appendix D), the manufacturer's inspection sheets, or a checklist designed by the holder of an IA, that includes the scope and detail of the items listed in appendix D, to check the condition of the entire aircraft. This includes checks of the various systems listed in **14 CFR Part 43, section 43.15.**

15. Is routine servicing part of the 100-hour or annual inspection?

No. Routine servicing is **NOT** a part of the annual inspection. The inspection itself is essentially a visual evaluation of the condition of the aircraft and its components and certain operational checks. The manufacturer may recommend certain services to be performed at various operating intervals. These can often be done conveniently during an annual inspection, and in fact should be done, but are not considered to be a part of the inspection itself. **CFR 43.11** inspection only.

16. Are there any other manual of guides an A&P/IA should use for and 100-hour or annual inspection?

Yes. It is very important that the holder of an IA be familiar with the manufacturer's service manuals, bulletins, and letters for the product being inspected. Use these publications to avoid overlooking problem areas. AC 43-16, Aviation Maintenance Alerts, is also an important source of service experience. The articles for the alerts are taken from selected service difficulties reported to the FAA on FAA Form 8010-4, Malfunction or Defect Reports. Monthly copies of the alerts are provided on the Internet at the following addresses: http://www.mmac.jccbi.gov/afs/afs600 or http://fedworld.gov/pub/faa-asi. Comments may be sent by letter, with name and address typed or legibly printed to the Federal Aviation Administration, Designee Standardization Branch, AFS-640, P.O. Box 25082, Oklahoma City, OK 73125.

17. Is the A&P/IA responsible for the record entries of the AD's?

Yes and No. During an **inspection** you are required to perform a record and AD check. Remember you are only required to do an inspection. If the owner wants you to perform the AD now you become responsible to comply with the required record entry after completion. A statement in the records such as "Record compliance with all AD's actually accomplished" may not provide sufficient information for the owner to comply with **14 CFR Part 91, section 91.417(a)(2)(v).** A general statement, such as "All AD's complied with" is NOT an adequate entry and should be avoided. Many owners keep a separate record of AD compliance in the back of the logbook or in a section specifically provided for this record. This is a good place to identify the AD's of a recurring nature and show when the next compliance is required. **Reference CFR 43.11.**

18. Previous AD's signed off. Does an A&P/IA have to accomplish all the AD's at each inspection?

No. If the maintenance records indicate compliance with an AD, the holder of an IA should make a reasonable attempt to verify the compliance. It is not uncommon for a component to have compliance with an AD accomplished and properly recorded then later be replaced by another component on which the AD has not been accomplished. The holder of an IA is not expected to disassemble major components such as cylinders, crankcases, etc., if adequate records of compliance exist.

When the maintenance records **DO NOT** contain indications of AD compliance, the holder of an IA should:

1. Make the AD an item on a discrepancy list provided to the owner, in accordance with **14 CFR Part 43, section 43.11(b)**.
2. With the owner's concurrence, do whatever disassembly is required to determine the status of compliance; or
3. Obtain concurrence of the owner to comply with the AD.

19. Is the A&P/IA responsible for all required inspections?

No. Remind the owners or operators that they are responsible for operational requirements, such as:

1. VOR equipment checked in accordance with **14 CFR Part 91, section 91.171**.
2. Altimeter and altitude reporting equipment test and inspections in accordance with **14 CFR Part 91, section 91.411**.
3. ATC transponder inspection in accordance with **14 CFR Part 91, section 91.413**. These tests and inspections are not part of the annual inspection.

20. How long is the annual inspection good for?

Only until the ink dries on the paper!!!

The aircraft may not be operated unless the annual inspection has been performed within the preceding 12 calendar months. A period of 12 calendar months extends from any day of a month to the last day of the same month the following year. However, an aircraft with the annual inspection overdue may be operated under a special flight permit issued by the FAA for the purpose of flying the aircraft to a location where the annual inspection can be performed.

CFR Part 91 section 91.409 Inspections. (a) Except as provided in paragraph (c) of this section, no person may operate an aircraft unless, within the preceding 12 calendar months. What this means is if the annual was completed on November 1, 2003 the next annual is due by the end of the month November 30, 2004, remember (preceding 12 calendar month).

21. Are A&P/IA's held responsible for previous inspections completed by another IA?

No. CFR Part 91 section 91.417(b) The owner or operator shall retain the following records for the periods prescribed: The records specified in paragraph 91.417(a)(1) of this section shall be retained until the work is repeated or superseded by other work or for 1 year after the work is performed. You are not labile for someone missing something it is your responsible to inspect and look for items that may not of been accomplished. You will be held liable if you don't find them on your inspection. Such items could be improper repairs, improper alterations, AD signed off and not accomplished.

22. Airworthiness and registration certificates. Is the airworthiness and registration certificates part of the inspection?

No. They are **operational rules** under **CFR 91 Section 91.203** Civil Aircraft: Certifications required. No person may operate a civil aircraft unless it has within it the following: An appropriate and current airworthiness certificate or an authorization under section 91.611 must have on it the registration number assigned to the aircraft under Part 47 of this chapter. However, if you notice them missing you should note it on your discrepancy list and provide it to the owner.

23. Does a current 100-hour or annual inspection mean that the aircraft is in "first class" condition?

No. It indicates only that the aircraft was found to be in airworthy condition at the time of inspection. **CFR 43, Section 43.15**.

24. Does the 100-hour or annual inspection require the IA to inspect for the AFM/POH or flight manual?

Yes. In most cases the placards are in the flight manual or listed on the TCDS. Some, but not all TCDS will have the most current AFM/POH listed and its revision date. Certain parts of the manual are FAA approved and without the current manual an IA cannot check everything that must be checked. The aircraft specification or type certificate data sheet indicates when a flight manual is required. It also identifies limitations, which must be displayed in the form of markings and placards. If the AFM/POH is out of date the placards in these manuals may not be current. Reference CFR Part 91, section 91.7, 43.13, and **23.1581**.

So be advised not all aircraft will have a flight manual, but have placards and specifications. Make sure and check the TCDS. On aircraft for which no approved flight manual is required, the operating limitations prescribed during original certification, and as required by 14 CFR Part 91, section 91.9, must be carried in or be affixed to the aircraft. Range markings on the instruments, placards, and listings are required to be worded and located as specified in the type certificate data sheet.

Reading CFR 91.9 says the aircraft must have an AFM/POH but **CFR 21 Section 21.5** says this is only required only for aircraft certified after 1979.

25. **What should I do when performing a 100-hour or annual inspection and cannot find the flight manual?**

On aircraft for which no approved flight manual is required, the operating limitations prescribed during original certification, and as required by 14 CFR Part 91, section 91.9, **must be** carried in or be affixed to the aircraft. Range markings on the instruments, placards, and listings are required to be worded and located as specified in the type certificate data sheet. If the aircraft has an AFM/POH it is required during the inspection in accordance with **CFR 23 Section 23.1581**.

26. **What AC's, CFR's and FAA guides should an IA have?**

    1. AC 43.13.1 and 2A as applicable.
    2. AC 43.9, AC 43.9-1, AC 39.7, AC 91.67, AC 43.11, AC 00.55 current revision.
    3. FAA-G-8082-11.
    4. CFR Parts 1, 21, 23, 27, 33, 35, 39, 43, 45, 47, 65, 91, 135 and 183.

27. **What responsibility does an A&P/IA have for operational requirements during an inspection?**

None. Remind the owners or operators that they are responsible for operational requirements, such as:

    a. VOR equipment checked in accordance with **14 CFR Part 91, section 91.171**.
    b. Altimeter and altitude reporting equipment test and inspections in accordance with **14 CFR Part 91, section 91.411**.
    c. ATC transponder inspection in accordance with **14 CFR Par t91, section 91.413**.

These tests and inspections are not part of the annual inspection.

28. **If you are performing a 100-hour or annual inspection are you responsible for major repairs or alteration done improperly?**

Yes. If you have found a major alteration or a major repair to be non-conforming with FAA-approved data you should review the FAA Form 337. All operating limitations affected by an alteration should be appropriately revised. Sometimes limitations are in the form of flight manual supplements, instrument range markings, placards, or combinations of these. You may have to remove the alteration or repair and re-accomplish it to sign off the aircraft as airworthy. Always notify the owner the aircraft is unairworthy until repairs can be made. Reference **CFR 43, Section 43.15**.

29. During a 100-hour or annual inspection does all the discrepancies have to be cleared by a mechanic?

No. A person who is authorized by 14 CFR Part 43.3 to do the work can clear the discrepancies. Preventive maintenance items could be cleared by a pilot who owns or operates the aircraft, provided the aircraft is not used under 14 CFR Parts 121, 127, 129, or 135; except that approval may be granted to allow a pilot operating a rotorcraft in a remote area under 14 CFR Part 135 to perform preventive maintenance.

30. What if I do not complete a 100-hour or annual inspection how do I sign it off?

If an inspection is not completed, the holder of an IA should:

1. Indicate any discrepancies found in the aircraft records.
2. **NOT** indicate that a 100-hour or annual inspection was conducted.
3. Indicate the extent of the inspection and all work accomplished in the aircraft records. **14 CFR 43, Section 43.9.**

31. Can the owner assist in performing the 100-hour or annual inspection?

No. The inspection cannot be delegated. The owner should be made aware that the inspection does not include correction of discrepancies or unairworthy items and that such maintenance will be additional to the inspection. Maintenance and repairs may be accomplished simultaneously with the inspection by a person authorized to perform maintenance if agreed on by the owner and holder of the IA. This method would result in an aircraft that is approved for return to service with the completion of the inspection.

Remember to document all repairs and maintenance prior to signing off the 100-hour or annual inspections. All persons who assisted in performing maintenance their names should also be in the spelled out in the maintenance entry as referenced in **CFR 43.9.**

32. An Airworthiness Directive required that a propeller be altered. Can a certificated mechanic perform this task?

Yes. A certificated mechanic could perform and approve the work for return to service if it is a **MINOR** alteration. **Reference CFR 1.1.**

33. Where are the required placards on aircraft found?

By checking the Aircraft Specification or Type Certificate Data Sheet. All are in the AFM/POH this is why they are required during inspections. **Reference CFR 23.1559.**

34. Maintenance Record Entries for Repair Stations. Are repair stations required to provide copies of work orders in addition to meeting the requirements of CFR 43.9 on serviceable parts tags? What does it take to meet the requirements of CFR 43.9? Are the terms "overhauled or rebuilt" sufficient to describe the work accomplished? (Overhaul and rebuilt as defined in CFR 43.2)

Repair stations are required to meet the requirements of CFR 43.9, which includes a description of the work performed. The requirements of Appendix B to CFR Part 43 must also be met when recording major repairs and major alterations. Repair stations often use a "yellow tag" as a maintenance release, and refer to a work order on file at the repair station. References to work orders by number only, or the term overhaul which has different meaning thru industry, does not satisfy the requirements of CFR 43.9(a)(1). The entry must say exactly what you did: what parts were replaced, service bulletins (S.B.) compliance, etc. Attachment of work orders, which list this data, will meet the requirements.

35. When do I need an Experimental Certificate?

Aircraft is going though modification, which will require flight-testing before final FAA approval, and then it will require an Experimental Certificate. Once the modification is FAA approved the Manufacturing Inspection District Office can return the aircraft back to "Standard" airworthiness certificate.

36. As a certificated A&P/IA can I be held liable for missing something on an experimental aircraft condition inspection?

Yes you can. Experimental aircraft are issued a Special Airworthiness certificate and are maintained to the standards outlined on their operational limitations. In most cases the required Condition Inspection follows **Part 43 Appendix D** requirements. To meet the intent of Part 21, Section 21.191 and to be eligible for an experimental airworthiness certificate the aircraft had to comply with acceptable aeronautical standards and practices. The Condition Inspection is the same as an Annual inspection as CFR as what is required to be inspected. The only difference is using the term "airworthy condition" for type certificated aircraft and Condition for safe operation for experimental aircraft.

Since you are certificated you are still held to **Part 43.15 and Part 65** requirements.

37. Are Experimental aircraft required to submit FAA Form 337's for major repair or alterations?

No. This requirement is for only type-certificated aircraft in accordance with **CFR 43, Section 43.1.**

38. What if I disagree with the FAA Inspector on what is considered a Major or Minor repair what should I do?

The person making the repair or alteration is primary responsible for making the determination major/minor. The FAA will follow the guidance in FAA Handbook Order 8900.1 Vol. 4, Chapter 9 and **CFR 1.1**. Contact the ASI supervisor and request an evaluation.

39. The aircraft I am inspecting has a fuel or oil leak and I cannot find any limitations in the service manual is it okay to return to service?

To make this clear there should be NO fuel leaks!!! However there are limits in some maintenance manuals. If the manuals **do not** call out how much leakage is allow then none is allowed. **CFR 43, Section 43.13.**

40. Part 43 Appendix D states check all systems for improper installation, poor general condition, apparent and obvious defects, and insecurity of attachment. What does this really mean?

Let's break this down some. Improper installation means does the radio fit the rack, is it held on with plastic tie strips, or is duck tape holding something on? Not good! Second poor general condition, this many times will be a judgment call. Say if the seat belt is fraying, the general condition would bad or several of the plastic interior moldings are cracked or missing the general condition is said to be poor. Obvious defects are things like holes in seat cushions, screws missing from cowling, rust on hardware.

And lastly insecurity of attachment pretty straightforward is the fasteners missing from cowlings, fairings, interior moldings, nose gear shimmy, wires hanging out from under the instrument panel.

41. Where is the latest revision to individual pages in type certificate data sheets indicated?

By a dash number following the type certificate data sheet number in the heading block of page 1. It is a recommendation only to list he latest T/C revision during the inspection.

42. Can the FAA Inspector require an IA perform a reexamination to hold there certificates and why?

The reconsideration of an airman's competence is a serious issue and requires that there be ample cause. In most cases, a reexamination will follow the investigation of an accident or incident apparently caused by the airman's incompetence. The aviation safety inspector (ASI) will determine whether a reexamination test is necessary based on personal knowledge, reliable reports, or evidence obtained through an accident, incident, or enforcement investigation. Reference **Order 2150.3 Chapter 8** Under **Section 609** of the Federal Aviation Act of 1958, as amended (FA Act), the Administrator is authorized to re-inspect any aircraft, aircraft engine, propeller, appliance, air navigation facility or air agency, and to reexamine any airman.

43. Can an A&P/IA place a lien on an aircraft?

Yes. There are generally two types of liens possessory and non-possessory. General Aviation Possessory Liens usually require that in addition to having a written agreement for the work to be performed, the service provider must retain possession of the aircraft for the lien to be effective. The aircraft may be sold to pay the bill if the customer does not fulfill his or her responsibilities. General aviation non-possessory liens may include a requirement that the written agreement be recorded with the Federal Aviation Administration Aircraft Registry, which will then give the service provider a statutory right to recover for repairs performed.

44. Is a "Yellow Tag" a proper return to service for a part?

Yes and No. The yellow tag attached to the product will be acceptable only if it has a maintenance release statement in accordance **Part 43.9**, dated, signed, certificate number and statement of work performed. If the yellow tag does not have this statement is means nothing and cannot be used for return to service.

45. During a 100-hour or annual inspection is the inspector required to have and check all the work orders if called out in the maintenance records?

Yes and No. All work orders should be kept by the owner/operator, as it is the history of work/ maintenance performed on their aircraft. Many times AD's may be listed as complied with on a work order and now the work order becomes part of the permanent maintenance records. Without the work order you may have to re-accomplish an inspection to show compliance.

46. After a major repair or alteration that may change the flight characteristics of an aircraft, other than an maintenance record entry required by Part 43.9, what must be entered in the aircraft records and by who?

A record of a flight test is required. If you re-rig the ailerons or any primary flight control the operator is now required to make an approved for return to service statement in the permanent maintenance records after the flight test. Without the flight test statement the aircraft has not been approved for return to service. Think of liability here if you do not notify the operator of the required flight test. You have a duty to warn the operator and I would write this in the aircraft maintenance record so there is no misunderstanding of what is required. **Reference CFR 91, Section 91.407.**

The law of **negligence** imposes a **duty of care** upon a person to take reasonable care to avoid causing foreseeable harm to another person or their property.

47. **Can FAA Airframe and Powerplant mechanics sign a maintenance release for a Canadian aircraft?**

YES, in accordance with **Part 43 Section 43.17**. This could be someone who holds a foreign license, which is deemed to be equivalent to that required to exercise maintenance release privilege for the Canadian registered aircraft. An example would be a Canadian aircraft requiring an annual inspection, where a Canadian AME isn't available to certify the work. However the FAA does Bilateral Agreements with most countries, but not all.

48. **An aircraft I have worked on has an accident can I be held responsible?**

Maybe. This is why you should make a maintenance record entry that states **"only for the work performed"** and explain only what maintenance you performed and provide a reference to the data you used in accordance with **CFR 43, Section 43.9.**

Limitation of Liability for General Aviation

While the Warsaw Convention and Federal Aviation Act rules limiting liability do not apply to general aviators, some states, such as South Dakota and Illinois have Guest Statutes, which limit the liability of a private plane owner. Guest statutes require that a plaintiff who suffers injuries while a guest on an owner's plane show wanton or willful conduct resulted in the plaintiff's injury. This standard represents a higher hurdle for a plaintiff than mere negligence. Wanton and willful conduct includes actions that purposefully caused an accident, as well as action that appeared so likely to cause the accident that any reasonable person would not have acted in that manner. In order for a Guest Statute to operate to protect an owner of a plane, the owner must show that he or she allowed the plaintiff to ride in the plane without charging CFRs, and that the accident did not result from purposeful or grossly irresponsible behavior. Furthermore, the plaintiff must have incurred his or her injury while a passenger on the owner's plane.

The law treats a general aviator much like the operator of a motor vehicle, requiring that the pilot use reasonable care to prevent accident or injury. Even in cases where a general aviator agrees to carry a CFRs-paying passenger, only the ordinary rules of negligence and due care applies with respect to the maintenance and inspection of the aircraft. Like the standard for commercial pilots, the pilot of a private aircraft must still comport with the standards of care and expertise of the average, qualified pilot in the operation of the plane.

There are many types of aviation accident legal claims many revolve around pilot error, manufacture and maintenance, or unsafe flying/weather conditions. Victims' families and survivors may file an aviation accident legal claim revolving around one or more of the following causes:

1. Defective Onboard Computers or Software
2. Fuel Tank Explosions
3. Poorly Maintained Equipment
4. Pilot Error

You can bet if an accident occurs you may be named in a lawsuit even if you did nothing to cause the accident. I would suggest you contact an aviation lawyer for legal assistance in matters that involve accidents where you are being sued.

Statute of Limitations

A statute of limitations requires a plaintiff to file suit within a certain number of years after the accident that caused the plaintiff's injuries. The length of the statute of limitations varies depending upon the state in which the plaintiff files the suit and the nature of the claim filed. In some cases, the statute of limitations can be as short as two years.

If you believe that you might have incurred injuries as the result of an aviation accident, you should contact a qualified attorney immediately to ensure that your claim is properly handled prior to the expiration of the statute of limitations.

49. What Happens After A Plane Crashes?

Most of the time, after a plane crashes, the airline's insurance company will contact survivors or the families of victims. The insurer may offer a settlement for your loss and your pain and suffering. They may also offer what is called a "cash advance" to help defray some of the costs you may be faced with as a result of the accident.

DON'T ACCEPT ANY OFFERS AND DON'T SIGN ANYTHING BEFORE YOU SPEAK TO AN ATTORNEY.

Immediately contact an attorney who handles plane crashes to review these documents. They may not be in your best interest and they may limit or jeopardize your legal rights. Accepting a settlement from the insurer will entail that you sign a document waiving your rights to any further action against the insurer or other parties involved in the cause of the accident.

Statutes of limitation restrict the amount of time a person has to file a claim. Because you are dealing with a complex area of the law involving state law and federal laws, you need to contact and experienced attorney immediately if you or a loved one has suffered injury or loss as a result to an aviation accident.

The Federal Aviation Act dictates the technical safety standards for aircraft operated in the United States. The Act does not, however, create a cause of action for plaintiffs injured as the result of a defendant's failure to meet those safety standards. A plaintiff must find a cause of action, therefore, in the individual states' laws. The causes of action that might exist as the result of an aviation accident depend upon the nature of the accident. In cases where controlled flight into terrain, approach and landing, loss of control, runway incursions, or weather (including turbulence) caused the accident, a claim of negligence against the airline and the pilots might exist. Such negligence claims include personal injury claims, injury to property claims, and wrongful death claims. In those cases, a plaintiff would need to establish that the pilot failed to act in a manner comporting with the skill of the average commercial pilot. If the plaintiff fails to establish that the average commercial pilot should have avoided the accident then a court will not find the airline liable.

In a personal injury or injury to property case, the plaintiff must show that the air carrier, or one of its employees acted negligently, and that as a result, the plaintiff incurred injury to him or herself or to his or her property. In injury to property claims, the jury can award a plaintiff damages in the amount of repairing or replacing the damaged property. In personal injury claims, the jury can award a plaintiff damages for pain and suffering, medical expenses, lost wages, both past and future, and inconvenience as a result of bodily injury.

Wrongful death claims have certain requirements that differ from personal injury claims. The individual suing for wrongful death must have a relationship to the decedent on whose behalf the suit is being brought. In some states only parents, children, spouses or executors of the decedent's estate may bring a wrongful death claim. As part of such a claim, the plaintiff must show that the decedent's death resulted from the negligent, wanton or willful actions of the defendant air carrier. In such cases, if the death occurred instantaneously, the jury can award the plaintiff from loss of consortium, lost wages, loss of future income or earning capacity. In cases where death does not occur instantaneously, and the plaintiff can prove the decedent's conscious suffering, the jury can also award damages for pain and suffering, bodily mutilation, and mental anguish.

In a case in which mechanical failure contributed to the accident, the plaintiff may have to establish that the **pilot's negligence** contributed to the accident or that a **mechanic negligently** failed to detect or properly repair a component of the plane. In such cases, the plaintiff can maintain a lawsuit against the common air carrier or the owner of the private plane. A few states may also allow an action for breach of implied warranty of a plane's airworthiness in such a case; however, many states do not allow an implied breach of warranty to support a wrongful death suit.

Where a mechanical failure results from a defect in the design or construction of an airplane or a component of the airplane, the plaintiff may establish a products liability claim against the manufacturer of the component or the airplane. In a products liability claim based on defective construction or manufacturing, the plaintiff must establish that the manufacturer of the component that caused the accident failed to detect a defect in the particular component that was used in the airplane that had the accident.

Products liability based on the premise that the design of the particular component was defective represents a unique hurdle for a plaintiff, in that the plaintiff must establish that the manufacturer could have used a reasonable, alternative design that would have prevented the injury. A plaintiff might incur great expense in pursuing a products liability case based on defective design. In order to establish a reasonable, alternative design the plaintiff will likely have to hire an engineer or other expert to critique the manufacturer's design and to suggest the alternative design. A products liability case faces a better chance for success if prior cases have already established that the design of the component is defective.

50. **Am I required to have my A&P/IA certificates on my person at all times?**

NO. However they have to be in the immediate area where you normally exercises your privileges of the certificate and SHALL present for inspection. **CFR 65, Section 65.89**.

51. **What is an Experimental Certificate?**

In order to legally operate an aircraft, it must have a current airworthiness certificate. Airworthiness certificates come in different classifications depending on the purpose of operation and the qualification of the aircraft. The Standard Airworthiness Certificates are issued to type-certificated aircraft; and

Special Airworthiness Certificates for aircraft that does not meet all the requirements of the Standard Airworthiness Certificate.

Special Airworthiness Certificates are "primary", "restricted", "limited", and "provisional" Airworthiness Certificates, "special flight permits" and "Experimental Certificates".

An Experimental Certificate is issued for the purpose of research and development, showing compliance with regulations, crew training, or market surveys, exhibition and air racing, operating amateur-built aircraft, and operating kit-built aircraft.

Federal Aviation Regulation §21.175 and subsequent speaks of Airworthiness Certificates and Experimental Certificate.
(The link to 14 CFR §21.175 can be found at the FAA website **http://www.faa.gov/ regulations_policies/**

52. **What will an FAA Inspector be inspecting with regards to a mechanic?**

The basic objective of Aviation Safety Inspectors (ASIs) surveillance of Airframe and Powerplant mechanics is to promote aviation safety by ensuring compliance with applicable Federal Aviation Regulations. Components of such surveillance include the following:

    a. Observation of airmen performing or supervising maintenance.
    b. Evaluation of airmen having completed maintenance.
    c. Review of maintenance records to determine compliance with the regulations.

The mechanic must be proficient in using various types of mechanical and visual inspection aids appropriate for the article being inspected, so the ASI will inspect to:

    i. Determine if the ratings are appropriate to the work performed. Ensure that the mechanic does not exceed the privileges and limitations of the certificate **part 65.81**.
    ii. Question the mechanic to ensure understanding of the manufacturer/maintenance manual(s) for the specific operation concerned **part 43.13.**
    iii. Determine if the mechanic meets the requirements for recent experience **part 61.83**.
    iv. Ensure that the airman certificate is within the immediate area where the airman normally exercises the privileges of the certificate **part 65.89**.

In some cases it may be appropriate to request an A&P give a demonstration he has the following available:

    a. A current and appropriate set of Airworthiness Directives (AD's).
    b. A current and appropriate set of type certificate data sheets.
    c. Current and appropriate Federal Aviation Regulations.
    d. Manufacturers' maintenance instructions, as required by CFR Part 43.
    e. Other data as needed. Recommended data may include maintenance alerts, service difficulty reports, etc.

The A&P has shown by experience as a journeyman that he understands:

    a. The inspection methods.
    b. The inspection techniques.

c. The equipment used in determining the air-worthiness of the article.

53. What should I do if a dispute comes up of the cost of the annual after the inspection?

One of the best insurance policies I know is **DO NOT** sign off the inspection until the owner provides you with payment. If the owner pays you in accordance with the work order or receipt they accept the cost of doing business.

If you do not have a written contract with the owner stating when and how to be paid for services you have made a fatal mistake. And your only course may be one in civil court. You can place a lien against the aircraft, but you may never get paid until he aircraft sells.

Once you have selected to perform an annual inspection your next step is to write a contract outlining exactly what the mechanic duties will be and what owner expects. This contract should include the complete aircraft maintenance records check, airworthiness directives (AD) compliance list with all AD's complied with, service bulletins complied with, major/minor repairs or alteration performed, service difficulty reports, engine borescope inspection, oil analysis, and a complete list of unairworthy items found during the aircraft inspection. You need to include who and how parts will be provided to make repairs.

The FAA **CAN NOT** help you in this matter.

54. Aircraft markings whom is responsible for them?

It is the *owner or operator's responsibility* to have the nationality and registration markings properly displayed on the aircraft **(14 CFR Part 91, section 91.9(c))**. The holder of an IA can, and should, offer advisory service to owners and operators in regard to any deficiencies in markings; however, such deficiencies are not cause to report an aircraft in "unairworthy" condition. However, placards are limitations and are required these should be brought to the attention of the aircraft owner in the form of written notice. Required aircraft identification markings are discussed in **14 CFR Part 45.29**.

55. AC 43.13-1B as applicable refers to the acceptable drill size for rivets may be found in Metallic Materials and Elements for Flight Vehicle Structure (MIL-HDBK-5) and if another alloy is being considered, refer to the information on the comparative strength properties of aluminum alloys contained in MIL-HDBK-5. Is the mechanic required to have a copy of MIL-HDBK-5?

Yes. Or have access to the required sections of MIL-HDBK-5 when making repairs. MIL-HDBK-5 is **required by reference**.

MIL-H DBK-5 is acceptable data accepted by the FAA for material allowable. The FAA is taking over control of the program, and the new document is called AR-MMPDS. The FAA say's they will eventually incorporate data from ESDU 00932 to make it universal in Europe and N.A. The complete book is 1,726 pages.

I found this out while reading page ii of MIL-HDBK-5J. Using the MMPDS-01 is no different than MIL-HDBK-5, which is a relief. So if you have a copy of MIL-HDBK-5J it should be acceptable. **Note** MIL-HDBK-5J was the current revision at time of this printing.

MIL-HDBK-5 used to be free to down load, at http://www.mil-hdbk-5.org/ at the time of this printing. The replacement for MIL-HDBK-5 is **MMPDS-01**. For a fee, you will be able to get the MMPDS is two formats, Microfiche at $116.50 and paper copy at $223.00. The second way to get the first version of the MMPDS is through the FAA Technical Center Web-Site: http://actlibrary.tc.faa.gov/. Through this web site, you can access the MMPDS, and in general all FAA Technical Center reports in PDF. The site is http://155.178.136.203/eosweb/opac/search/SimpleSearch.asp

The Handbook is the only publicly available source in the U.S. for material allowables that the Federal Aviation Administration generally accepts for compliance with Federal Aviation Regulations (CFR) for material strength properties and design values for aircraft certification and continued airworthiness. Moreover, it is the only publicly available source worldwide for fastener joint allowables that comply with the CFRs. This edition, MMPDS-01, incorporates the additions and changes to aircraft metallic material design properties and analysis guidelines approved at the 1st and 2nd MMPDS government/industry coordination meetings.

56. Can A&P shops do static, altimeter test (CFR 91.413/411)?

No. A Repair Station certificate and ratings is required even if the station only has "Specialized Services" ratings.

57. Are only Repair Stations able to legally install radios?

Yes/No. In most regions an A&P/IA with the proper manuals and tools can install radios and complete the installation paperwork. The FAA may require radio shops to do the testing after the installation. If a repair station has a limited airframe rating yes they can install radios, but they must have the airframe rating.

Part Replacement Questions

1. **Why did manufactures impose multiple inspections and ultimately place life limits on certain components?**

History and or analysis indicated a need to include additional inspections periods or life limits on certain parts.

2. **How does the mechanic know that he has the authority to install a superceded part not yet listed in the IPC?**

If the part is purchased from aircraft manufacture it will come with an FAA Form 8130 tag showing that it is approved.

3. **Who is responsible for making sure the standard and life limited parts is airworthy and the right part to install?**

The installer is held responsible if they install any part to make sure it is the correct part and is airworthy. 14 CFR Part 91, Section 91.417 establishes the record keeping responsibilities and requirements for the owner/operator of the aircraft while 14 CFR Part 43, Section 43.9 and 43.11 establish the record keeping responsibilities and requirements for the personnel who maintain the aircraft.

Section 91.417 requires the total time-in-service records for airframes, engines, rotors, and propellers to be retained by the owner. These records are used to schedule overhauls, retirement life limits, and inspections.

Life-Limited Parts Current Status Records. Part 91 requires retention by the owner of records for components of the airframe, engine, propellers, rotors, and appliances that are identified to be removed from service when the life limit has been reached.

(1) The current life-limited status of the part is a record indicating the life limit remaining before the required retirement time of the component is reached. This record must include any modification of the part according to AD's, service bulletins, or product improvements by the manufacturer or applicant.

(2) The following are not considered to be current life-limited status records:
   a. Work orders
   b. Purchase requests
   c. Sales receipts
   d. Manufacturers' documentation of original certification
   e. Other historical data

(3) Whenever the current status of life-limited parts records cannot be established or has not been maintained (e.g., a break in current status) and the historical records are not available, the airworthiness of that product cannot be determined, and it must be removed from service.

(4) Current status of life-limited parts records must be retained with the aircraft indefinitely. If selling the aircraft, the records must be transferred to the new owner.

The **owner must** retain a record identifying the current inspection status of each aircraft. This record must show the time-in-service since the last inspection required by the inspection program under which the aircraft and its appliances are maintained.

Mechanics remember it is your responsibility during the annual/100-hour inspection to check the current life limits on parts. During inspection you are held responsible in accordance with Part 43, Section 43.10 to determine the disposition of Life-Limited parts.

4. **You purchase a new battery for your ELT and the manufacture say's the new battery life limit is 5-years, however the rule in part 91 says to change the battery every 2-years. Which takes precedence the manufactures data or part 91?**

In all cases Title 49 Code of Federal Regulation take precedence over manufactures data. In many cases technology has exceeded the regulation and the regulations have not been update to reflect the changes.

5. **An owner wants you to repair his or her aircraft with parts they supply, is this acceptable and can the A&P or IA be held responsible if the parts are not traceable?**

In all cases the person who installs any part is responsible to make sure the part is an approved part and yes you can be help responsible if you install it. The installer must ensure it is an approved part. In most cases owner supplied parts and materials are **NOT** encouraged. Owners may supply their own parts; materials or other services providing they are OEM, FAA-PMA, and TSO approved from traceable legitimate sources or repaired by properly certificated repair facilities and have appropriate release documents.

1. What should I do if I cannot determine if a part is approved?

Refer to AC 21-29 for information that may help you make this determination. If the part is suspected of not meeting the requirements of an approved part, complete FAA From 8120-11, Suspected Unapproved Parts Report.

Effective July 24, 2007 all suspected unapproved parts are to be received by and processed through the Aviation Safety Hotline Office. All SUP reports must be submitted to the Aviation Safety Hotline Office, which will forward the reports to the appropriate personnel in AFS and AIR within the FAA.

To submit a report, you can:
Call the 24-hour Aviation Safety Hotline toll-free number: 1-800-255-1111.
Email a report to the Aviation Safety Hotline go to:
http://www.faa.gov/about/office_org/headquarters_offices/avs/offices/sup/

2. What information or documentation do I need to submit when I report a SUP?

Submit a detailed description of why the part is suspect and any documents that lead you to believe the part is suspect.

3. May I submit a SUP report anonymously?

Yes, but please ensure that you have provided all the requested information since the FAA will not be able to contact you with any follow-up questions.

4. What do I do with a purchased suspect part after I have reported it?

If at all possible, quarantine the part until a determination can be made regarding the part's status. The part may need to be evaluated and/or tested during the investigation.

5. Does the FAA investigate SUP involving foreign entities?

Yes, if the part was produced or repaired by an FAA certificate holder, or the part is installed on a U.S.-registered aircraft. Other situations may require evaluation or coordination with foreign civil aviation authorities.

6. Does the FAA investigate suspect parts used in a military application?

Generally, the FAA will investigate a suspect military part only if the part has a civil application. To report a suspect part used in a military-only application, contact the Defense Criminal Investigative Services, Product Substitution Program, at (703) 604-8607.

7. How can I get information about a SUP investigation?

You may request information about a closed SUP investigation through the Freedom of Information Act (FOIA) and receive all information eligible for release under FOIA.

8. Where can I get information regarding a specific technical issue relating to unapproved parts?

Send any technical questions to the SUP Program Office e-mail address, http://www.faa.gov/aircraft/safety/programs/sups/

9. Is the sale of unapproved parts allowed in the open market?

The FAA does not regulate the sale and/or distribution of parts. Parts represented "as is" and without documentation are not contrary to the regulations. It is important to note, however, that parts represented as being "airworthy" or eligible for installation on a type-certificated product—**and in fact are not**—could be fraudulent.

10. Does the FAA offer any type of SUP training?

Yes, a SUP Training CD has been produced for industry and can be requested at your local Flight Standard District Office.

Reference http://www.faa.gov/aircraft/safety/programs/sups/

INOP Instruments Questions

1. How do you get my Weight & Balance FAA approved?

The Aircraft Certification Office or the Flight Standard District Office of the FAA must approve weight and Balance document. The related Flight Manual Supplement must also be approved by the ACO or FSDO. DER approved data may be used.

2. Where can you find the requirement in the Code of Federal Regulations (CFR) and Civil Air Regulations (CAR) for weight and balance?

CAR 3.73 *Empty weight.* The empty weight and corresponding center of gravity location shall include all fixed ballast, the unusable fuel supply (see § 3.437), undrainable oil, full engine coolant, and hydraulic fluid. **The weight and location of items of equipment installed when the airplane is weighed shall be noted in the Airplane Flight Manual.**

CFR Sec. 23.29 Empty weight and corresponding center of gravity.
(a) The empty weight and corresponding center of gravity must be determined by weighing the airplane with—
   (1) Fixed ballast;
   (2) Unusable fuel determined under **Sec. 23.959**; and
   (3) Full operating fluids, including—
      i. Oil;
      ii. Hydraulic fluid; and
      iii. Other fluids required for normal operation of airplane systems, except potable water, lavatory precharge water, and water intended for injection in the engines.
(b) The condition of the airplane at the time of determining empty weight must be one that is well defined and can be easily repeated.

To arrive at an answer, we need to examine CFR Part 91.213(d) in detail. Let's start with, "Who Is Affected By The Rule?" Individuals affected are those, under Part 91, operating:

   1. Rotorcraft, nonturbine-powered airplanes, gliders, or lighter-than-air aircraft for which a Master Minimum Equipment List (MMEL) has **not** been developed **(91.213(d)(1)(i))** and
   2. Small rotorcraft, nonturbine-powered small airplanes, gliders, or lighter-than-air aircraft for which a MMEL **has** been developed **(91.213(d)(1)(ii))**.

3. What does the rule provide for INOP instruments?

The rule provides that Part 91 operators of the kinds of aircraft may operate without an approved minimum equipment list provided the inoperative instruments and equipment are not:

a. Part of the VFR-day type certification instruments and equipment prescribed in the applicable airworthiness regulations under which the aircraft was type certificated; **(91.213(d)(2)(i)**. This would require the pilot to look at the applicable regulations such as CAR 3, Par t 23, etc. and the applicable Type Certificate Data Sheets.

b. Indicated as required on the aircraft's equipment list or on the Kinds of Operation Equipment List for the kind of flight operation being conducted; (91.213(d)(2)(ii). The equipment list can normally be found with the weight and balance report; and a generic equipment list can be found in the applicable section of your Airplane Flight Manual (AFM) or Pilot Operating Handbook (POH).

c. Required by **CFR Section 91.205** or any other rule of this Part for the specific kind of flight operation (day/night VFR, IFR, etc.) being conducted; (91.213(d)(2)(iii). This is usually the first place a pilot or mechanic would look.

d. Required to be operational by an airworthiness directive, **91.213(d)(2)(iv).** This is an area generally overlooked by everyone.

If you answer **YES** (required) to any of the conditions above, the aircraft is considered to be unairworthy, **should not** be flown, and the performance of maintenance is required. However, if you answer **NO** (not required), then the aircraft may continue to operate provided the inoperative instruments and equipment are:

a. Removed from the aircraft, the cockpit control placarded, and the maintenance recorded in accordance with **CFR Part 43.9 (91.213(d)(3)(i)**; OR

b. Deactivated and placarded "Inoperative." If deactivation of the inoperative instrument or equipment involves maintenance, it must be recorded in accordance with **CFR Par t43.9 (91.213(d) (3)(ii); AND

c. A determination is made by a pilot, who is certificated and appropriately rated under Part 61 of this chapter, or by a person, who is certificated and appropriately rated to perform maintenance on the aircraft, that the inoperative instrument or equipment does not constitute a hazard to the aircraft.

An aircraft with inoperative instruments or equipment as provided in paragraph (d) of **section 91.213** is considered to be in a properly altered condition acceptable to the Administrator.

4. **How long may the aircraft fly with inoperative instruments and equipment?**

Each owner or operator of an aircraft **shall have** any inoperative instrument or item of equipment, permitted to be inoperative by section **91.213(d)(2)** repaired, replaced, removed, or inspected at the next required inspection. (Part 91.405(c)).

The bottom line is, you can operate with inoperative instruments and equipment forever if the following conditions are met:

a. It is in a rotorcraft, non-turbine powered airplane, or lighter-than-air aircraft.
b. It is conducted under Part 91 flight rules.

---

c. The aircraft doesn't already have an Approved MEL under any flight rule.

d. The inoperative instrument or equipment isn't required by the certification basis, regulation, equipment lists, or Airworthiness Directive.

e. The inoperative instrument or equipment is removed from the aircraft or deactivated.

f. The cockpit control and/or equipment/instrument is placarded "Inoperative".

g. A maintenance record entry is accomplished by an appropriately rated airman in accordance with **Part 43 section 43.9.**

h. A determination is made, by an appropriately rated pilot or mechanic, that the inoperative instrument or equipment does not present a safety hazard to the aircraft.

i. The inoperative instrument or item of equipment shall be repaired, replaced, removed, or inspected at the next required inspection.

If an aircraft comes in for a 100-hour or annual inspection with inoperative instruments or equipment and they are properly placarded with a record entry. At the end of the inspection the aircraft can be returned-to-service with the inoperative instruments or equipment.

The inspector job is to determine if the inoperative instruments or equipment is deferred properly and can be in accordance with CFR 91 section 91.213. This should also be explained to the owner he now has to operate under certain restrictions.

Deferred Maintenance Questions

1. What does inoperative mean?

Inoperative means that a system and/or component has malfunctioned to the extent that it does not accomplish its intended purpose and/or is not consistently functioning normally within its approved operating limits or tolerances. **Reference CFR 91, Section 91.213**.

2. Deferred maintenance what is it?

Deferred maintenance is the postponement of the repair or replacement of an item of equipment or an instrument. To defer a repair will require the aircraft to have a Master Equipment List (MEL). **Reference CFR 91, Section 91.213**.

3. If I am performing a 100-hour or annual inspection and find deferred items, are they required to be fixed before I perform a return to service?

No. However, when inspecting aircraft operating **without** an MEL, the rule "**14 CFR Part 91, section 91.213(d),**" allows certain aircraft not having an approved MEL to be flown with inoperative instruments and/or equipment. These aircraft may be presented for annual or progressive inspection with such items previously deferred or may have inoperative instruments and equipment deferred during an inspection. In either case, the holder of an IA is required by 14 CFR Part 43, section 43.13(b) to determine that:

1. The deferrals are eligible within the guidelines of that rule.
2. All conditions for deferral are met, including proper recordation in accordance with 14 CFR Part 43, sections 43.9 and 43.11; and
3. Deferral of any item or combination of items will not affect the intended function of any other operable instruments and/or equipment, or in any manner constitute a hazard to the aircraft. When these requirements are met, such an aircraft is considered to be in a properly altered condition with regard to those deferred items.

Minimum Equipment List—Deferred Maintenance. The operator's FAA-approved MEL allows the operator to continue a flight or series of flights with certain inoperative equipment. The continued operation must meet the requirements of the MEL deferral classification and the requirements for the equipment loss.

Operators frequently use a system to monitor items that have been inspected and found within serviceable limits. These items are still airworthy, yet warrant repair at a later time or when items no longer meet serviceable limits. This method of deferral may require repetitive inspections to ensure continuing airworthiness of the items. Examples of items that are commonly deferred in this manner are fuel leak classifications, dent limitations, and temporary (airworthy) repairs.

4. **During a 100-hour or annual is the mechanic required to comply with special inspections?**

Yes and No. This will depend on the inspection program the aircraft is on. If the owner is following the aircraft manufacture inspection program and it calls out a 200, 300, 400 or 500 hour inspection for some components they they you are required to comply with that hourly inspection. The only way to know what inspection program the aircraft is on is to ask the owner/operator and have it noted in the airframe maintenance records. This is a requirement of Part 91.409 the owner has to pick a program and the mechanic has to inspect to that program. Take note Part 43 Appendix D does not cover all inspection programs and signing an aircraft referencing Part 43 Appendix D may fall short of the inspection requirements in Part 43.15 Additional Performance Rules for Inspections.

Remember you have to use a checklist as referenced Part 43.15 the manufacturer's inspection sheets, or a checklist designed by the holder of an IA, that includes the scope and detail of the items listed in Part 43 Appendix D, to check the condition of the entire aircraft. **This includes checks of the various systems listed in 14 CFR Part 43, section 43.15.**

Some special inspections may be spelled on FAA Form 337's as a result of a major repair or field approval. In block 8 on the 337 form it should explain inspection/maintenance periods in which each of the major alteration components are inspected, cleaned, lubricated, adjusted, tested, including applicable wear tolerances and work recommended at each scheduled maintenance period. This section can refer to the manufacturers' instructions for the equipment installed where appropriate (e.g., functional checks, repairs, inspections.) To lessen your liability during an inspection complying with any special inspections and record them in your maintenance entry.

5. **Do any items on the deferred list have to be listed on a discrepancies list as unairworthy?**

No. When the requirements are met, such an aircraft is considered to be in a properly altered condition with regard to those deferred items. CFR 91 section 91.405 Maintenance required. (c) Shall have any inoperative instrument or item of equipment, permitted to be inoperative by **91.213(d)(2)** of this part, repaired, replaced, removed, **or inspected at the next required inspection**; and (d) When listed discrepancies include inoperative instruments or equipment, **shall ensure** that a placard has been installed as required by 43.11 of this chapter.

6. **Minimum Equipment List (MEL) are they required?**

Yes and No. The minimum equipment list (MEL) is intended to permit operations with certain inoperative items of equipment for the minimum period of time necessary until repairs can be accomplished. It is important that repairs are accomplished at the earliest opportunity in order to return the aircraft to its design level of safety and reliability. The owner has to request a MEL and have it approved by the FAA now it becomes mandatory.

a. When inspecting aircraft operating with an MEL, the holder of an IA should review the document where inoperative items are recorded. (aircraft maintenance record, logbook, discrepancy record, etc.) to determine the state of airworthiness with regard to those recorded discrepancies. Inspections of aircraft with approved MEL's will be in accordance with 14 CFR under which the MEL was issued.

b. Those MEL's specifying repair intervals through the use of A, B, C, D codes require repairs of deferred items at or prior to the repair times established by the letter designated category. In such instances, some items previously deferred may not be eligible for continued deference at the inspection or may require additional maintenance. Where repair intervals are not specified by codes in the MEL, all MEL-authorized inoperative instruments and/or equipment should be repaired or inspected and deferred before approval for return to service.

c. Aircraft established on a progressive inspection program require that all MEL-authorized inoperative items be repaired or inspected and deferred at each inspection whether or not the item is encompassed in that particular segment.

d. When inspecting aircraft operating without an MEL, the rule "14 CFR Part 91, section 91.213(d)," allows certain aircraft not having an approved MEL to be flown with inoperative instruments and/or equipment. These aircraft may be presented for annual or progressive inspection with such items previously deferred or may have inoperative instruments and equipment deferred during an inspection. In either case, the holder of an IA is required by 14 CFR Part 43, section 43.13(b) to determine that:

1. The deferrals are eligible within the guidelines of that rule.
2. All conditions for deferral are met, including proper recordation in accordance with 14 CFR Part 43, sections 43.9 and 43.11; and
3. Deferral of any item or combination of items will not affect the intended function of any other operable instruments and/or equipment, or in any manner constitute a hazard to the aircraft. When these requirements are met, such an aircraft is considered to be in a properly altered condition with regard to those deferred items.

Unauthorized Repairs Questions

1. **The owner says the compass is low on fluid. Can I service the compass and change the O-ring as an A&P or IA?**

No. A compass is an instrument you cannot service it only a repair station with the proper ratings can. In accordance with **CFR 65.81(a)** General Privileges and limitations A&P/IA is prohibited because the rules states: "excluding major repairs to and major alterations of, propellers, and any repair to, or alteration of instruments".

2. **If you remove and replace a compass or install addition electronic equipment must the compass be swung?**

Yes. Compass swing must be performed whenever any ferrous component of the system (i.e. flux valve compensator, or Standby Compass) is installed, removed, repaired, or a new compass is installed. The magnetic compass can be checked for accuracy by using a compass rose located on an airport. The compass swing is normally affected by placing the aircraft on various magnetic headings and comparing the deviations with those on the deviation cards. Conduct a ground compass swing and record deviations from correct magnetic headings at 15-degree intervals. Be particularly attentive for errors induced by intermittently operated electrical equipment that is not removable by compass compensation plates. Don't forget to make a maintenance record entry in the airframe records. Reference to **CFR 14, 23.1327 and 23.1547**, and the equipment or aircraft manufacturer's manual.

3. **I am performing a 100-hour inspection and find a repair to the flight control surfaces that does not meet the sheet metal requirement of AC 43.141B Chapter 4 Para 4.57(f) metal repairs and the surfaces have several blind rivets installed?**

As a mechanic you have a duty to inspect and provide the owner with a list of discrepancies of stuff you find that does not meet the requirements of the CFR's. **Blind rivets** are used under certain conditions when there is access to only one side of the structure. Blind rivets shall not be used on aircraft in air intake areas where rivet parts may be ingested by the engine, on aircraft control surfaces, hinges, hinge brackets, flight control actuating systems, wing attachment fittings, landing gear fittings, on floats or amphibian hulls below the water level, or other heavily-stressed locations on the aircraft.

CAUTION
For metal repairs to the airframe, the use of blind rivets must be specifically authorized by the airframe manufacturer or approved by a representative of the FAA.

1. **When you submit a FAA Form 337 to the FSDO does it have to be original?**

Yes. The person who performed or supervised the major repair or major alteration prepares the original FAA Form 337 (two original copies). The holder of an IA then further processes the forms when they are presented for approval. Reference Part 43 Appendix B (a)(1). One copy to the FAA and the second copy to the owner. **14 CFR Appendix A.**

2. **Is the replacement of fabric on fabric-covered parts such as wings, fuselage, stabilizers, or control surfaces considered a major repair?**

Yes. Reference **CFR 43 Appendix A (b) Major repairs (1)(xxvii).**

3. **I inspect an aircraft and find addition stuff installed and no FAA Form 337 documentation what do I do?**

Without the required documentation the aircraft does not meet its type design **CFR 21, Section 21.31** and is considered unairworthy. You can do one of two things:

   1. Perform a maintenance record entry stating the aircraft is unairworthy and provide a list written list to the owner explaining what is not airworthy. The inspection can be signed off as UNAIRWORTHY in the maintenance record.
   2. Inspect the installation and prepare a FAA Form 337 for field approval to your local FSDO.

4. **If you inspect an aircraft that a STC was installed and do not have a copy of the STC can you inspect the item in accordance with Part 43 Appendix D?**

No. CFR 43, Section 43.13 says you have to have the current manufactures data. All STC's are FAA approved and so is the continued airworthiness section contained in the STC. Without the STC data you cannot properly inspect the item and would not know what to inspect for.

5. **If you deviate from a Supplemental Type Certificate will it require addition approval?**

Yes and No. Making minor deviations from the approved data is permissible if the change is one that could be approved as a minor alteration when considered by its self. And make sure to record it on the FAA Form 337 you will submit to the FAA.

6. **How many copies of a FAA Form 337 should I submit to the FAA for a field approval?**

Two originals. Both copies will be signed in Block 3 and returned for completion of the alteration. After completion of work sign Block 7 and return one copy to the local FSDO. Remember if you install a field approval using a STC the data is all ready approved. In this case you only have to submit one copy to the FAA to be forwarded to aircraft records in Oklahoma City by the local FSDO. **CFR 43, Appendix A**.

7. **As an IA can I issue an Airworthiness Approval Tag (FAA Form 8130-3) for parts I inspect and overhaul?**

NO. You cannot issue a FAA Form 8130-3. This is reserved for PMA, TSO, and repair stations. **Reference FAA Order 8130.21.**

8. **How do I get a modification FAA approved?**

Contact your local Flight Standards District Office (FSDO) for a field approval, or contact your local Aircraft Certification Office (ACO) for a Supplemental Type Certificate (STC).

9. **Is a copy of a DER approval Form 8110-3 from a previous FAA approved data acceptable?**

No. Only the original is considered FAA approved. Copies are submitted to the FSDO, but the DER must create an original for each specific aircraft or project. Furthermore, a Form 8110-3 is only an approval of specific data; it is that data, which shows compliance with the regulation, and the data must be specific to each modification and available to the FSDO inspector to determine acceptability. It is common practice for modifiers to sell kits and enclose copies of previous field approvals to be shown to the FSDO.

Often field approvals are granted on this data, but this data alone does not entitle the applicant to a field approval. It should be remembered that the FSDO inspector is making the determination of safety in this instance, and may deny approval. Generally the FAA takes a dim view of shipping parts with copies of field approvals to aid in another field approval.

10. **Does the Aircraft Certification Office (ACO) have a role in the Field Approval process?**

Yes, if the FSDO inspector is willing to grant a Field Approval, but would like an engineering review of data, which is outside their field of expertise, they may request support from the ACO. The request is usually in writing, and the appropriate ACO engineer may then contact the applicant to obtain necessary data in order to write a statement of engineering approval back to the FSDO. This statement is to be kept with the Field Approval data.

11. **What is acceptable data?**

Acceptable data can be used as an approval basis; however, it cannot be used alone as substantiating data to support the mod. The acceptance of the data is at the FAA's discretion to ensure its applicability to the mod.

Acceptable data can come from many sources, i.e., **ADVISORY CIRCULAR 43.13-1B or ADVISORY CIRCULAR 43.13-2A,** OEM's Service Bulletins, modification drawings, ASTM, Mil-Specs, CMM, ICA, or other means. (Advisory Circulars on this and related subjects can be found in the following FAA website http://www.faa.gov/regulations_policies/advisory_circulars/

12. **What does DER approved data mean?**

DER approved data, via Form 8110-3, can be used to support the modification. However, it is not an FAA approval for the aircraft installation, return to service, or a field approval.

Be advised that DER approved data may not encompass or cover all aspects of the modification, therefore, an additional approval from other discipline(s) may be required by other DER(s) or FAA to ensure that the data is compatible and integrated for the modification.

13. Can I use previously approved data?

Previously approved data may be used as substantiation data to support the new modification. However, acceptance is at the FAA's discretion to determine if previously approved data is applicable to the modification and its adequacy for showing compliance to the regulations.

If previously STC approved data is used to support the modification, written permission is required from the STC holder that authorizes the use of the data.

14. Can you use AC 43.13 as approved data?

Maybe, AC 43.13 Acceptable Methods, Techniques, and Practices (Aircraft Inspection and Repair), may be used directly as approved data **(for repairs only)** without further approval **only when** there is no manufacturer repair or maintenance instructions that address the repair and the user has determined that it is:
   a. Appropriate to the product being repaired.
   b. Directly applicable to the repair being made; and N-number.
   c. Not contrary to manufacturer's data.

Caution: Contact your local FSDO Inspector and discuss AC 43.13 data you want to use before cutting metal of wires.

15. How do I get data from an inactive STC/TC? (Owner cannot be located, or the owner is not supporting the STC/TC)

Under the Freedom of Information Act (FOIA), the applicant owner/operator can request this information by submitting a letter to the local Aircraft Certification Office (ACO) in stating that the data is strictly use for aircraft maintenance and restoration.

Once the letter is received, an internal coordination is required through the FAA's legal for review and release. There will be some service fees to cover the data retrieval and other associated resources that the FAA has to allocate under the FOIA.

16. How do I get a "Flight Manual Supplement" FAA approved?

The Supplement must be submitted to the FAA for review and approval by the Manager of the Flight Test Branch of the Aircraft Certification Office (ACO).

If the flight manual is being revised in conjunction with a Field Approval (i.e. FAA Form 337), submit the Flight Manual Supplement to the FSDO inspector assigned to your modification. The inspector will contact the ACO and request approval of the Supplement. If the flight manual is being supplemented in conjunction with a Supplement Type Certificate (STC) project at the ACO, submit the Flight Manual Supplement through your ACO Project Manager using the process for submission of all your substantiating data.

If a Flight Manual Supplement is not the result of a hardware change to the aircraft (i.e. a change to a normal operating procedure), it may be submitted with an appropriate explanation directly to the Manager of the Flight Test Branch for processing.

Once approved, the originally signed pages will be returned to the applicant by regular mail. If you request it, a copy of the signed pages may be faxed to you so the aircraft can be operated.

17. When do I need an Aircraft Flight Manual Supplement?

The purpose of an aircraft flight manual is to provide clear, concise and technically accurate information to the flight crew necessary for safe aircraft operation. When an aircraft has been modified such that the basic limitations, procedures, or performance data have changed, a flight manual supplement is required.

18. If I complete the installation of my modification and then tell the FSDO about it, will they be angry and less likely to approve my modification?

Typically, yes. The best procedure, if you are unsure if your modification is appropriate, is to let the FSDO know that you are going to make the modification before you install it, and ask for any advice or assistance. If a FSDO inspector can look at your modification while the aircraft is disassembled, they are much more comfortable with the integrity of the work. If you are open with the FAA they are more likely to trust your modification.

19. I have copies of all the Field Approval data for another aircraft of the same model as mine with the same modification, am I entitled to a field approval based on this data?

No. Each field approval stands alone, and one is never entitled to it. The previously approved data will of course help the FSDO inspector make a decision whether the modification is acceptable.

20. What do I do if I ask for a Field Approval, and my local FSDO says no?

First, ask why they denied your application. If the FSDO has good reasons for a denial, you may contact a DER or other engineering organization for advice on the suitability of the modification. You may also apply to the ACO for an STC.

21. I got this seat; how do I get it installed?

14 CFR parts 23, 25, 27 and 29 contain the regulatory requirements for seats and their installation. _TSO C-39B_ and _TSO C-127A_ also provide standards for seats. A seat installation can impact many other regulatory requirements such as emergency evacuation, material flammability, and pilot visibility. Contact the local FSDO or ACO and discuss the details of the installation. You will be given additional information on how to proceed.

22. What is the role of ACO/FSDO/MIDO/AEG?

ACO—Responsible for the certification of TC, STC, PMA, and TSO. Also responsible for the continued operational safety of the certificated products which include the issuances of AD's and AMOC (Alternative Method of Compliance to an AD). Provide technical engineering support to the FSDO's on major modifications and repairs and administer the designees (DER) and delegated organizations: DAS, DOA, SCFR 36.

MIDO—Responsible for the conformity inspection, airworthiness approval, and production approval of the type design. Provides surveillance inspection on the production holders to ensure the manufacturing requirements are met.

Oversight the designees (DAR) and other delegated organizations (APIS, TSO and PMA holders).

AEG—Responsible for the evaluation and conformance of the operation and maintenance requirements. Review and approve the MEL and MMEL for aircraft carriers. Support the ACO and FSDO in the review and acceptance of ICA.

FSDO—Responsible for aircraft surveillance and inspection for aircraft operators/owners. Also has the responsibility to issue field approvals for major modifications and repairs. Oversee the designees (DAR's) and other delegated organizations (Part 121, 145, 147, etc.)

23. How do I get a modification FAA approved?

Contact your local Flight Standards District Office (FSDO) for a field approval, or contact your local Aircraft Certification Office (ACO) for a Supplemental Type Certificate (STC).

24. Is a copy of a DER approval Form 8110-3 from a previous FAA approved data acceptable?

No. Only the original is considered FAA approved. Copies are submitted to the FSDO, but the DER must create an original for each specific aircraft or project. Furthermore, a Form 8110-3 is only an approval of specific data; it is that data, which shows compliance with the regulation, and the data must be specific to each modification and available to the FSDO inspector to determine acceptability. It is common practice for modifiers to sell kits and enclose copies of previous field approvals to be shown to the FSDO.

Often field approvals are granted on this data, but this data alone does not entitle the applicant to a field approval. It should be remembered that the FSDO inspector is making the determination of safety in this instance, and may deny approval. Generally the FAA takes a dim view of shipping parts with copies of field approvals to aid in another field approval. The modifier should have made application for STC, since this assures that the modification has been reviewed by engineers from all disciplines and flight tested if necessary.

25. Does the ACO have a role in the Field Approval process?

Yes, if the FSDO inspector is willing to grant a Field Approval, but would like an engineering review of data, which is outside their field of expertise, they may request support from the ACO. The request is usually in writing, and the appropriate ACO engineer may then contact the applicant to obtain necessary data in order to write a statement of engineering approval back to the FSDO. This statement is to be kept with the Field Approval data.

26. What does DER approved data mean?

DER approved data, via Form 8110-3, can be used to support the modification. However, it is not an FAA approval for the aircraft installation, return to service, or a field approval.

Be advised that DER approved data may not encompass or cover all aspects of the modification, therefore, an additional approval from other discipline(s) may be required by other DER(s) or FAA to ensure that the data is compatible and integrated for the modification.

27. Who can I get to help me with my modification certification?

You can hire a DER who can advise you on how to show compliance with the applicable airworthiness rules. Also, a properly qualified DER can approve on behalf of the FAA certain compliance data in support of a STC or field approval by the FAA Form 337.

28. How do I find a DER?

Advisory Circular 183.29-1HH found on the FAA website below will provide a link to the lists of consultant DER's and their approval authorities by the charts included in Order 8110.37C.

(Advisory Circulars on this and related subjects can be found in the following FAA website **http://www. faa.gov/regulations/index.cfm**

29. How do I get an engine FAA approved?

Review Code of Federal Regulations 14, Part 33 Regulations and <u>Advisory Circular 33-2</u> which is entitled "Aircraft Engine Type Certification Handbook". Also, review CFR 14 Part 21; Subpart B entitled "Type Certificates". When you are familiar with these regulations, set up a meeting with the local Aircraft Certification Office and present your plans for your engine design. In this meeting your will be given additional information on how to proceed.

(Advisory Circulars on this and related subjects can be found in the following FAA website **http://www.airweb.faa.gov/Regulatory_and_Guidance_Library/rgAdvisoryCircular.nsf/MainFrame?OpenFrameSet**

30. How do I get an increase in Gross Weight FAA approved?

Increased Gross Weight Approvals may require significant structural, acoustical and flight test analysis and/or testing. An STC will be required. Please contact your local Aircraft Certification Office. Please also see "How to obtain a STC" above.

31. Who do I contact about TSO/TC/PMA/AC/STC/Orders?

For TSO—ADVISORY CIRCULAR 20-110J is available at the local ACO or on the FAA Website. The last date that ADVISORY CIRCULAR 20-110 was updated was 1997 and therefore is out of date.

For PMA—Order 8110.42A
Depending on the nature of the PMA, different Branches of the ACO will received the application (i.e. Structures, Propulsion, etc.).

TC—Order 8110.4B

STC—Advisory Circular 21-40

Other FAA's Orders/Advisory Circulars/Notices:

(Advisory Circulars and FAA Orders on this and related subjects can be found in the following FAA website **http://www.faa.gov/regulations_policies/**

32. Why do I care about Noise?

Aircraft that produce significant noise pollution for a community can become a cause for action by a community to reduce their exposure to the noise. Those actions may include restrictions on flight operation times; noise level limits monitoring sites (leading to citations), etc. That will affect your ability to fly into or out of your local airport whenever you want. In addition, exposure to high levels of noise for extended or repeated times can be damaging to the quality of life for those exposed.

33. When do I need a noise approval?

As required by 14CFR §21.93, anytime a voluntary change has occurred to an aircraft that may increase the noise levels an acoustical (Noise) evaluation must be conducted by the applicant and approved by the ACO.

Some changes that increase the noise levels include changes or additions to noise sources, increase in power, propeller/rotor tip speeds, drag from all sources (including landing gear), gross weight, or any other changes that affect aircraft performance.
(The lead to 14CFR §21.93 can be found at FAA website.

34. How do I get a Supplemental Type Certificate (STC)?

Talk to the FAA before you modify your aircraft. Develop your modification; conduct necessary research and development to determine airworthiness of modification. Guidance and other information about the certification process may be obtain from Advisory Circular 21-40, Application Guide for Obtaining a Supplement Type Certificate, and The FAA and Industry Guide to Product Certification. Your local ACO will be able to provide additional information relating specifically to your modification.

(Advisory Circulars and FAA Orders on this and related subjects can be found in the following FAA website **http://www.faa.gov/regulations_policies/**

The FAA and Industry Guide to Product Certification can be found in the follow FAA **website: http://www.faa.gov/aircraft/air%5Fcert/**

35. Why can't I get a STC for my replacement parts?

The FAA group "replacement parts" into two categories depending on how it is FAA approved:

1. Parts Manufacturer Approval (PMA)
2. Others:
   * Parts produced under a *type* or *production certificate*,
   * Parts produced by an owner or operator for maintaining or altering his own product,
   * Parts produced under an FAA Technical Standard Order,
   * Standard pars (such as bolts and nuts) conforming to established industry or U.S. specifications.

If you make replacement parts that have identical installation and maintenance instructions to the original parts then a STC is not appropriate. STC's are applicable to a major change in type design and normally replacement parts do not qualify as a major change. FAA policy, as presented in Order 8110.4A, Type Certification Process, states that a STC will not be issued for approval of replacement parts except under unique circumstances.

In order to make replacement parts and be able to sell them to others, a Parts Manufacturer Approval (PMA) will be required. Review Code of Federal Regulations 14, part 21. §21.303 entitled "Replacement and modification parts" and FAA Order 8110.42A entitled "Parts Manufacturer Approval Procedures". Guidance is also provided in Advisory Circular 20-62, Eligibility, Quality, and Identification of Aeronautical Replacement Parts.

36. How do I obtain FAA approval for an antenna installation on a Damage Tolerance aircraft (aircraft approved using the newer damage tolerance technology)?

Contact and contract a Designated Engineering Representative (DER) with the authority to approve damage tolerance Analysis.

37. How do I install a required instrument?

Essential instruments must be TSO'd prior to installation. Then approved for location and function prior to approval of the AFMS/RFMS. Depending whether previously approved, some instruments may require flight-testing prior to AFMS/RFMS approval.

38. How do I get a different propeller model installed on my aircraft FAA approved?

The propeller must be found to be compatible with the engine, structural and acoustical requirements. For single engine tractor (propeller in front) applications the propeller/engine vibration compatibility may be located in propeller Type Certification Data Sheet (TCDS). Even if the engine is listed on the propeller TCDS as being compatible, the installation in the airframe must be evaluated for changes in vibration effects on the structural components. If the propeller provides different thrust or weight, weight and balance as well as structural considerations must be made. A revision to the Airplane Flight Manual or Pilots Operating Handbook is usually required and comes in the form of an Airplane Flight Manual Supplement (AFMS) or Supplement Airplane Flight Manual (SAFM). Continued compliance with the noise regulations is required. The local Aircraft Certification Office must be contacted for guidance on noise compliance.

39. How do I get vortex generators FAA approved?

Vortex Generators and other aerodynamic/ engineering analysis including before and after flight-testing. A STC will likely be required. (Please see STC or Modification above.)

40. Can I put vinyl fabric on my old seats?

Yes, provided the vinyl fabric and the new interior material meet the applicable flammability requirements for your airplane. Testing to demonstrate compliance with the flammability standards may require the assistance of a DER for flammability test laboratory. Contact the local FSDO or ACO and discuss the details of the installation.

41. What type of modification is too large or complex for a Field Approval?

That depends entirely on the experience of the inspector and the policy of the FSDO involved. Generally, if the flight characteristics of the aircraft are affected, if a large part of the structure or system is modified, or if a noise finding/approval is required, then an STC should be pursued. The FSDO inspector makes this determination.

42. When do I need an Aircraft Flight Manual Supplement?

The purpose of an aircraft flight manual is to provide clear, concise and technically accurate information to the flight crew necessary for safe aircraft operation. When an aircraft has been modified such that the basic limitations, procedures, or performance data have changed, a flight manual supplement is required.

43. How do I get my Weight & Balance FAA approved?

Weight and Balance document must be approved by the Aircraft Certification Office or the Flight Standard District Office of the FAA. The related Flight Manual Supplement must also be approved by the ACO or FSDO. DER approved data may be used.

44. Where can you find the requirement in the Code of Federal Regulations (CFR) and Civil Air Regulations (CAR) for weight and balance?

CAR 3.73 *Empty weight.* The empty weight and corresponding center of gravity location shall include all fixed ballast, the unusable fuel supply (see § 3.437), undrainable oil, full engine coolant, and hydraulic fluid. **The weight and location of items of equipment installed when the airplane is weighed shall be noted in the Airplane Flight Manual.**

CFR Sec. 23.29 Empty weight and corresponding center of gravity.
(a) The empty weight and corresponding center of gravity must be determined by weighing the airplane with—
   1. Fixed ballast;
   2. Unusable fuel determined under **Sec. 23.959**; and
   3. Full operating fluids, including—
      i. Oil;
      ii. Hydraulic fluid; and
      iii. Other fluids required for normal operation of airplane systems, except potable water, lavatory precharge water, and water intended for injection in the engines.
(a) The condition of the airplane at the time of determining empty weight must be one that is well defined and can be easily repeated.

45. If an item is installed on a Form 337 does it have to be removed on a Form 337 or will a logbook entry be enough?

Major alterations are changes to the type design of the aircraft and documented on FAA Form 337 for installation. Now you want to remove an item and the only way to undo an alteration is to document it on another Form 337. The alteration may have had wires that cannot be removed, but were capped off and left in the aircraft this will be documented on the removal. Also holes may have been drilled in the structure they may have to be plugged again this will be documented on the removal in block 8 of the Form 337.

In most cases it is impossible to totally remove an alteration and what is left has to be documented. If it goes in with a Form 337 it comes out with a Form 337.

46. **You are performing a filed approval and the aircraft does not have a current registration for the new owner or the address is not correct what should you do?**

Inform the owner you cannot release the aircraft until you have a correct address to fill in the FAA From 337. The registered owner of an aircraft is responsible registration. The registration has to be current to maintain a current airworthiness certificate. Before an aircraft can be legally flown, it must be registered with the FAA Civil Aviation Registry and have within it a Certificate of Aircraft Registration issued to the owner as evidence of the registration with a current address. Reference FAA-H-8083-25 and CFR 47.

The Certificate of Aircraft Registration will expire when:
- The aircraft is registered under the laws of a foreign country.
- The registration of the aircraft is canceled at the written request of the holder of the certificate.
- The aircraft is totally destroyed or scrapped.
- The ownership of the aircraft is transferred.
- The holder of the certificate loses United States citizenship.
- Thirty days have elapsed since the death of the holder of the certificate.

Aircraft RVSM Compliance/Airworthiness Questions and Answers

1. **Conformity Inspections. Is an FAA conformity inspection required on an airframe prior to the issuance of RVSM authority (i.e., Operations Specifications or Letter of Authorization (LOA))?**

While it is the prerogative of the FAA to inspect any US registered aircraft, an inspection is not required if the airworthiness inspector is able to determine RVSM compliance from aircraft documentation.

2. **Equipment List. Where should the RVSM required equipment list be published?**

The required equipment list should be documented in the approved RVSM Data Package along with any associated drawings. This list should be published in documents readily available to the operator and approving inspector (i.e., Instructions for Initial and Continuing Airworthiness (IICA), approved Service Bulletins, Illustrated Parts Catalog (IPC). The list should clearly show equipment required for RVSM operations.

3. **Field Approvals. In lieu of an STC, can I obtain a field approval for RVSM airworthiness approval of my aircraft?**

No. An applicant for RVSM airworthiness approval for both group and non-group aircraft shall submit an RVSM Data Package to the appropriate Aircraft Certification Office. The RVSM Data package must contain the items listed in 14 CFR Part 91 Appendix G, Section 2(b). IG 91-RVSM Section 9 provides detailed guidance on the development of RVSM Data Packages. RVSM Data Package approval is the responsibility of FAA Aircraft Certification Offices or in some cases an appropriately authorized designee. RVSM Data Package approval may not be accomplished using the field approval process.

4. **BITE Testing. Is BITE testing acceptable for returning an aircraft to RVSM service following maintenance on an RVSM required system?**

Unless the airframe manufacturer addresses the use of BITE testing in its instructions for RVSM continued airworthiness, BITE is not an acceptable method or means, by itself, for returning an aircraft to RVSM service. BITE can be used for fault isolation and troubleshooting.

5. **Contract Maintenance. When contract maintenance is used, does the operator still need an approved RVSM maintenance program?**

Yes.

6. Can RVSM maintenance be contracted out to an FAA approved repair station?

Yes. RVSM maintenance can be contract out to an FAA approved repair station. When RVSM maintenance is contracted out, the operator's approved maintenance program will contain provisions for that and the operator will ensure that the repair station or maintenance contractor complies with the provisions of its approved maintenance program by:

    a. Documenting in its maintenance program that RVSM maintenance will be contracted only to FAA certificated repair stations that are appropriately rated to perform the required maintenance tasks.

    b. Supplying the repair station with aircraft maintenance requirements and

    c. Reviewing completed work records.

7. Functional Flight Test. When are functional flight tests required?

A functional flight test is an element of continued airworthiness programs. It is only performed by the operator after repairs or modifications that are deemed to warrant such testing to confirm that the maintenance action was effective. Functional flight tests generally do not require the installation of specialized flight test equipment.

8. Maintenance Program Elements. What are the required elements of an RVSM maintenance program?

Airworthiness Inspector's Handbook (FAA Order 8900.1), Volume 4, Chapter 10 "FAA Inspector Guidance". Section 1, paragraph 9D lists the required RVSM maintenance program elements. It is reproduced below.

Paragraph 9D. Each RVSM maintenance program must include the following:

    (a) Identification of components considered to be RVSM critical, and identification of structural areas noted as RVSM critical areas.

    (b) The name or title of the responsible person who will ensure that the aircraft is maintained in accordance with the approved program.

    (c) The method the operator will use to ensure that all personnel performing maintenance on the RVSM system are properly trained, qualified, and knowledgeable of that specific system.

    (d) The method the operator will use to notify the crew if the aircraft has been restricted from RVSM but is airworthy for an intended flight.

    (e) The method the operator will use to ensure conformance to the RVSM maintenance standards, including the use of calibrated and appropriate test equipment and a quality assurance program for ensuring continuing accuracy and reliability of test equipment, especially when outsourced.

    (f) The method the operator will use to verify that components and parts are eligible for installation in the RVSM system, as well as to prevent ineligible components or parts from being installed.

    (g) The method the operator will use to return an aircraft to service after maintenance has been performed on an RVSM component/system or after the aircraft was determined to be non-compliant.

    (h) Periodic inspections, functional flight tests, and maintenance and inspection procedures with acceptable maintenance practices for ensuring continued compliance with the RVSM aircraft requirements.

        • These elements may be listed in detail or described by reference to an acceptable program that is identified and controlled by revision or issue number

- The need for functional flight tests may be limited to only after repairs or modifications that are deemed to warrant such testing and may be accomplished through monitoring height-keeping performance
(i) The maintenance requirements listed in Instructions for Continued Airworthiness (ICA) associated with any RVSM associated component or modification.
(j) Any other maintenance requirement that needs to be incorporated to ensure continued compliance with RVSM requirements

9. **Manuals Is it a requirement to list all the RVSM components by part number in the FAA approved RVSM maintenance manual?**

Answer: It is recommended that the operator identify all RVSM critical components by part number and either include this list in their program or make reference to it. An operator that does not develop a list must ensure that the Service Bulletins, STC's or other documents that identify RVSM critical components are made available to all maintenance providers.

10. **Minimum Equipment Lists. What is the guidance for MEL development?**

Global Change (GC-59) provides guidance material for development of MEL's for RVSM. It is posted on the RVSM Documentation web page under "Documents Applicable to All Approvals".

11. **Minimum Equipment Lists. Is it a requirement to have a MEL before being issued RVSM authorization?**

Operators are not required to adopt an MEL. If the operator chooses, however, to adopt an MEL, then the MEL must be developed using the Global Change 59.

12. **Mixed Fleets. Will there be additional procedures required for handling fleets where some aircraft are RVSM compliant and others are not?**

Procedures should be developed to ensure that only RVSM compliant aircraft are dispatched and filed into RVSM airspace.

13. **Monitoring Related to Maintenance. Does an aircraft need to be re-monitored, if maintenance is performed on an RVSM component or system?**

No. It is imperative, however, that the ICA and any additional maintenance program elements are consulted.

14. **RVSM Return To Service Checks. What steps should be required to return an aircraft to RVSM service following maintenance to required RVSM equipment?**

Part 91, Appendix G, section 3 (b) (i) requires that an operator develop and obtain approval of maintenance and inspection procedures for ensuring continued compliance to the RVSM requirements. The specific steps may vary for different operators but must be approved by the FAA and included in the approved RVSM maintenance program.

15. **RVSM Return-to-Service Checks. Can any maintenance personnel or maintenance organization perform these checks?**

The approved maintenance program must include provisions for maintenance personnel to be properly trained, qualified, and authorized to perform RVSM return to service checks following maintenance to RVSM required systems.

16. **Skin Waviness Checks. When are skin waviness checks required for RVSM initial and continued airworthiness?**

If skin waviness checks are required for initial and/or continued airworthiness, the requirement will be documented in the Instructions for Initial and Continued Airworthiness (ICA's) and incorporated into the operator's approved RVSM maintenance program.

    a. **Who will be authorized to perform skin waviness checks besides the airframe manufacturer?**

Criteria for authorized inspection personnel are contained in the operator's approved maintenance program. Generally, this criteria is limited to RVSM-specific inspection training.

    b. **What is CFD?**

CFD is the acronym for Computational Fluid Dynamics. CFD is a computer simulation used for analyzing the effects of skin waviness, static ports/plates, etc. and their contribution to static source error. CFD analysis is generally performed by the airplane manufacturer or design authority responsible for the RVSM airworthiness approval.

17. **Scale Error Tolerances: 14 CFR Part 43. Can I use Part 43, Appendix E to maintain my altimetry systems to RVSM standards?**

No. The specifications listed in Part 43, Appendix E are not adequate to ensure RVSM altitude keeping performance. Operator responsibilities are:

    a. An operator that is required to comply with part 91 Section 91.411 must ensure that the requirements of part 43, Appendix E are accomplished and . . .

    b. If that operator is authorized to operate in RVSM airspace, it must also ensure that the requirements and tolerances stated in the approved RVSM maintenance program are met.

In some instances procedures in an approved RVSM maintenance program may include all the requirements of Part 43 appendix E. The operator of an RVSM aircraft should ensure that work records indicate specifically which (or both) requirements have been met.

GA Operator RVSM Maintenance Programs

18. **Part 91 Letters of Authorization. Is it required to record the serial numbers of RVSM required components on the LOA?**

No. There is no requirement to record or list the serial numbers of the RVSM components on the LOA. If the components' serial numbers were recorded on the LOA, then the LOA would become invalid if a component were replaced.

19. **Manuals. For part 91 operators, is an RVSM maintenance manual required to document policy and procedures for maintaining RVSM required aircraft systems?**

The development of an RVSM maintenance manual is a preferred method for a part 91 operator to document its RVSM maintenance program.

20. **Minimum Equipment Lists. Is it a requirement to have a MEL before being issued RVSM Authorization?**

Operators are not required to operate under an MEL. However, if an operator operates under an MEL, the operator must incorporate the provisions of Global Change 59. See "Documents Applicable to All RVSM Approvals".

21. **Program Requirements. Must a Part 91 operator obtain approval of their entire maintenance program?**

No. Only the elements required to maintain RVSM required aircraft systems must be approved.

22. **Program Requirements. General aviation operators are already subject to an inspection program required by the operating rules. Will I need an additional program to support the RVSM maintenance provisions?**

Yes. RVSM maintenance provisions must be reflected in the operator's approved RVSM maintenance program. RVSM maintenance requirements are beyond the inspection requirements that are outlined in an inspection program.

23. **Program Requirements what is the difference between an inspection program required for general aviation operators and an approved maintenance program required for air carriers?**

Not all inspection programs are FAA approved. An approved maintenance program exceeds the scope and detail of an inspection program by including maintenance procedures, training requirements, parts control, responsibility for implementing and maintaining the RVSM requirements, RVSM airworthiness release procedures, etc.

The goal of RVSM is to reduce the vertical separation between flight level (FL) 290 and FL 410, inclusive, from the current 2000 feet minimum to 1000 feet minimum, in order to gain fuel savings and operational efficiencies. The process of safely changing this separation standard requires a study to assess the actual performance of airspace users under the current separation (2000-ft) and potential performance under the new standard (1000-ft). In 1988, the ICAO Review of General Concept of Separation Panel (RGCSP) completed this study and concluded that safe implementation of the 1000-ft separation standard was technically feasible.

Inspection Limitations
Q&A

FAA Extends Inspection Authorization Renewal Period To Two Years

FAA has amended the regulations for the Inspection Authorization (IA) renewal period. The current IA regulation has a one-year renewal period. This rulemaking changes the renewal period to once every two years. "This will reduce the burden on both FAA and on the mechanic holding the IA," says (AFS-350). The amendment to § 65.92(a) changes the expiration date of an inspection authorization from March 31 of each year to March 31 of each odd-numbered year. The rulemaking change is in response to concerns regarding the administrative burden associated with the renewal of inspection authorizations under § 65.93. The final rule is posted with an effective date of March 1, 2007, the same date that comments close.

In a Direct Final Rule, the FAA has extended the Inspection Authorization ("IA") renewal period under CFRs 65.92 and 65.93 from one year to two years. The FAA believes the final rule will reduce the renewal administrative costs for both the FAA and mechanics holding the IA by 50%. The final rule does not change the requirements of the prior rule for annual activity (work performed, training, or oral examination).

The final rule is effective March 1, 2007.

1. **I am working on aircraft that is maintained on a Part 135 9 or less certificate Approved Aircraft Inspection Program (AAIP). Are the inspections required to be signed off using my Airframe and Powerplant (A&P) certificate or Inspections Authorization (IA) certificates?**

Your Inspection Authorization (IA) is required to sign off required inspections on aircraft under an AAIP maintenance program. Title 49 Part 65 Section 65.85 states an A&P may perform the 100-hour inspection required by Part 91. Section 65.95 states and IA Perform an annual, or perform or supervise a progressive inspection according to section 43.13 and 43.15. CFR 43.15 states: Each person performing an inspection required by part 91, 125, or 135 of this chapter, shall—
(1) Perform the inspection so as to determine whether the aircraft, or portion(s) thereof under inspection, meets all applicable airworthiness requirements; and
(2) If the inspection is one provided for in part 125, 135, or 91.409(e) of this chapter, perform the inspection in accordance with the instructions and procedures set forth in the inspection program for the aircraft being inspected

2. **I am performing a progressive phase inspection do I have to sign off each phase inspection with my IA certificate?**

Yes, Part 65.95 states: you may perform an annual, or perform or supervise a progressive inspection according to Sections 43.13 and 43.15 of this chapter. Under Section 65.85 it states and A&P can only perform a 100-hour inspection and not progressive inspections.

3. **The CFRs specifically requires that an annual inspection on a piston aircraft include a compression check and an inspection of the engine oil filter or screen (as applicable) for metal. Do I as a mechanic have to record it in the aircraft records?**

Yes, CFR Part 43 Appendix D specifically spells out the scope of annual and 100-hour inspections. Both cylinder compression checks and inspection of the engine oil filter or screen for metal are specifically called out. All inspections must be recorded CFR 43.11.

4. **Can Canadian mechanic ("Aircraft Maintenance Engineer") perform maintenance, repairs, and 100-hour inspections on U.S.-registered aircraft when they are in Canada?**

Yes, CFR 43.17 specifically provides for maintenance of U.S.-registered aircraft by Canadian AMEs. However, annual inspections are specifically excluded—a U.S.-certificated inspector must inspect U.S. aircraft.

5. **Can Canadian mechanic ("Aircraft Maintenance Engineer") perform maintenance, repairs, and 100-hour inspections on U.S.-registered aircraft when they are in the United States?**

Yes and No, CFR 43.17 specifically provides for maintenance of U.S.-registered aircraft by Canadian AMEs. If they hold an A&P certificate the answer is yes, or if they work for a repair station with the proper ratings and are allowed to perform work away from the repair station. If not then the answer is No. However, annual inspections are specifically excluded—a U.S.-certificated inspector must inspect U.S. aircraft.

Owner Mechanic Issues

1. **I have provided the owner with an estimate to repair his aircraft can I be held to the estimate price once I start the work?**

The author is not a lawyer and **CANNOT** give legal advice. Having said that estimates for aircraft repairs are very difficult to do accurately. If you use the auto industry standard estimates are only guesses and when addition repairs are required they are required to contact the owner and have verbal acceptance or may even require the owner to resign authorizing the addition repairs before work proceeds. You can fax a letter to the owner with the new items and have the owner sign, date, and fax the letter back to you. All work must be completed in an uncompromising airworthy manner. Many previous repairs may be unacceptable. Parts supplies are inconsistent and prices may of gone up. The reality is the total can double the estimate without any intended deception on your part. Tell the owner do not expect accurate estimates for their aircraft without out a full inspection and availability of parts.

2. **You are performing an inspection or repair and find a repair that is not in accordance with the manufacture date or you cannot find a FAA Form 337 to cover a major repair or alteration what should you do?**

In all cases if you find something you are required by law to inform the owner or you could be charged with negligence if something goes wrong and you did not warn the owner. Remember CFR 43.11 (b) Listing of discrepancies and placards. If the person performing any inspection required by part 91 or 125 or 135.411(a)(1) of this chapter finds that the aircraft is unairworthy or does not meet the applicable type certificate data, airworthiness directives, or other approved data upon which its airworthiness depends, that persons must give the owner or lessee a signed and dated list of those discrepancies.

The simple answer you are required to give the owner a statement saying the aircraft is unairworthy. Let the owner make a decision on how they want to take care of unairworthy items. Airworthiness is the owner responsibility your job is to fix things and make them airworthy.

3. **While performing an inspection or repair you find an unairworthy item and want to notify the owner is a verbal statement enough in accordance with CFR 43.11?**

NO!!! You **must** give the owner or lessee a signed and dated list of those discrepancies (CFR 43.11(b)). This can be an aircraft record entry or a written statement in a letter signed and dated. If you provide the owner with a letter I would suggest you make an aircraft record entry indication the date you provided the owner with a list of discrepancies. This is no time to trust anyone it is your certificates on the line not theirs.

4. **The owner wants to assist with the annual inspection to save money can the A&P/IA allow this?**

Yes and No. No inspections can be delegated. You have to perform the inspection yourself however maintenance is something different. **Yes** owners can perform certain maintenance as cited in CFR 43

Appendix A Preventive Maintenance or work under the direct supervision of a certificated mechanic. Just remember if someone does any maintenance it has to be signed off in the aircraft records (CFR 43.9).

Owners can open inspection plates, remove seats, carpet, cowling, change oil, remove spark plugs, and etc. If they remove it there should be an entry saying what they did. After the inspection is completed the owner can reinstall stuff again maintenance entry saying what they did. After all the stuff is reinstalled and the A&P/IA must perform the run up inspection then the annual can be signed off as airworthy or unairworthy as the case may be. Keep in mind an annual inspection is an inspection only to determine the condition at that time. If some maintenance is required it should be signed off as maintenance.

If may be good or even welcome or encouraged to have the owners observe the inspection, servicing and repairs of their aircraft. It is convenient for them to make decision on various service options.

5. **The owner wants a daily update on the process of his aircraft should I do this or just tell them when it is done I will contact them?**

I would recommend daily contact while their aircraft is undergoing servicing in your shop to keep the communication lines open. Is also good business to have the owner stop by the shop during servicing as it keeps them in the loop if unforeseen maintenance items come up or other diagnostics has to be performed to find resolve a problem.

a. **The owner wants to trade (barter) for maintenance can the mechanic do this?**

Yes you can. However you may want to get this in writing to protect yourself incase something comes up later. **Know your customer!!!**

6. **An owner comes into your shop and states they only want to pay X-amount for an annual inspection based on what a dealer is compensated for. Is there a set standard for inspections?**

No! Most annual inspections are flat rated with an additional percent added depending on the aircraft. The recommended inspection time for many aircraft is published by the manufacturer reflecting the amount the dealer is compensated for the **first initial 100-hour/annual inspections.** Remember new aircraft are cleaner, which makes them easier to see things and inspect for. This inspection is based on a new aircraft. Other aircraft inspection times may be determined by aircraft history such as accidents, industry standards, and comparison to similar aircraft.

7. **As an independent A&P/IA an owner wants me to perform warranty work and bill another fix based operator can you bill someone else for work you perform?**

I would seriously consider contacting the other fix base operator and explain the situation. If they agree to reimburse you for work make sure and get it in writing how much they are willing to pay and when payment is to be received.

8. **You are performing an inspection or maintenance and the owner decides they do not want to use your services anymore how should you handle this situation?**

The owner has the right to stop work at any time and take their aircraft somewhere else. However you are required to be paid for the service you have performed. You expect to receive a fee for services rendered.

One way to collect your fee is to have part of the fee paid in advance for older or high performance complex aircraft. If repair or part cost more than your estimate the prepaid fee will help with that.

If the owner says stop work and button it up you should do what the owner requests and make an aircraft record entry only for the work performed and describe what you did. If you discover unairworthy items it should be noted on your record entry. It now becomes the owner's responsibility to obtain a Special Flight Permit from the FAA if needed to relocate the aircraft.

9. **If an owner refuses to pay for services rendered what can a mechanic do about it?**

In every state you can and should take the owner to small claims court and get a judgment for lack of payment for services rendered. This is why a contract such as a work order is a must before starting work. Also you have the right to file a mechanics lien on the aircraft through the FAA certification branch for lack of payment.

10. **An owner wants to know how long your warranty is on parts or serviced you perform. After two or three months they return the aircraft for warranty work for something they said you caused. How should you handle this situation?**

This is why a work order or contract is very important. All warranty work should be spelled out on the work order or contract. If you performed an inspection the warranty is only good until the ink dries on the logbook. Once an aircraft leaves your facility and you have no control over it you cannot be held responsible for it. However it is good practice to provide a 25-hour or more or even 6-months warranty only for work performed.

Most PMA, OEM and TSO new parts come with a warranty for a certain period of time. You cannot be responsible for parts warranty, but only the installation of those parts. This is why when you make a maintenance record entry you should state "only for the work performed" then explain the work you performed. Documentation is everything in aviation and I would highly suggest you keep a computer record of every record entry you perform.

11. **As a fixed base operator (FBO) I sign off maintenance releases and states see work order XYZ. Do I have to provide a copy of the work order to the owner?**

Yes. To comply with the requirement in CFR 43.9 the work order now becomes part of the required maintenance record entry by reference. Part 145 repair stations are required to keep work order for two years and fix base operator do not. Maintenance providers are required to provide the owner with a copy of the work order to show compliance with the CFR's. Also owners are required to make sure A&P and IA's make the proper maintenance record entries in accordance with part 91.417

12. **An owner brings his aircraft to your shop and requests an annual inspection be performed. Do I have to provide copy of the inspection checklist I am going to use to the owner?**

No. However it may be a good idea so there is no miss communication on what you are going to inspect. CFR 43.15(c)(1) states each person performing an annual or 100-hour inspection shall use a checklist while performing the inspection. The checklist may be of the person's own design, one provided by the manufacturer of the equipment being inspected or one obtained from another source. This checklist must include the scope and detail of the items contained in appendix D to this part and paragraph (b) of this section.

13. **An owner brings his aircraft in for an annual inspection how does the mechanic know what inspection program to follow?**

CFR 43.11(a)(7) the entry must identify the inspection program, which part of the inspection program accomplished, and contain a statement that the inspection was performed in accordance with the inspections and procedures for that particular program. It is the owners responsible to inform you the mechanic what inspection program they are under in accordance with CFR 91.409. Also there should be an airframe record entry indicating what inspection program the aircraft is under reference CFR 43.15. As part of the aircraft records inspection you should be able to find this if not bring it to the attention of the owner.

14. **The owner says he want his annual inspection performed in accordance with the aircraft manufacturer's manual. You explain you will perform the inspection in accordance with CFR 43 Appendix D isn't it the same thing?**

No!!! CFR 43 Appendix D is the minimum you have to inspect in addition CFR 43.15 may have some additional items to inspect that are not listed in Appendix D. Second the manufacture inspection checklist has many more items over and above Appendix D. They may require you to perform certain Service Bulletins, Service Communiqué, Service Instructions or Service Letters to meet the requirement of their inspection procedures over and above what Appendix D will require. Remember manufactures and Appendix D are two different inspections, but both meet the requirement for the annual/100-hour inspection.

15. **The owner wants me to sign off the annual/100-hour inspection in accordance the manufactures checklist procedures. However you use your own in house checklist can you still sign off the entry in accordance with CFR 43.11?**

No!!! If you use your own checklist it is not the same as the manufactures see question 17 answer. If you use your own checklist you can sign off the inspection in accordance with CFR 43 Appendix D. If you follow the manufactures checklist you must sign it off stating the manufactures checklist and procedures were used. These are two different sign off's, remember CFR 91.409 makes it the owners responsibly to decide what inspection program they are on. Don't make decisions for the owner it may cost you.

16. **After an inspection or repair on the owner's aircraft he claims several personal items are missing from his aircraft upon return. How do you protect yourself in this situation?**

When an aircraft is received note location of all personal effects and loose equipment, box, identity and store. Notify the owner of the personal effect found in the aircraft and attach the list on the work order or have the owner come pick them up and sign a hand receipt (CYA). If you don't have a digital camera now is a good time to purchase one.

17. **After the annual or 100-hour inspection the owner doesn't want to pay for some of the items you noted on your inspection checklist and says they did not need repair. How do you handle this situation?**

I you haven't purchased a digital camera yet this is another good time. I would suggest upon receiving the aircraft that several pictures be taken of the outside, interior and other compartments. Items that may come up as a dispute later should be documented with pictures before any work is performed. Contact the owner before proceeding with repairs. If you have to go to court pictures say it all.

18. **The owner doesn't think an item isn't bad enough to be changed or repaired and doesn't want it fixed. Who makes this determination?**

You the inspector make the determination of allowable limits in accordance with the manufactures maintenance manual. If the owner doesn't want something repaired you can still sign off the inspection as **UNAIRWORTHY** and provide the owner a list of the items in writing in accordance with CFR 43.11.

19. **The owner does not like the record entry I pasted in his airframe or engine logbooks and wants the mechanic to replace it by pasting another entry over the top of the old one. How do you handle this?**

Reference Aircraft Records on page 41 for proper record entries. Second you **CANNOT** past over a record entry they are stand alone entries. The proper way is to draw a line through the entry and write VOID, date it and sign. The new entry should reference back to the voided entry indicating entered in error and why. Never remove a pasted in record entry, as it is an official entry.

Preventive Maintenance & Related Questions

1. **Is cleaning an aircraft maintenance or preventative maintenance?**

Answer: The regulations do not consider physical cleaning of an aircraft as maintenance or preventative maintenance. However, when preparing the aircraft for cleaning requires removal of components or protection of components, which may fall under the definition of maintenance or preventative maintenance. For example, before cleaning an aircraft, it may be necessary to close and secure the upper and lower fan cowl doors on a transport category aircraft. The FAA considers the closing and securing of the engine fan cowl doors maintenance. Additionally, after the cleaning process, it may be necessary to reapply lubrication compounds and preservatives to aircraft components, both of which could be considered maintenance/preventative maintenance. Conversely, the FAA does not consider cleaning seat cushions/covers maintenance or preventative maintenance.

2. **Is painting an aircraft maintenance or preventative maintenance?**

Answer: 14 CFR Part 43, Appendix A, defines the "refinishing of decorative coating of fuselage, cabin, or cockpit interior" as preventative maintenance. Keep in mind if flight controls or the weight and balance of the aircraft change this will require addition maintenance and possible test flight under Part 91.

3. **How can an employer be sure that the work being performed qualifies as maintenance or preventive maintenance?**

Answer: It is the employer's responsibility to evaluate the duties of its employees and make a determination of whether the work being performed is a safety-sensitive function (i.e., maintenance or preventive maintenance). When making this determination, employers should refer to the definitions of maintenance and preventive maintenance, which are found in 14 CFR Part 1 §1.1 and Part 43. Additionally, we suggest employers access FAA's Flight Standards Service's Guidance Alert on Maintenance. If further clarification is necessary, we recommend you consult directly with your local Flight Standards District Office (FSDO), as they are the expert in clarifying maintenance or preventive maintenance duties. Please visit FAA's website to find the FSDO closest to you.

4. **Do non-certificated helpers, who perform some maintenance duties on part 135 or 121 as part of a process under direct supervision, need to be covered under a drug and alcohol-testing program even though they will not sign off the work?**

Answer: Yes. All employees who conduct maintenance or preventative maintenance are required to be covered by an FAA drug and alcohol testing program regardless of whether they sign off the work or not.

5. **Do non-certificated helpers, who perform some maintenance duties as part of a process under direct supervision, need to be covered under a drug and alcohol-testing program even though they will not sign off the work?**

Answer: No. The person who physically manufactures a part does not have to be a covered employee because manufacturing is not considered maintenance or preventative maintenance. However, the person who takes that manufactured part and consumes it while repairing the next higher assembly must be covered under a program.

6. **Are people who repair or maintain cargo containers loaded on the aircraft in cargo operations included in the requirement for a drug and alcohol-testing program? (Note: Cargo containers are considered part of the aircraft.)**

Answer: Yes. 14 CFR Part 43 covers these types of repairs/maintenance, and they must be performed by individuals covered under a drug and alcohol-testing program.

7. **If an air carrier arranges for an outsource maintenance provider to perform maintenance on its aircraft, or the aircraft's components, and that provider contracts out portions of that maintenance (third level), does the third level contractor have to be covered under a drug and alcohol program?**

Answer: Yes. The regulations require any person, at any level, to be covered under a drug and alcohol-testing program. It is the air carriers' responsibility to ensure that any maintenance contracted out is done by an individual covered by a drug and alcohol program. The air carrier cannot delegate this regulatory responsibility.

8. **How much aircraft maintenance can a U.S. commercial carrier outsource?**

Answer: The FAA does not restrict the amount of outsourced maintenance if the carrier has a maintenance audit program in place. We will inspect the carrier's audit program, as well as individual contract vendors.

Supplemental Inspection Document (SID) Questions and Answers

1. How can the issuance of a Supplemental Inspection Document (SID) that has not been approved and adopted by the FAA Administrator under Section §91.415 be made mandatory?

Answer: There are four inspection program options that an owner or operator must select, identify in the aircraft maintenance records, and use under § 91.409(f). 1 We must assume for the purposes of this question that the inspection program being modified by the SID is either the applicable "current inspection program recommended by the manufacturer "that is referenced in 14 C.F.R. § 91.409(f)(3), or "[a]ny other inspection program established by the registered owner or operator of that airplane . . . and approved by the Administrator," which is referenced in § 91.409(f)(4). It is this fourth option that provides that the Administrator may require revisions in accordance with the provisions of § 91.415, the section referenced in the question.

NOTE: The first two options apply to a person that holds an air carrier operating certificate or an operating certificate [ref. 14 C.F.R. parts 121 or 135].

To the extent that an owner or operator has already selected and identified in the aircraft maintenance records a "current inspection program recommended by the manufacturer," or has selected and identified "any other inspection program . . . [that has been] approved by the Administrator," a SID issued by the manufacturer after the date of selection and identification in the aircraft maintenance records of the then current program would not be mandatory unless the FAA had mandated the SID requirements by issuing an Airworthiness Directive (AD) or through another rulemaking adopted through notice and comment procedures required by the Administrative Procedure Act (AP A); or, in the case of an approved inspection program selected under § 91.409(f)(4), the Administrator required the revision in accordance with the provisions of § 91.415.

2. How can a SID (or any government rule) that has never been approved under the Administrative Procedure Act (APA) by a governmental agency ever be made mandatory on an owner?

Answer: The way a SID issued by a manufacturer (not the FAA) would be mandatory for an aircraft owner or operator would be if it had already become a part of the manufacturer's recommended inspection program when the aircraft owner or operator selected and identified the program (ref. § 91.409(f)(3)); if the SID was already included in an inspection program established by the registered owner or operator of the airplane and approved by the Administrator (ref. § 91.409(f)(4)); or if the Administrator found that the SID should be incorporated into the previously approved program because it was necessary for the continued adequacy of the program (ref. § 91.409(f)(4) and § 91.415).

I am not sure what is mean by the phrase "or any government rule" that had not been approved under the APA. Generally, any "government rule" that was issued by an agency without comporting with the APA requirements could, if challenged, likely be invalidated by a competent court of law.

3. **Aircraft manufactures have stated to some: owners that unless they comply with the SID their aircraft will be "'grounded" by them. It has always been my understanding that such powers could not be delegated by the FAA to a private, non-governmental entity. How can any private entity ground an aircraft or fleet of aircraft for non-compliance with their program?**

Answer: Your understanding that "'such powers," *i.e.,* to "ground" an aircraft cannot be delegated by the FAA to a private, non-governmental entity is correct. Not only does the FAA not have the authority to delegate its rulemaking authority to manufacturers or other private entities. Neither does the agency have authority to delegate particular orders, such as the "grounding" of an airplane. If, however, any person, including a manufacture, had knowledge that an aircraft might be in an unairworthy condition, that person could so advise the owner or operator of that opinion, and could also report the suspected condition to the FAA, which could then conduct an inspection of the aircraft to determine its condition.

4. **I select a maintenance program that did not have a SID at the time of selecting it. The manufacture has since developed a SID program and they state no change has been approved or mandated for the manufactures Inspection program, that if an owner engages in the SID inspection program it is their personal election to do so. Are they correct?**

Answer: Consistent with what was said above, if an aircraft owner or operator had selected and identified in the aircraft maintenance records a current inspection program recommended by the manufacturer before the date the manufacture issued the SID at issue, then the program was current without the SID when the owner or operator adopted it. Therefore, for that owner or operator the SID is not mandatory. However, the owner or operator who adopted the program before the SID was incorporated into it may elect to incorporate the additional requirements of the SID into the previously adopted program. In that case, the inspection program with the SID would be the "current inspection program recommended by the manufacturer," and it would be mandatory for that owner or operator.

5. **Since the manufactures SID has not gone through final FAA and APA approval and adoption, can you state with assurance that it will ultimately be adopted in total without additions or deletions of particular inspection items?**

Answer: As of the date of this letter, the FAA has not issued an AD mandating the SID requirements for previously adopted inspection programs. Any inquiries should be directed to the FAA's Small Airplane Directorate in Kansas City, Missouri. If the FAA decides to make all or part of the manufactures SID mandatory for those previously-adopted inspection programs, the most likely mechanism would be through the AD process. Absent an emergency determination requiring immediate adoption (in accordance with the APA), the AD process would be done through notice and comment rulemaking, also in accordance with the APA procedures. If the FAA does decide to issue an AD based on the SID, whether it would "ultimately be adopted in total without additions or deletions of particular inspection items" would depend in large part both on the FAA's analysis of the SID requirements and on comments received in response to the published notice.

6. **If the SID implemented by the manufacture has applicability to all new owners after the date of the SID (August 2007) and if the FAA cannot relinquish it's authority to a private entity, then**

how is it that manufacture is able to grant an extension to an owner on a mandatory inspection? If the inspection is mandatory, isn't the FAA the only authority to grant an extension?

Answer: In general, once a current inspection program is adopted under § 91.409(f)(3) that program is mandatory under that regulation, and its intervals must be followed. However, the underlying factual predicate is not clear from the question. Assuming the inspection program at issue is one adopted under § 91.409(f)(3), and an interval extension is "granted" by manufacture to an individual owner or operator based on a particular set of applicable circumstances, the now-modified inspection program would be considered the most "current" one recommended by the manufacturer for that owner or operator. That is the program (with the extended interval) that the owner or operator must follow. Under the facts and circumstances assumed here, that interval extension would apply only to that owner or operator; it would not extend automatically to other owners or operators who had adopted the manufacture inspection program containing the SID.

In the case of an inspection program approved under § 91.409(f)(4), the program, as approved, would be mandatory, and the inspection intervals contained therein would have to be followed-unless the program itself contains provisions allowing the manufacture to grant extensions. Absent such a provision, however, if the manufacture were to "grant" an interval extension to an owner or operator who was using such an approved program, the owner or operator would have to seek approval from the FAA to make that change to the program; alternatively, the FAA, under the provisions of § 91.415, could unilaterally make the revision if the FAA found it necessary for the continued adequacy of the program.

Note: The **Administrative Procedure Act** (**APA**) (P.L. 79-404) is the United States federal law that governs the way in which administrative agnecies of the federal government of the United States may propose and establish regulations. The APA also sets up a process for the United States federal courts to directly review agency decisions. It is one of the most important pieces of United States administrative law. The Act became law in 1946.

SAMPLE IA TEST QUESTIONS AND ANSWERS

1. **Where can the major items to be inspected be found that must be included in a checklist used while performing an annual inspection on a fixed-wing aircraft?**
   a. FAA Form 8130-10.
   b. 14 CFR Part 43, Appendix D.
   c. Advisory Circular 43.13-1B.

Answer B-Subject Matter Knowledge Code: K49. 14 CFR Part 43, section 43.15(c) states:
"Sec. 43.15 Additional performance rules for inspections . . . . c. Annual and 100-hour inspections.

   i. Each person performing an annual or 100-hour inspection shall use a checklist while performing the inspection. The checklist may be of the person's own design, one provided by the manufacturer of the equipment being inspected or one obtained from another source. This checklist must include the scope and detail of the items contained in appendix D to this Part and paragraph (b) of this section . . . ."

2. **Airworthiness Approval Tags (FAA Form 8130-3) may be used by which maintenance entity for approving class II and III products for return to service after maintenance or alteration?**
   a. Inspection Authorizations.
   b. 14 CFR Part 145, Certified Repair Stations.
   c. Either A or B.

Answer B-Subject Matter Knowledge Code KO5. Order 8130.21A. The work must be accomplished by a certificate holder under 14 CFR Part 121 or 135, having continuous airworthiness maintenance program or by a repair station certificated under Part 145.

3. **When installing additional equipment in an aircraft, if not otherwise specified, the ultimate load factor used in the static load test is?**
   a. Four times the weight of the equipment.
   b. Variable, depending on the direction of applied force.
   c. The limit load factor multiplied by 1.5.

Answer C-Subject Matter Knowledge Code: K50. AC 43.13-2A, Chapter 1, Paragraph 3.
Ultimate load factors are limit load factors multiplied by a 1.5 safety factor.

4. **Which Code of Federal Regulations (CFR's) provides for the fabrication of aircraft replacement and modification parts?**
   a. 14 CFR Part 21.303. 14 CFR Part 23, Appendix B.
   b. 14 CFR Part 45.21.

Answer A-Subject Matter Knowledge CodeA112. CFR part 21, subpart K, section 21.303, defines who may produce modification and replacement parts for sale and those persons to which the part does not apply.

5. **A proposed airframe alteration will require a section of Mil-H-8788-10 hydraulic hose to flex through 60° of travel. The system will operate at 210° centigrade and 1200 p.s.i. What is the minimum bend radius for this installation?**
   a. 30 inches.
   b. 7 inches.
   c. 5½ inches.

Answer B-Subject Matter Knowledge Code: K49. Acceptable Methods, Techniques, and Practices—Aircraft Inspection and Repair, Chapter 10, Paragraph d; and figure 10.5.

6. **Where would you find the marking and placards required for Cessna Model 208, serial number 20800044?**
   a. Type Certificate Data Sheet No. A37CE.
   b. Airplane Flight Manual, Cessna P/N D1286-13PH.
   c. Model 208 Series Maintenance Manual.

Answer B-Subject Matter Knowledge Code: A157. 14 CFR Part 23, Sub Part C "Operating limitations and Information."

7. **Which of the following aircraft, operating under 14 CFR Part 91, could the holder of an inspection authorization approve for return-to-service after a major alteration has been made in accordance with technical data approved by the administrator?**
   a. A commuter category, multiengine, turbopeller airplane.
   b. A transport category, multiengine, turbojet airplane.
   c. Either A or B.

Answer C-Subject Matter Knowledge Code: A45. 14 CFR Part 65, Section 65.95(a).
"Sec. 65.95 Inspection authorization: privileges and limitations.

a. **The holder of an inspection authorization may—**
1. Inspect and approve for return to service any aircraft or related part or appliance (except any aircraft maintained in accordance with a continuous airworthiness program under Part 121 or 127 of this chapter) after a major repair or major alteration to it in accordance with Part 43 of this chapter, if the work was done in accordance with technical data approved by the Administrator; and
2. Perform an annual or perform or supervise a progressive inspection according to CFR 43.13 and 43.15 of this chapter."

8. **An owner brings you his light twin-engine airplane operating under Part 135. Where would you find the appropriate instructions for inspecting the aircraft?**
   a. Flight manual
   b. Operations Specifications
   c. CFR 43, Appendix D

Answer B

9. **For an appliance, the manufacturer's manual could be used as approved data for which of the following?**
   a. Major repairs
   b. Major alterations
   c. Both A and B

Answer A, AC65.19 par. 2 g.

10. **For an appliance major alteration, which of the following could be used as approved data without further approval?**
    a. Advisory Circulars
    b. Manufactures Manual
    c. Neither A or B

Answer C, AC 65.19 par 2.f(9)

11. **Title 14, Part 43 requires persons performing maintenance to make entries in the maintenance records. If the logbook entry is made per the requirements of CFR 91.417, does this entry also meet the requirements of CFR 43?**
    a. No, it would not be sufficient
    b. Yes, if it is for an inspection only
    c. Yes, it would be sufficient for maintenance and inspections

Answer A, CFR 91.417 does not require the name of the person performing maintenance.

12. **The completion and signing of block 6 (conformity statement) of FAA Form 337 indicates?**
    a. FAA approval of the work only
    b. Agency approval for return to service
    c. The work accomplished to FAA approved data

Answer C, AC 43.9

Chapter 5

MECHANIC GENERAL KNOWLEDGE

FAA IA RENEWAL PROCEDURES

The FAA Inspector should have prior knowledge of the following references:
- CFR 65.91 through 65.95
- FAA Order 8900.1 Volume 5 Chapters 5(As Amended)

1. Upon contact with applicant the FAA Inspector will ensure FAA Form 8610-1 is properly completed, **in duplicate (two copies)**, in accordance with FAA Order 8900.1, Vol. 5, Chap 5, (RENEW INSPECTION AUTHORIZATION).

2. FAA will verify applicant's status utilizing reports for prior or active enforcements, and A&P Certificate status, (active, suspended, revoked, not issued, etc).

3. FAA will request and verify applicant's activity record. This record at a minimum should contain a list of annuals, major alterations, major repairs and/or progressive inspections by date, aircraft registration number, make, model and type of activity.

4. If renewal is based on CFR 65.93(a)(4) ensure a copy of the Certificate of Attendance is made. (FAA approved eight hour course)

5. FAA will verify the applicant has documents to substantiate the renewal eligibility IAW Order 8900.1 Volume5 Chapter 6 and CFR 65.93. *Reminder: The requirements of CFR 65.91(c 1-4) must still be met by the applicant.*

6. If any requirement of CFR 65.91(c 1-4) cannot be substantiated, a visit to the applicant's facility would be recommended. In lieu of a personal visit, request that the applicant present other documents or physical evidence that they do meet the CFR 65.91(c 1-4) requirements.

7. Upon satisfactory application, presentation of supporting evidence, review of material, case file and then evaluate the applicant's eligibility and qualifications.

8. FAA will complete the renewal process by following the instructions in Order 8900.1 Volume 5, Ch 5 Section 2 Paragraph 5.

After completing the renewal process, FAA will ensure one copy of the 8610-1 is forwarded to OKC, AFS-760. Ensure one copy of the 8610-1 along with the activity report (or copy of the Certificate of

Attendance) and a photocopy of the applicants Inspection Authorization Card (FAA Form 8310-5) is placed in the applicant's case file.

IA Eligibility

To be eligible for renewal of an inspection authorization for a one-year period an applicant must present evidence at an FAA Flight Standard District Office during the month of March that he/she still meets the requirements of Section 65.91(c)(1) through (4), and by showing that during the current period that he/she held the inspection authority. They must show:

1. Has performed at least one annual inspection for each 90 days that he has held the current authority;
2. Has performed inspections of at least two major repairs or major alterations for each 90 days that he held the current authority; or
3. Has performed or supervised and approved at least one progressive inspection in accordance with standards prescribed by the Administrator.

Application for renewal may be required to comply with following:

1. Complete FAA form 8610-1, Mechanic's Application for Inspection Authorization, in duplicate; and
2. Show evidence of meeting the requirements of CFR 65.93(a).

Meeting the requirements of CFR 65.93(a) does not mean that the applicant has to meet all five (5) of the listed requirements. There are several ways to meet the requirement. To be eligible for renewal of an inspection authorization for a one-year period, the applicant **must** show evidence of having performed four annual inspections during the 365-day period prior to renewal date to be able to qualify for renewal. The same logic applies for major repairs and alterations. However, the number of annual inspections, major repairs and alterations performed cannot be mixed simply because the 14 CFR section does not provide for such combinations.

Mixing annual inspections, major repairs, and alterations is not permissible.

NOTE

An inspection program required under 14 CFR part 91, Section 91.409(e) is not acceptable as IA activity. Partial inspections such as phases or events on more than one aircraft are not acceptable as activity. A progressive inspection is a complete inspection on one identified aircraft.

Successful completion of an eight-hour refresher course, acceptable to the Administrator, during the 12-month period preceding the renewal application.

The refresher course must contain subjects directly related to aircraft maintenance, inspection repairs, and alterations. In addition, some non-technical subjects, such as human factors or professionalism as they relate to aviation maintenance personnel, may be acceptable. The raining must not be used to promote a new or existing product.

The instructional requirements of CFR 65.93(a)(4) may be met by accumulating at least 8 hours of maintenance training. Each course or seminar must be at least one hour long and completed in the 12-month period between April 1 and March 31 prior to inspection authorization renewal.

Each person who intends to use 8 hours of instruction to meet **14 CFR 65 section 65.93(a)(4)** must provide proof of attendance for instruction received at the time of renewal. Acceptable proof of attendance consists of a Certificate of training or similar document showing:

1. The name of the course
2. Name of attendee
3. Course identification number assigned by the RSPM A/W
4. Expiration date
5. Description of the course content
6. Time in hours
7. The date
8. Location
9. Course instructor's name and affiliation.

The proof of attendance should be reviewed by FAA Inspectors at renewal time to ensure that both:

1. The training organization and the IA have met the appropriate requirements.
2. The training organization must keep a list of all attendees for a period of two (2) years.
3. This list must be provided by the training organization to FSDO inspectors upon request.

A lastly take an oral test given by an FAA Aviation Safety Inspector (ASI) to ensure that the applicant's knowledge of regulations and standards is current. **Reference 14 CFR 65 section 65.93(a)(5).**

NOTE

If the applicant applies for renewal at an office other than the jurisdictional office, the receiving office should withhold renewal until the applicant's activities can be verified.

IA Suspensions

Inquiries have been made in the field as to the effect of the amendment of Section 65.91 (Amendment 65-22; 42 FR 46278; September 15, 1977) on the renewal of an inspection authorization (IA) under Section 65.93.

Section 65.93 provides that, to be eligible for the renewal of an IA an applicant must present evidence that, among other things, he still meets the requirements of Section 65.91(c)(1) through (4). The question arises whether an applicant whose mechanic certificate was suspended, and subsequently restored, during a year in which he held an IA can show that he meets the requirements of Section 65.91(c)(1), when he applies for renewal of the IA.

Before Amendment 65-22, Section 65.91(c)(1) provided that to be eligible for an IA, an applicant had to be "a certificated mechanic who has held both an airframe rating and a powerplant rating for at least 3 years before the date he applies. "Section 65.91(c)(1) now requires that the applicant hold "a currently effective mechanic certificate with both an airframe rating and a powerplant rating, each of which is currently effective **AND HAS BEEN CONTINUOUSLY IN EFFECT** for not less than the three year period immediately before the date of application." (Emphasis added.)

Under the old rule, the holder of an IA whose mechanic certificate was suspended could still be said to have "held" that certificate during the time of suspension. However, under the new rule, the certificate cannot be said to be "in effect" while it is suspended. Accordingly, although the IA becomes effective again at the end of the suspension of the mechanic's certificate, it may not be renewed at the end of the year because at that time the mechanic certificate will not have been continuously in effect during the preceding three years. The mechanic will not be eligible again for an IA until three years after the end of the suspension of the mechanic certificate.

Security Investigations

Answers to field questions regarding security investigations:

1. **When interviewed by a Security Agent will my answers be confidential?**

First of all, the Report of Investigation (ROI) is provided to personnel (those who determine suitability or action) on a need to know basis. Secondly, the entire ROI (including all statements and/or testimony) is provided to the subject of the investigation upon request in compliance with privacy act requirements. Lastly, the ROI can be released under the Freedom of Information Act (FOIA); however, information pertaining to national security or an individual's privacy may not be released.

In accordance with the Human Resources Policy Manual (HRPM) for non-bargaining unit employees and the Federal Aviation Personnel Manual, Letter 2635, Chapter 2, Paragraph 209 (For bargaining unit employees); it is the duty of every employee to give to any superior or official conducting an official investigation or inquiry, all information and testimony about matters inquired of, arising under the law, and regulations administered by the FAA.

2. **Can I refuse to answer a Security Agent's questions?**

Yes and No. If the investigation involves criminal conduct you may refuse to answer on the grounds it may incriminate you. Your invoking of this "right" will be considered in determining corrective action. For investigations not involving criminal allegations the answer is no. The agencies current table of penalties for bargaining unit employees recommends that employees who refuse to give testimony in connection with employment or any investigation be given a 10-day suspension to removal on the first offense and removal on the second offense.

3. **May I request a representative to attend my interview with Security?**

Yes, you may bring a representative of your choosing as long as it does not cause an inordinate delay in the completion of the interview. Your representative is allowed to observe but not answer for you or otherwise participate in the interview.

4. **What if I want to make sure my interview/statement is captured accurately?**

Upon completion of the interview, the Security Agent will show you your statement and have you initial or sign your statement to certify it's accuracy.

Threats Against Government Employees

The 1996 Anti-Terrorism Act, passed in the wake of the Oklahoma City tragedy, requires the U.S. Attorney General to collect data "relating to crimes and **incidents of threats of violence** and acts of violence" against government employees and their families in the performance of official duties. A centralized government tracking system is needed, given the poor track record of federal agencies in maintaining reliable data on incidents against public employees.

The FBI investigates assaults, **threats** and killings of federal employees pursuant to Title 18 U.S.C. Sections 111 (Assaulting, Resisting or Impeding Certain Officers or Employees); 115 (Influencing, impeding, or retaliating against a Federal Official by **threatening** or injuring a family member); 1111 (Murder); 1112 (Manslaughter); 1114 (Protection of officers and employees of the United States); 1116 (Murder or manslaughter of foreign officials, official guests, or internationally protected persons); 1117 (Conspiracy to murder in violation of Section 1114); 2231 (Assault or resistance); and 1201 (a)(5) (Kidnapping in violation of 1114). Additionally, U.S. Supreme Court Justices, members of Congress, and the heads of executive branch departments are afforded protection under Title 18 U.S.C. Section 351 (Congressional, Cabinet, and Supreme Court Assassination, Kidnapping, and Assault).

The safety of all federal employees and their family members is a top priority of the FBI. For the purposes of this hearing, the term "federal employee" includes the class of employees defined by Title 18 U.S.C. Section 1114,

> "Any officer or employee of the United States or of any agency branch of the United States Government (including any member of the uniformed services) while such officer or employee is engaged in or on account of the performance of official duties."

Each reported incident is aggressively pursued and referred to the Department of Justice for prospective consideration. In those incidents where the FBI acts as the primary investigative agency, coordination is closely established with the victim employee's agency. Nevertheless, each threat creates tremendous strain on the victims and their families, and therefore requires and receives appropriate attention.

PROSECUTION OF SUBJECTS WHO ASSAULT FEDERAL OFFICERS

The FBI encourages aggressive Federal prosecution of those who threaten federal employees. Generally speaking, Federal prosecutors require actual injury, or substantial overt acts before prosecuting a case in which a law enforcement officer is the victim. Agents and officers who carry firearms and possess arrest powers are viewed as somewhat less vulnerable than prosecutors, judges and elected officials.

Making threats

- Display weapons as a way of making you afraid or directly threaten you with weapons.
- Use his anger or "loss of temper" as a threat to get you to do what he wants.

Data and Specifications Sources

Specifications, Standards, Drawings

Defense Printing Service
Attn.: Customer Service
700 Robbins Ave.
Bldg. 4, Section D
Philadelphia, PA 19111-5094

Phone assistance only:
(215) 697-2179 or 4107
FAX: (215) 697-1462

This agency provides all the MIL Specifications and Standards. Most are free on the inter net at: http:// www.dodssp.daps.mil/ Look under Quick Assist.

National Airspace System Specifications and Standards
The FAA's NAS specifications and standards relating to the CIP Capital Investment Plan are available to government personnel, FAA contractors, and respondents to FAA RFP's Requests for Proposals from:

TRW Thompson, Ramo, and Woodridge
NAS Documentation Control Center
FAA
Seta/ TRW
800 Independence Ave., SW
Washington, DC 20591
Phone: (202) 651-2392
Fax: (202) 484-1257

Contractors and RFP respondents should be prepared to provide their name, company name, address, phone number, their FAA contract number or RFP number, and the routing symbol of the FAA group being supported.

Standards referenced in FAA specifications are available from:
Federal Supply Services Bureau
Specifications Section
470 E. L'Enfant Plaza, S.W.
Suite 8100
Washington, D.C. 20407
Phone: (202) 755-0325
FAX: (202) 755-0285

NTIS
National Technical Information Service
U.S. Department of Commerce
5285 Port Royal Rd.
Springfield, VA 22161

Order desk: (703) 487-4650
Research library: (703) 487-4780
Rush/express order desk:
Phone: (800) 553-6847
FAX: (703) 321-8547

The NTIS National Technical Information Service provides many FAA and aviation-related scientific, technical, and business reports at cost. Included are printed reports, videotapes, computer software, data files and tapes, diskettes, and CD-ROM. A free copy of the NTIS Products and Services Catalog is available upon request from the NTIS.

FAA Information

Designee Reference Library

http://www.faa.gov/other_visit/aviation_industry/designees_delegations/
http://www.faa.gov/other_visit/aviation_industry/designees_delegations/tools/forms/

This site list all the required FAA Handbook and Orders for aircraft certifications, import, export, and inspection requirements and bilateral agreements.

FAA Career Opportunities

http://jobs.faa.gov

This site lists FAA vacancies nationwide. You can search for jobs by job series, location, and grade level. Also included are vacancies with the International Civil Aviation Organization (ICAO) and Executive Career Opportunities. Job application forms are also available at the site.

FAA Catalog of Training Courses

http://www.academy.jccbi.gov/catalog

Course listings and descriptions for training offered by the FAA Academy, Center for Management Development, Transportation Safety Institute, and the Civil Aero medical Institute. Includes resident courses, correspondence training, CBI and IVT training, information for students, and how to receive college credit for some of the FAA training courses.

MMAC Office of Human Resource Management (AMH)

http://www.oklahoma.feb.gov/FEBKids/MikeMonroneyAeronauticalCenter.htm

This is the best place to start if you have a human resources question. There is an abundance of information available on local Aeronautical Center policies and procedures as well as information applicable FAA wide. You can find a list of AMH personnel and their job functions, links to online personnel regulations, information on Employee Express, an order form for national job announcements, a list of labor unions and their officers at the Aeronautical Center, and other useful information.

Job Listings

USA Jobs

http://www.usajobs.opm.gov

Here you will find a current list of Federal Government job openings nationwide. You can search the listing by type of job, agency, or job series. You can also find general information on applying for Federal jobs, salary schedules, Veterans benefits, and job scams. You can also access this site through a link at the main Office of Personnel Management site.

Fedworld Federal Job Search

http://www.fedworld.gov/jobs/jobsearch.html

This site is maintained by the National Technical Information Service, a part of the Department of Commerce. It is very similar to USA Jobs. The job listings are searchable. If you would like to work at Fedworld, you are able to sign up for free e-mail delivery of job announcements for jobs at Fedworld in certain career fields.

Federal Jobs Central

http://www.fedjobs.com

This is an automated version of the Federal Research Service publication Federal Career Opportunities. Job postings are searchable by occupation, pay level, or location. Although some areas of the site are free, this is a fee based subscription service.

*** Note ***

The Internet is a very dynamic environment. Although addresses presented here were verified as correct at the time this paper was written (March 2005), some of the addresses may no longer be valid.

Experience Requirements For None A&P

1. Can you as a certificated A&P mechanic sign a letter attesting to the work experience of non A&P's?

Yes, you can, however be very careful what you sign your name to.

To answer this question better, let's examine the following scenario: You, an FAA certificated mechanic are asked one day by your buddy you to write or sign a letter verifying they have the necessary experience and skills to meet the qualifications for both mechanic ratings. This is your buddy, so you may think there is nothing wrong with writing or signing a letter of this nature. Besides, they could get a pay raise.

Think back to those late nights, when you were studying for your exams. Do you remember studying a regulation that might address this particular situation or something similar?

Hopefully, at this point, you are now reviewing Title 14 Code of Federal Regulations (CFR) Part 65. Specifically, subpart A, section 65.20(a) which states: "No person may make or cause to be made—any fraudulent or intentionally false statements on any application for a certificate or rating under this part." Therefore, if you write or sign that letter, you may be <u>causing</u> fraudulent or intentionally false statements to be <u>made</u> on an application for the mechanic certificate.

Now the question becomes, "What can happen to me?" For the answer to this question, let's look at section 65.20(b) which states: "The commission by any person of an act prohibited under paragraph (a) of this section is a basis for <u>suspending</u> or <u>revoking</u> any airman or ground instructor certificate or rating held by that person."

For the sake of this scenario, let's suppose your certificate is <u>revoked</u> and you would like to get it back, then read section 65.11(d)(2) which states: "A person whose mechanic or repairman certificate is revoked <u>may not</u> apply for either of those kinds of certificates for one year after the date of revocation." After the year has passed, you must again seek authorization to retest for the mechanic certificate. That means you must present documentary evidence to the local FSDO. If the authorization to retest is granted; then you will have to retake all the written, oral, and practical exams.

Now, suppose that your mechanic certificate was suspended. What effect could that have on you? If you've had your mechanic certificate for at least three years, maybe you were considering obtaining the Inspection Authorization. Section 65.91(c)(1) requires that the applicant hold "a currently effective mechanic certificate with both an airframe rating and a powerplant rating, each of which is currently effective and has been <u>continuously</u> in effect for not less than the three year period immediately before the date of application.

Your mechanic certificate was suspended, therefore it cannot be said to be "in effect" while it is suspended and you will not be eligible for the IA until three years after the end of the suspension of the mechanic certificate.

As you can see from the above scenarios, by writing or signing that letter documenting maintenance experience <u>could</u> jeopardize your mechanic certificate and maybe your job. Think about it hard and serious before verifying their experience and your responsibilities before you write or sign that letter

An individual can work for an FAA Repair Station or FBO under the supervision of an A & P mechanic for 18 months, for each individual airframe or powerplant rating, or 30 months for both ratings. The FAA considers a "month of practical experience" to contain at least **160 hours**. This practical experience must be documented. Some acceptable forms of documentation are: Pay receipts, a record of work (log book) signed by the supervising mechanic, a notarized statement stating that the applicant has at least the required number of hours for the rating(s) requested from a certificated air carrier, repair station, or a certificated mechanic or repairman who supervised the work. The practical experience must provided you with basic knowledge of and skills with the procedures, practices, materials, tools, machine tools, and equipment used in aircraft construction, alteration, maintenance, and inspection. If you have a repair station or certificated mechanic provide a letter, it should be original and should state that you meet the minimum 30-months experience required by Part 65 Section 65.71 and 65.77. Also they must provide their name, signature and mechanic certificate number.

In evaluating documented part-time practical aviation mechanic experience, an equivalent of 18 months (or 30 months) based on a standard 40-hour workweek is acceptable. The months need not be consecutive. *A standard workweek has 8 hours per day for 5 days per week, thus totaling 40 hours per week and approximately 160 hours per month.*

A&P Experience Requirements

Below are the requirements you will have to meet before making an appointment with the FAA to have your FAA Form 8610-2 application signed authorizing you to take the written tests.

Eligibility Requirements

Applicants for a mechanic certificate must meet the requirements of 14 CFR Part 65, subparts A and D. (For the certification of foreign applicants physically located outside the United States as per Part 65.3, see FAA Order 8900.1, Airworthiness Inspector's Handbook, vol. 5, ch. 5, Certificate Foreign Applicants Located Outside the United States for Mechanic Certificates/Ratings.)

1. All applicants must be at least 18 years of age. An applicant under 18 may take the tests, but no mechanic certificate will be issued until the applicant's 18th birthday.

2. All applicants must be able to read, write, speak, and understand English. See Advisory Circular (AC) 60-28, English Language Skill Standards Required by 14 CFR Parts 61, 63, and 65, which states for all certification testing, applicant will be required to read a section of a technical manual, and then write and explain their interpretation of the reading. (An appropriate technical manual in this sense means an airplane flight manual, a maintenance manual, or other publication as appropriate for the certificate or rating sought.)

Experience Requirements

Part 65, Section 65.77 requires the applicant to have practical experience in maintaining airframes and/or powerplants. At least 18 months of practical experience is required for the appropriate rating requested. For a certificate with both ratings, the requirement is for at least 30 months experience concurrently performing the duties appropriate to both ratings. If the 30 months concurrently performing the duties appropriate to both ratings has not been met, then calculate each rating separately using the 18-month requirement for each.

The practical experience must provide the applicant with basic knowledge of and skills with the procedures, practices, materials, tools, machine tools, and equipment used in aircraft construction, alteration, maintenance, and inspection.

For foreign applicants located in the United States, all of the requirements for a citizen of the United States apply. This includes applicants who come to the United States just to take the mechanic test. The following are types of documents that will be acceptable to establish the required record of time and experience:

The application process for the Airframe and Powerplant (A&P) authorization may require between one and two hours. We suggest you review FAA Order 8900.1 Volume 5, with emphasis on chapter 5. In addition, you should review the Code of Federal Regulations (CFR) Part 65, with particular emphasis on subparts A & D. You can peruse these orders and regulations at the following Internet address:

http://www.faa.gov/regulations_policies

All applicants **must be able to read, write, speak, and understand English**. See the current version of Advisory Circular (AC) 60-28, English Language Skill Standards Required by 14 CFR parts 61, 63, and 65, which states for all certification testing, the applicant will be required to read a section of a technical manual, and then write and explain their interpretation of the reading. (An appropriate technical manual in this sense means an airplane flight manual, maintenance manual, or other publication as appropriate for the certificate or rating sought.) The responsibility for ensuring applicants meet the English language requirements is based on the aviation safety inspectors. Ultimately the aviation safety inspector are required to evaluate each applicant's eligibility, including English fluency, prior to beginning the practical test or accepting an application for an airman certificate or rating.

In order to meet the FAA Experience Requirements you must provide the FAA with documentary evidence, satisfactory to the Administrator (FAA).

Please bring the following documents with you to your interview:

1. A letter/resume stating that you have documented practical experience in maintaining airframes and/ or powerplants and the time periods by month and year. If you work at an FAA Repair Station or FBO under the supervision of a certified mechanic for 18 months for each certificate, or 30 months for both. You must document your experience, a log book signed by your supervising mechanic, a notarized statement from your employer, or other proof you worked the required time.
2. The practical experience must provided you with basic knowledge of and skills with the procedures, practices, materials, tools, machine tools, and equipment used in aircraft construction, alteration, maintenance, and inspection.
3. The above letter/resume should be original and should state that you meet the minimum 30-months experience required by Part 65 Section 65.71 and 65.77.
4. The letter/resume should also show details of type aircraft, type maintenance performed and length of time you have been performing that type of practical experience concurrently performing the duties appropriate to the rating. Provide the month, year of experience and where experience received.
5. If you are applying for only the airframe rating, indicate type of aircraft, type maintenance performed and length of time you have been performing that type of work. Provide the month, year of experience and where experience received.
6. If you are applying for only the powerplant rating, indicate type of engine, type maintenance performed and length of time you have been performing that type of work. Provide the month, year of experience and where experience received.
7. If you can get a letter from the local CAA with a raised seal it is acceptable indicating your work experience.
8. If you have a CAA-66 license please bring it with you.

- **The FAA will give you credit for your practical experience only after they review your paperwork and you have a satisfactory interview with an FAA Airworthiness inspector.**

- All documents presented to the inspector or advisor **must be** a signed, dated original and traceable to the initiator.

- Each FAA inspector has the authority to accept or deny your letter of experience.

- Suggest you bring all documentation to verify your experience, including military, aviation schooling, and training certifications. In addition, if you keep a daily log of work performed, suggest you bring these logs with you for review after having them appropriately certified by your employer.

NOTE:

Be advised that all experience provided to an FAA Inspector must be truthful and verifiable in accordance with Section 65.20 that you performed the work.

NOTE

Appropriate action is whatever the inspector deems appropriate to determine that the experience is valid, i.e., review supporting documentation presented to satisfy authorization, without expending an excessive amount of time or resources on behalf of the applicant.

A&P Knowledge, Skills, and Abilities:
1. Must possess required knowledge, skills, abilities and experience and be able to explain and demonstrate, with or without reasonable accommodations, that the essential functions of the job can be performed.
2. Knowledge of General Orders, Policies and Procedures
3. Knowledge of maintenance materials, manuals, service bulletins, airworthiness directives and advisory circulates.
4. Knowledge of **aircraft** maintenance safety procedures
   - Skill in the use of power and hand tools.
   - Skill in oral and written communication
   - Ability to use tools (e.g., power shears, sheet metal cutters, rivet guns and pneumatic or electrical Drills) to rebuild or replace airframe ports or components.
   - Ability to operate **aircraft** measuring instruments.
   - Ability to work with a team or independently with minimal supervision.
   - Ability to interpret wiring and schematic diagrams and technical instruction.

Sample Reference Letter For A&P

USE ONLY AS A GUIDE

New World Airlines
Anywhere, USA
January 1, 2010

To: Flight Standard District Office

Dear FAA Inspector:

I have known Good for over 5 years and find him to be of good character. For the past three years, January. 2004 to present, he has worked under my direct supervision on small aircraft of various makes and models, including but not limited to Cessna 150, 152, 172, 182, 210, 310, Beach craft A35, A36, and engines including Continental 0-300, 0-320, O-300, IO-502, TISO-520, Lycoming IO-320, O-360, etc Or turbine engines EG 101, T-201 and etc. He has performed airframe maintenance including inspection, removal, repair and replacement of control surfaces, windows and windshields, installation of rivets and fasteners, rigging of controls, repair of landing gear, shock struts, brakes, wheels, tires, hydraulic, and steering systems, removal and installation of aircraft instruments, inspection and repair of fuel systems, and inspection and service of taxi, landing and strobe lights.

He has performed powerplant maintenance including inspection, removal, repair and replacement of aircraft engines, cylinders, pistons and related parts. Inspection, troubleshooting and service of ignition systems. Inspection removal and replacement of carburetors, fuel metering, intake and exhaust manifolds, engine exhaust system components and heating systems. Inspection, removal, service and replacement of propellers and governors. Since Mr. Good meets the eligibility requirements of CFR 65.71 and experience requirements of CFR 65.77, I recommend him for his A&P certificates.

Sincerely,

I. B. Good
A&P
Certificate No. #1234567

Replacement of Certificates

Application for Replacement of Lost, Destroyed, or Paper Airman Certificate(s) and Knowledge Test Report(s)

For replacement of lost, destroyed, or paper certificates, submit a signed, written request stating your name, date and place of birth, social security number and/or certificate number, and the reason for replacement to the mailing address below.

FAA
Airmen Certification Branch, AFS-760
PO Box 25082
Oklahoma City, OK 73125-0082

Or go to http://www.faa.gov/licenses_certificates/aircraft_certification/aircraft_registry/

Include a check or money order for $2 (U.S. Funds) for each certificate, made payable to the FAA. If your current address is listed as a Post Office Box (POB), General Delivery, Rural Route, or Star Route, please provide directions or a map for locating your residence. Allow 4 to 6 weeks for processing. Only one copy of each certificate can be issued. The original date of issue cannot be placed on a replacement certificate. Expired certificates cannot be issued; however, an expired CFI letter can be requested at no charge.

*NOTE: In compliance with the policy dated July 23, 2002, airmen applying for a replacement certificate issued on the basis of a foreign license under 14 CFR Part 61, Section 61.75 or 14 CFR Part 63, Section 63.42, must complete and submit a Verification of Authenticity of Foreign License, Rating, and Medical Certification form to the Airmen Certification Branch and appear at a FSDO for positive identification to make application for a replacement certificate.

Change Your Airman Certificate Number

All new original airmen certificates will be issued with a unique certificate number. The Airmen Certification Branch no longer assigns your Social Security Number (SSN) as your certificate number. If your certificate uses your SSN as the certificate number we will continue to issue you that number unless you request a unique number.

If your airman certificate uses your SSN as your certificate number and you would like to change it, or you would like to remove your SSN completely from our official records, please fill out a **Request for Change of Certificate Number** form. You can mail the completed form to:

Federal Aviation Administration
Airmen Certification Branch, AFS-760
P.O. Box 25082

http://www.faa.gov/licenses_certificates/airmen_certification/change_certificate_number/

Airmen Online Services
To utilize the online services, you must first create an account with the Airmen Certification Branch. After you create an account log in to your account to:

- Change your address
- Order a replacement certificate
- Remove SSN as certificate number
- Request temporary authority to exercise certificate privileges
- Request verification of certificate privileges

After you register with the site you can receive notices of FAA safety meetings via email. The FAA will provide your email address to the FAA Safety Program Airmen Notification System (SPANS) so that they can communicate with you on vital safety matters. Due to security requirements, the FAA will not provide your Registry password to the SPANS site, so you will need to register to take full advantage of the site. If you do not wish to receive safety notices by email, you can change your preferences by registering with the SPANS site.

http://www.faa.gov/licenses_certificates/airmen_certification/airmen_services/

Enforcements and Re-Examinations

Competency Examinations/Reexaminations

Title 49 of the United States Code (49 U.S.C.), § 44709 (formerly Section 609 of the Federal Aviation Act of 1958) provides for reexamination. The aviation safety inspector (ASI) will determine whether a reexamination test is necessary based on personal knowledge, reliable reports, or evidence obtained through an accident, incident, or enforcement investigation.

A. An airman demonstrating questionable competency while exercising the privileges of the certificate and ratings may be reexamined.
B. Questions of airman competency may arise from any source.
C. Inspectors must consider airman competency as a factor in the following:
- Complaint investigations
- Surveillance
- Unairworthy aircraft notice issuance
- Incident investigations
- Accident investigations
- Enforcement investigations
- Hearings, both formal and informal

Based on the results of a reexamination, the FAA must approve, amend, suspend, or revoke the airman's certificate. The reconsideration of an airman's competence is a serious issue and requires that there be ample cause.

In most cases, the office issuing the reexamination letter conducts the reexamination test and undertakes any needed enforcement action. However, an airman may contact a different district office. In such a case, the receiving district office must contact the requesting office.

- Immediately upon scheduling the reexamination test, the ASI must inform the requesting office of the appointment and request a copy of the original reexamination letter;

- After completion of the test, the receiving office forwards a copy of the test results to the requesting office; and

- If enforcement action is necessary as a result of the test, the ASI who conducted the reexamination advises the office manager. The requesting and receiving office managers should coordinate responsibility for the enforcement action. See FAA Order 2150.3.

Airman Scheduling Appointment at a Later Date. An airman may request an appointment for the reexamination beyond the time limit stated in the letter. The airman either must schedule the reexamination within a reasonable time, or place the certificate and/or rating on temporary deposit at the district office.

If the airman chooses temporary deposit, an ASI issues a 30-day temporary airman certificate with specific limitations. The Airmen Certification Branch, AFS-760, should be notified if the certification or authorization is placed on temporary deposit.

Airman Refusal to Submit to Reexamination. If the airman does not submit to a reexamination within the stated time limit, the investigating district office shall initiate emergency enforcement action to suspend the airman's certificate.

This emergency order suspends the certificate, ratings, or authorization until the airman agrees to reexamination and proves qualified to continue to hold the certificate and exercise its privileges.

Voluntary Cancellation of Certificate, Rating, or Authorization. The airman may volunteer to surrender the certificate in question for cancellation. If this occurs, the airman has no re-issuance rights other than passing all knowledge, oral, and practical tests.

Standards. The airman must meet the appropriate practical test standards for the applicable certificate or rating. The airman cannot be tested to a more difficult standard than initial certification requires. The field office conducting the reexamination may select a Designated Mechanic Examiner (DME) to conduct the test, for appropriate compensation.

Satisfactory Reexamination. If the airman's performance was satisfactory, the FAA will issue a letter of results indicating the satisfactory status of the rating or certification. However this reexamination will remain part of your records in Oklahoma City on file.

Falsification, fraudulent reproduction, or alteration of documents.

Persons, who falsify, fraudulently reproduce, or **alter certificates or other documents** required to support the issuance of a certificate are subject to suspension or revocation of any airman or ground instructor certificate held by that person. Mechanics' should also be reminded that Title 18 of the United States Code (18 U.S.C.) § 1001 applies, which states that whoever, in any matter within the jurisdiction of any department or agency of the United States, knowingly and willfully falsifies, conceals, or covers up by any trick, scheme, or devise a material fact, or makes any false, fictitious, or fraudulent statements or representations, or makes or uses any false writing or document knowing the same to contain false, fictitious, or fraudulent statements or entries, shall be fined under 18 U.S.C. or imprisoned, or both.

Part 65.91 Amendment (Docket No. 24233; Amendment No 65-30)
Before Amendment 65-22, Section 65.91(c)(1) provided that to be eligible for an IA, an applicant had to be "a certificated mechanic who has held both an airframe rating and a powerplant rating for at least 3 years before the date he applies. "Section 65.91(c)(1) now requires that the applicant hold "a currently effective mechanic certificate with both an airframe rating and a powerplant rating, each of which is currently effective AND HAS BEEN CONTINUOUSLY IN EFFECT for not less than the three year period immediately before the date of application." (Emphasis added.)

Under the old rule, the holder of an IA whose mechanic certificate was suspended could still be said to have "held" that certificate during the time of suspension. However, under the new rule, the certificate cannot be said to be "in effect" while it is suspended. Accordingly, although the IA becomes effective again at the end of the suspension of the mechanic's certificate, it may not be renewed at the end of the year because at that time the mechanic certificate will not have been continuously in effect during the preceding three years. The mechanic will not be eligible again for an IA until three years after the end of the suspension of the mechanic certificate.

Amendment No 65-30 permits persons who have had their mechanic certificates or ratings suspended to be eligible for issuance or renewal of inspection authorizations (IA's) if their mechanic certificates or ratings have been reinstated. This amendment will remove a requirement that is unnecessary as a means of ensuring that only responsible persons exercise IA privileges.

When renewal was sought under the old rule, the holder of an IA whose mechanic certificate or rating was suspended could still be said to have "held" that certificate during the time of suspension. However, the certificate could not be said to be "in effect" while it was suspended. Accordingly, after Amendment 65-22, the IA could not be renewed at the end of the year because at renewal time (authorization expires on March 31) the mechanic certificate or rating would not have been continuously in effect during the preceding 3 years. Therefore, the mechanic would not be eligible again for an IA until 3 years after the end of the suspension of the mechanic certificate. Moreover, because the eligibility requirements for issuance of a certificate are considered to be continuing requirements which must be met as long as certificate is held, an IA does not "become effective" again under Section 65.91 at the end of the suspension of the mechanic certificate.

At the time Amendment 65-22 was adopted, the FAA was aware that adding the words "continuously in effect" to Section 65.91(c)(1) would have this result. It was considered appropriate because the privileges and responsibilities that a person is charged with while holding the IA are greater than those of a certificated mechanic. Under § 65.95, the holder of an IA may inspect and approve for return to service certain aircraft or related parts or appliances after a major repair or major alteration to it in accordance with Part 43 of the CFR and perform annual and progressive inspections. Although a mechanic is authorized to perform much of the associated maintenance work underlying these functions, the IA holder is ultimately responsible for ensuring that the work is done in accordance with the CFR.

This 3-year-long period of ineligibility, however, has had an unintended inhibiting effect on the FAA's enforcement program. Amendment 65-22 has had a significant impact on the action taken against a mechanic for relatively minor to moderate violations. As a result of Amendment 65-22, a short-term suspension of a certificate or rating for a relatively minor offense effectively revokes an IA for a period of 3 years. Further, this creates the unusual situation where an action for revocation of an IA could have less of an impact on the mechanic involved than a 5-day suspension of a single rating on his or her mechanic certificate. (In most cases, a mechanic whose IA has been revoked may reapply after 1 year.) Not every action that warrants the suspension of a mechanic certificate evidences a lack of responsibility sufficient to justify such a long-term ineligibility for an IA. As a result, enforcement personnel have been reluctant in some cases to produce such results.

In attempting to resolve this problem, the FAA has reviewed the requirement of Section 65.91(c)(1) and has determined that it is unnecessary as a means of ensuring that only responsible persons continue to exercise IA privileges. First, the suspension or revocation of a mechanic certificate or rating does result in loss of IA privileges. Section 65.92(a) provides that the holder of an IA may exercise the privileges of that authorization only while he or she holds a currently effective mechanic certificate with both a currently effective airframe rating and a currently effective powerplant rating. In addition, the cause that gave rise to suspension of the IA holder's mechanic certificate or rating may also warrant suspension of an IA for a longer period of time and may even justify revocation of the IA. Revocation of the IA may be justified when the person's actions evidence a lack of responsibility indicating that the mechanic should not be allowed to exercise the inspection and other privileges prescribed by § 65.95. Also, section

609 of the Federal Aviation Act of 1958, as amended (FAAct), provides that the FAA may reexamine any civil airman, including the holder of an IA. The FAA may reexamine, for instance, when there is reason to believe that the holder of an IA may not be qualified to exercise his or her privileges. If, as a result of this reexamination, the FAA determines that safety in air commerce or air transportation and the public interest require, the FAA may issue an order suspending or revoking the IA. Thus, the cause that gave rise to the suspension of the IA holder's mechanic certificate may also warrant reexamination to determine his or her qualification to hold an IA. The results of this reexamination may warrant suspending or revoking the IA.

Accordingly, the FAA had amended Section 65.91 to return to the requirements, which existed prior to Amendment 65-22 and is clarifying these requirements to provide that an otherwise eligible applicant need only hold a currently effective mechanic certificate with both an airframe rating and a powerplant rating which have been in effect for a total of at least 3 years. This revision will remove any inequity associated with the renewal process and will provide more flexible and fair enforcement program for IA holders, without derogation of the original certification standards.

This rule will relax an unnecessary requirement for original issuance or renewal of an IA. It also will eliminate a double penalty currently imposed on any IA holder who, as a result of a suspension, becomes ineligible for renewal solely because his or her mechanic certificate or ratings were not continuously in effect during the 3-year period preceding the annual IA renewal.

Immediate adoption will permit persons who have had their mechanic certificates or ratings suspended since the last IA renewal date (March 31) to be eligible again on the following year's renewal date provided they meet all of the requirements of Section 65.91, 65.92 and 65.93 of the CFR.

This amendment will also permit persons who had previously become ineligible for a 3-year period, because of suspension of their mechanic certificates or ratings, to immediately become eligible for issuance of IA's provided that their mechanic certificates or ratings have been reinstated and they meet the requirements of Section 65.91 of the CFR.

Most if not all applications for employment we fill out will come with the following statements:

"The information I have provided on this application is true, complete and correct to the best of my knowledge and belief and is provided in good faith. I understand that a knowing and willful false statement on this application can be punished by fine or imprisonment or both under Section 1001 of Title 18 United States Code.

Federal Regulation Under TSR 49 1542.209 (l) impose a continuing obligation to disclose to the Airport Operator within 24 hours if you have been convicted of any disqualifying criminal offense that occurs while you have unescorted access authority.

By my signature below, I certify that I (check one and initial) have _____ (initial) _____or have NOT _____ (initial) _____ been convicted or found guilty by reason of insanity any of the above listed disqualify crimes.

The information I have provided on this application is true, complete and correct to the best of my knowledge and belief is provided in good faith. I understand that a knowing and willful false statement on this application can be punished by fine or imprisonment or both."

If you are planning on working at an airport that requires an airport badge be aware you will have to provide background information to obtain access for badging. The Transportation Safety Administration (TSA) has certain rules about airport badging and criminal offenses you must be aware of. This is a serious matter and if you have committed a criminal offense you must list it on any government application of serious results may happen under Title 18. I have provided a list of criminal offenses you should be aware of below.

Title 49 Code of Federal Regulations

TSR 1544

Disqualifying criminal offenses

Federal Register / Vol. 71, No. 102 / Friday, May 26, 2006 / Rules and Regulations

49 C.F.R. §1544.229 Fingerprint-based criminal history records checks (CHRC): Unescorted access authority, authority to perform screening functions, and authority to perform checked baggage or cargo functions.

§1544.229 Fingerprint-based criminal history records checks (CHRC): Unescorted access authority, authority to perform screening functions, and authority to perform checked baggage or cargo functions.

Link to an amendment published at 71 FR 30511, May 26, 2006.

(d) *Disqualifying criminal offenses.* An individual has a disqualifying criminal offense if the individual **has been convicted, or found not guilty by reason of insanity**, of any of the disqualifying crimes listed in this paragraph in any jurisdiction during the **10 years before the date of the individual's application for authority to perform covered functions**, or while the individual has authority to perform covered functions. The disqualifying criminal offenses are as follows:

(1)   Forgery of certificates, false marking of aircraft, and other aircraft registration violation; 49 U.S.C. 46306.

(2)   Interference with air navigation; 49 U.S.C. 46308.

(3)   Improper transportation of a hazardous material; 49 U.S.C. 46312.

(4)   Aircraft piracy; 49 U.S.C. 46502.

(5)   Interference with flight crewmembers or flight attendants; 49 U.S.C. 46504.

(6)   Commission of certain crimes aboard aircraft in flight; 49 U.S.C. 46506.

(7)   Carrying a weapon or explosive aboard aircraft; 49 U.S.C. 46505.

(8)   Conveying false information and threats; 49 U.S.C. 46507.

(9)   Aircraft piracy outside the special aircraft jurisdiction of the United States; 49 U.S.C. 46502(b).

(10) Lighting violations involving transporting controlled substances; 49 U.S.C. 46315.

(11) Unlawful entry into an aircraft or airport area that serves air carriers or foreign air carriers contrary to established security requirements; 49 U.S.C. 46314.

(12) Destruction of an aircraft or aircraft facility; 18 U.S.C. 32.

(13) Murder.

(14) Assault with intent to murder.

(15) Espionage.

(16) Sedition.

(17) Kidnapping or hostage taking.

(18) Treason.

(19) Rape or aggravated sexual abuse.

(20) Unlawful possession, use, sale, distribution, or manufacture of an explosive or weapon.

(21) Extortion.

(22) Armed or felony unarmed robbery.

(23) Distribution of, or intent to distribute, a controlled substance.

(24) Felony arson.

(25) Felony involving a threat.

(26) Felony involving—

    (i)   Willful destruction of property;

    (ii)   Importation or manufacture of a controlled substance;

    (iii)   Burglary;

    (iv)   Theft;

    (v)   Dishonesty, fraud, or misrepresentation;

    (vi)   Possession or distribution of stolen property;

    (vii) Aggravated assault;

    (viii) Bribery; or

    (ix)   Illegal possession of a controlled substance punishable by a maximum term of imprisonment of more than 1 year.

(27) Violence at international airports; 18 U.S.C. 37.

(28) Conspiracy or attempt to commit any of the criminal acts listed in this paragraph (d).

Airport Badges

Most Airport issues two (2) main types of badges;

1. The Security Identification Display Area (SIDA) badge, which provides unescorted access to the secured areas of the Airport, including the Air Operations Area (AOA), commonly called the ramp; and

2. The Non-SIDA badge, which authorizes an employee through the screening process at the security checkpoints, but does not authorize unescorted access to the SIDA or the AOA. Some badges may require U.S. Customs clearance based upon the employee's job responsibilities. This clearance may be added to either type of badge. In addition, certain Airport employees or contractors may apply for badges that provide access to various facilities that do not require SIDA or Non-SIDA badges.

Security definitions:

Security Identification Display Area (SIDA)

Access Control Office (ACO)

Air Operations Area (AOA)

Staring Your Own Business

You want to start your own aviation business where do you start and where can you find information.

First, anyone can start an aviation business and you do not have to have any FAA certificates to start a business. However you do need a FAA certificate to perform a return-to-service of U.S. registered aircraft.

Each state requirement is different how they regulate certificated persons (professionals). Some states for example; Washington State requires A&P mechanics to pay a use fee (TAX), most states do not require this. County run airports in some states require mechanics to carry liability insurance some don't. Some county and cities will require you to obtain a business license before working on a local airport some don't. Some airports do not allow major work in certain hangars most do.

Owning a business is the dream of many Americans starting that business converts your dreams into reality. However, there is a gap between dreams and reality. Your dreams can only be achieved with careful planning. As an entrepreneur, you will need a plan to avoid pitfalls, to achieve your goals and to build a profitable business.

It is helpful to begin with a business plan. A business plan is a blueprint of every aspect of your business. Sales, Marketing, Advertising, Promotion and Location are just some of the aspects of creating a plan.

The following seven key components should be considered:

- Identify Your Reasons;
- Self Analysis;
- Personal Skills and Experience;
- Finding a Niche;
- Market Analysis;
- Planning Your Startup; and,
- Finances.

Before starting a business go to the local county/city government office and inquire about the rules and requirements for your jurisdiction. Most businesses require licenses or permits in order to operate. A person in business is not expected to be a lawyer but each business owner should have a basic knowledge of laws affecting the business.

Once you decide to establish a business, a primary consideration is the type of business entity to form. Tax and liability issues, director and ownership concerns, as well as state and federal obligations pertaining to the type of entity should be considered when making your determination. Personal needs and the needs of your particular type of business should also be considered.

The following is a brief overview of various business structures. The information is intended to provide a basic understanding of the different business structures and is not intended to provide legal advice.

It is strongly recommended you consult with a legal representative and accountant before making a determination as to the type of business entity to form.

- **Sole Proprietorship**
- **Corporation**
- **Limited Liability Company**
- **Limited Partnership**
- **General Partnership**
- **Limited Liability Partnership**

Sole Proprietorship

A sole proprietorship is set up to allow an individual to own and operate a business by him/herself. A sole proprietor has total control, receives all profits from and is responsible for taxes and liabilities of the business. If a sole proprietorship is formed with a name other than the individual's name (example: John Smiths Fishing Shop), a Fictitious Business Name Statement must be filed with the County Clerk or County Recorder where the principal place of business is located. If the principal place of business is located outside California, the name will be filed with the Sacramento County Clerk-Recorder. No formation documents are required to be filed with the Secretary of State. Other state filings may be required depending on the type of business.

Corporation

A domestic corporation (Articles of Incorporation)) generally is a legal entity, which exists separately from its owners. While normally limiting the owners from personal liability, taxes are levied on the corporation as well as on the shareholders. The sale of stocks or bonds can generate additional capital and the longevity of the corporation can continue past the death of the owners. Legal Counsel should be consulted regarding the variety of options available for formulation.

Limited Liability Company

A domestic limited liability company (Domestic—LLC-1/Foreighn—LLC-5) generally offers liability protection similar to that of a corporation but is taxed differently. Domestic limited liability companies may be managed by one or more managers or one or more members. In addition to filing the applicable documents with the Secretary of State, an operating agreement among the members as to the affairs of the limited liability company and the conduct of its business is required. The limited liability company does not file the operating agreement with the Secretary of State but maintains it at the office where the limited liability company's records are kept. Professional limited liability companies are restricted in California at this time.

Limited Partnership

A domestic limited partnership (Certificate of Partnership _ LP-1) may provide limited liability for some partners. There must be at least one general partner that acts, as the controlling partner while the liability of limited partners is normally limited to the amount of control or participation they have engaged in. General partners of a limited partnership have unlimited personal liability for the partnership's debts and obligation.

General Partnership

A general partnership (Statement of Partnership Authority—GP-1) must have two or more persons engaged in a business for profit. Except as otherwise provided by law, all partners are liable jointly and severally for all obligations of the partnership unless agreed by the claimant. Profits are taxed as personal income for the partners. Filing at the state level is optional.

Limited Liability Partnership

A limited liability partnership (Registration of Limited Liability Partnership—LLP-1) is a partnership that engages in the practice of public accountancy, the practice of law or the practice of architecture, or services related to accountancy or law. A limited liability partnership is required to maintain certain levels of insurance as required by law.

Where to Obtain Business Licenses

1. Alabama—http://www.ador.state.al.us/licenses/authrity.html
2. Alaska—http://www.dced.state.ak.us/occ/buslic.htm
3. Arizona—http://www.revenue.state.az.us/license.htm
4. Arkansas—http://www.state.ar.us/online_business.php
5. California—http://www.calgold.ca.gov/
6. Colorado—http://www.state.co.us/gov_dir/obd/blid.htm
7. Connecticut—http://www.state.ct.us/
8. Delaware—http://www.state.de.us/revenue/obt/obtmain.htm
9. District of Columbia—http://www.dcra.dc.gov/
10. Florida—http://sun6.dms.state.fl.us/dor/businesses/
11. Georgia—http://www.sos.state.ga.us/corporations/regforms.htm
12. Hawaii—http://www.hawaii.gov/dbedt/start/starting.html
13. Idaho—http://www.idoc.state.id.us/Pages/BUSINESSPAGE.html
14. Illinois—http://www.sos.state.il.us/departments/business_services/business.html
15. Indiana—http://www.state.in.us/sic/owners/ia.html
16. Iowa—http://www.iowasmart.com/blic/
17. Kansas—Not available at this time
18. Kentucky—http://www.thinkkentucky.com/kyedc/ebpermits.asp
19. Louisiana—Not available at this time
20. Maine—http://www.econdevmaine.com/biz-develop.htm
21. Maryland—http://www.dllr.state.md.us/
22. Massachusetts—http://www.state.ma.us/sec/cor/coridx.htm
23. Michigan—http://medc.michigan.org/services/startups/index2.asp
24. Minnesota—http://www.dted.state.mn.uss
25. Mississippi—http://www.olemiss.edu/depts/mssbdc/going_intobus.html
26. Missouri—http://www.ded.state.mo.us/business/businesscenter/
27. Montana—http://www.state.mt.us/sos/biz.htm
28. Nebraska—Not available at this time
29. New Hampshire—http://www.nhsbdc.org/startup.htm
30. New Jersey—http://www.state.nj.us/njbiz/s_lic_and_cert.shtml
31. New York—http://www.dos.state.ny.us/lcns/licensing.html
32. New Mexico—Not available at this time
33. Nevada—Not available at this time
34. North Carolina—http://www.secstate.state.nc.us/secstate/blio/default.htm
35. North Dakota—http://www.state.nd.us/sec/
36. Ohio—http://www.state.oh.us/sos/business_services_information.htm
37. Oklahoma—http://www.okonestop.com/
38. Oregon—http://www.filinginoregon.com
39. Pennsylvania—http://www.paopenforbusiness.state.pa.us
40. Rhode Island—http://www.corps.state.ri.us/firststop/index.asp

41. South Carolina—http://www.state.sd.us/STATE/sitecategory.cfm?mp=Licenses/ Occupations
42. South Dakota—Not available at this time
43. Tennessee—Not available at this time
44. Texas—http://www.tded.state.tx.us/guide/
45. Utah—http://www.commerce.state.ut.us/web/commerce/admin/licen.htm
46. Vermont—http://www.sec.state.vt.us/
47. Virginia—http://www.dba.state.va.us/licenses/
48. Washington—http://www.wa.gov/dol/bpd/limsnet.htm
49. West Virginia—http://www.state.wv.us/taxrev/busreg.html
50. Wisconsin—http://www.wdfi.org/corporations/forms/
51. Wyoming—http://soswy.state.wy.us/corporat/corporat.htm

Agreement for Services of Independent Contractor

This agreement is made this _____ day of _____, 200_____ between, _____ _____**(Your company)**, and _____ _____, whose address is _____ _____, ("Contractor").

1. Contractor agrees to perform the services described on Exhibit A attached hereto for the compensation stated therein, subject to the terms and conditions set forth below. Services rendered must meet **(Your company)** standards and will be subject to its right of inspection and approval as a condition of payment.

2. Contractor is an independent contractor and will have sole authority to control and direct the details of his or her performance of the services. Contractor will not be the employee of, **(Your company)** under the meaning or application of any federal or state laws, including but not limited to unemployment insurance or workers' compensation laws, and will not be entitled to any of the benefits of a **(Your company)** employee. Contractor assumes all liabilities and obligations imposed by any such laws. Contractor will have no authority to act as the agent of **(Your company)** and will not hold himself or herself out as such.

3. Contractor hereby assigns to **(Your company)** the entire right, title and interest for the entire world in and to all work performed, including inventions conceived, made or reduced to practice by Contractor during the performance of this agreement. **(Your company)** information and materials are its exclusive property. Contractor will safeguard all such property entrusted to it and will return it upon completion of services.

4. Contractor agrees not to disclose any confidential information received from **(Your company)** or otherwise acquired while performing the services. Contractor agrees not to use **(Your company)** name or logos for any advertising or other commercial purpose, or disclose the terms of this agreement, without **(Your company)** prior written consent.

5. Contractor agrees to comply with all applicable federal, state and local laws and regulations. Contractor will not discriminate on the basis of race, religion, age, sex, color, disability, sexual orientation, political affiliation, national or ethnic origin, or veteran status.

6. (Your company) may terminate this agreement if (a) funding for the services is withdrawn or curtailed, (b) Contractor fails to perform the services to (Your company) satisfaction or within the time specified in Exhibit A or any (Your company), or (c) Contractor becomes insolvent or otherwise unable to pay its obligations as they become due. If no time is specified in Exhibit A, then this agreement will terminate one year after the last date written below. Death of Contractor will automatically terminate this agreement.

7. This agreement will be governed by and construed in accordance with the laws of the State of California. No modification of this agreement may be made without the written consent of both parties.

8. In witness whereof, **(Your company)** and Contractor have executed this agreement as of the first date written above.

<u>**Your Company Name**</u>　　　　　　　　<u>**Contractor**</u>

_____　　_____

By: _____　　**By:** _____

Your Name: _____　　**Printed name:** _____
Date: _____　　**Date:** _____

AD Compliance Record

AIRWORTHINESS DIRECTIVE COMPLIANCE RECORD

Make Piper   **Model** PA28-161   **S/N** 28-7410669

AD Number	Subject	Date and Hours of Compliance	Method of Compliance	One time	Recurring	Next Comp. Due.	Authorized Signature
62-19-03 08-28-62	Prop Bolt failure	1044.8 12-01-77	N/A by S/N	X			Stache Air AP 272182 IA
64-06-06 04-06-64	Control Wheel failure	1044.8 12-01-77	N/A by S/N	X			Stache Air AP 272182 IA
67-20-04 09-27-67	Main landing gear torque link failure	1044.8 12-01-77	N/A by Torque links not drilled for lube fittings	X			Stache Air AP 272182 IA
67-26-02 05-22-68	Various Modifications	1044.8 12-01-77	N/A by S/N	X			Stache Air AP 272182 IA
77-23-03 11-14-77	Control Rod Binding	1044.8 12-01-77	C/W by installing new style rod end	X			Stache Air AP 272182 IA
79-02-05 01-29-79	Fuel Flow Interruption	1308.7 12-30-79	N/A by S/N	X			Stache Air AP 272182 IA
79-13-03 06-08-79	Prevent Potential Fire Hazard	1352.2 01-05-80	N/A by S/N	X			Stache Air AP 272182 IA
79-22-02 10-26-79	Prevent Possible Fuel Leakage and Fire Haz.	1352.6 01-05-80	N/A by S/N	X			Stache Air AP 272182 IA
80-14-03 07-01-80	Disruption of Radio Communication	1422.3 01-05-81	N/A by S/N	X			Stache Air AP 272182 IA
81-23-05 03-08-82	Prevent In-Flight Fire	1615.4 05-25-82	C/W by inspection and by installing Piper kit P/N 764-303V	X			Stache Air AP 272182 IA

AIRWORTHINESS DIRECTIVE COMPLIANCE RECORD

Make _____ Model _____
S/N _____

AD Number	Subject		Method of Compliance	One time	Recurring	Next Comp. Due.	Authorized Signature

Sample Letter to Owner Unairworthy Items

March 31, 2010

I.B Good Aviation
Hangar 87
Oakland Airport
Oakland, CA 95402

Mr. Johnny Broke
1400 Main Street USA
Oakland, CA 12009

Dear Mr. Broke:

This is to certify that on March 31, 2010, I completed an annual inspection on your aircraft, Cessna 172-N, Serial Number 172912009, N1234, and found the following unairworthy items:

1. Compression in Number #3 cylinder read 30 over 80, which is below the manufacturer's recommended limits.
2. The muffler has a broken baffle plate that is blocking the engine exhaust outlet.
3. There is a 6-inch crack on bottom of wing just aft of main landing gear attach point.
4. Seat belt is missing the plastic ring on the metal stud.

I.B Good
A&P 1234567 IA

Repair Stations & Air Carriers Privileges and Limitations

1. As a certificated Airframe and Powerplant mechanic working at a repair station am I protected if I make a mistake in return to service?

   Answer: No you are not protected under the repair station certificate number. CFR 43.9 (a) (4) If the work performed on the aircraft, airframe, aircraft engine, propeller, appliance, or component part has been performed satisfactorily, the signature, certificate number, and kind of certificate held by the person approving the work. **The signature constitutes the approval for return to service only for the work performed.** Your signature is the return to service. Be very careful if you are signing off the final return to service for several other inspections, as you are responsible to ensure the work was performed properly. Reference part 65 Section 65.85 and 65.87 addition limitations.

   The repair station may and can be held responsible as well under part 145 for not following procedures as well.

2. As a certificated Airframe and Powerplant mechanic working for an air carrier am I protected if I make a mistake in return to service?

   Answer: No same as above. You are not protected under the air carrier certificate number. CFR 43.9 (a) (4) If the work performed on the aircraft, airframe, aircraft engine, propeller, appliance, or component part has been performed satisfactorily, the signature, certificate number, and kind of certificate held by the person approving the work. **The signature constitutes the approval for return to service only for the work performed.** Your signature is the return to service. Be very careful if you are signing off the final return to service for several other inspections, as you are responsible to ensure the work was performed properly. . Reference part 65 Section 65.85 and 65.87 addition limitations.

3. As a certificated Airframe and Powerplant mechanic working at a repair station and I don't follow all the procedures in the maintenance manual and use a cheat sheet provided by the repair station am I protected if the FAA find out?

   Answer: No you are not protected by the repair station. Part 43 Section 43.13(a) states you must follow the current manufactures procedures. Not doing so is a violation of the Code of Federal Regulations. In accordance with Part 145 all repair stations must also follow part 43.

4. As a mechanic I an told to sign off a maintenance function or return to service to get the aircraft out the door or risk loosing my job, what should I do?

   Answer: Do **NOT** sign your name and certificate number to something you did not do this is considered FRAUD and is a crime. I would recommend you contact your local Flight Standard District Office (FSDO) and request assistance. Or you can file a whistle blower complaint. Keep in mind you will most likely be fired, but under the whistle blower laws you are protected and the Federal Government will stand behind you.

Sorry to say this is where your personal ethics comes in to play. Do you really want to work for someone the wants you to break the law?

5. If an out side shop non-certificate or certificated repairs an item and it comes back into a repair station are you accountable for installing it if all the process was not completely accomplished during the repair at the out side shop?

Answer: Yes as the installer you are held accountable to ensure the repair work was properly performed. This can be accomplished by reviewing the return to service for the work performed by the other shop. If the record entry doses not meet Part 43 Section 43.9 then it will not pass the smell test **DO NOT** install.

You can write a Malfunction and Defect report against the part as an Airframe and Powerplant mechanic. Repair Stations and Air Carriers will have procedures in their manuals that must be followed when defects (improper repairs) or improper sign offs are found. Your job is to inspect the part and paperwork before installation to ensure all the work is accomplished.

6. If I have an FAA Form 8110-3 for a DER for a major repair or major alteration can I perform the work?

Answer: Yes/maybe keep in mind all FAA Form 8110-3's are approved data only for the part, to install the part or repair you will need to complete a FAA Form 337 and have block 3 signed by your local FSDO authorization to install. Attached the 8110-3 to the 337 and complete the ICA, submit it to the local FSDO before proceeding. In some cases you may need more than one 8110-3, as one DER may not have the proper function codes to complete the entire repair or alteration. Make sure and check the DER approved function codes.

7. I work for a repair station and make a mistake what should I do fist?

Answer: All repair station will have a Repair Station Manual (RSM) and Quality Control Manual (QCM) that will have procedures to reports defects. Under part 145 you must follow the RSM and QCM procedures first. However is this fails contact your local FSDO for assistance your local Inspector will be more than happy to assist. Keep in mind your boss will not like this, again it's an ethics issue to deal with.

100-Hour/Annual Inspection
Checklist (GA)
Part 23 & CAR 3 Aircraft

Reference Data:

Order 8130.2, CAR-3, CFR 21 Certification, CFR 23 Airworthiness Standards, CFR 43 Maintenance, CFR 45 Markings, CFR 47 Registered properly, CFR 91 Pilot Responsibility, CFR 36 Noise, CFR 33 engines, CFR 39 AD's, CFR 145 Repair Stations and AC 43.13-1B & 2A Major Repair and Alterations, Manufacture Maintenance Manuals.

INTERPRETATION OF THE TERM "AIRWORTHY"

1) **The aircraft must conform to its type certificate.**
   a. **When aircraft configuration and the components installed are consistent with drawings, specifications, and other data that are part of the type certificate (T/C), and include any supplemental T/C and field approval alterations incorporated into the aircraft.**
2) **The aircraft must be in condition for safe operation.**
   a. *Aircraft relative to wear and deterioration i.e., corrosion, fluid leaks, tire wear, window delimitation/crazing.*

NOTE: *If one or both of these conditions are not met, the aircraft would be considered unairworthy.* **Order 8130.2**

NOTE: This is only a guide and should not be considered FAA approved data for 100 hour or annual inspection checklist. Consult CFR 43 subpart D, for scope and detail of items to be included for 100 hour or annual inspections. **This checklist is not exhaustive and does not supersede Manufacture's publications and is up-dated periodically!**

The owner or operator is responsible for the maintaining the aircraft in an airworthy condition, including compliance with all applicable Airworthiness Directives as specified in Part 39 of the Code of Federal Regulations and "Airworthiness Limitations" of the applicable manufactures manual. It is also the responsibility of the owner to insure that the aircraft is inspected in compliance with the requirement of Part 21, 43, and 91 of Code of Federal Regulations.

Aircraft Data

1. N-Number: N_____
2. Airframe Type Certificate No. _____ Rev. _____ Specification sheet _____
3. ASTM No._____ Rev. _____ N/A ☐
4. Aircraft Model _____ Model No. _____
5. Aircraft Serial No. _____ Year manufactured _____
6. Certification Basis: CAR or CFR _____

Airman Attitude

1. Has Constructive attitude toward Compliance Order 2150.3A par. 205   Yes ☐ No ☐ N/A ☐
2. Verify A&P/IA certificate number and picture ID   CFR 65.91   Yes ☐ No ☐ N/A ☐

---

3. Verify Pilots certificate number and picture ID   CFR 61.3   Yes ☐ No ☐ N/A ☐

Data

1. FAA-approved maintenance manuals available   CFR 43.13.   Yes ☐ No ☐ N/A ☐
2. Alterations IAW approved STC/TSO/PMA/Field approval or other FAA data, (337's)
                                                     CFR 21.97/101/113   Yes ☐ No ☐ N/A ☐
3. Instructions for Continued Airworthiness   CFR 21.31, 21.50, 23.1529 Yes ☐ No ☐ N/A ☐
4. Type Certificate Data Sheet (TCDS)   CFR 21.41/ CAR 3.   Yes ☐ No ☐ N/A ☐
5. Data plate aircraft   CFR 45.13   Yes ☐ No ☐ N/A ☐
6. Data plate aircraft MFG before **March 7, 1988** Make/model & S/N CFR 45.11(d)
                                                                         Yes ☐ No ☐ N/A ☐
7. Data plate engine on engine make and model/serial number CFR45.11 & 21.182
                                                                         Yes ☐ No ☐ N/A ☐
8. Data plates critical components   CAR 3.18 CFR 45.15 Yes ☐ No ☐ N/A ☐
9. Data plates Life Limited Parts   CFR 45.16   Yes ☐ No ☐ N/A ☐
10. Data plates critical components   CAR 3.18 CFR 45.15 Yes ☐ No ☐ N/A ☐
11. Data plates Life Limited Parts   CFR 45.16   Yes ☐ No ☐ N/A ☐

Records

1. Registration current and in aircraft **(NO photo copy)**   CFR 91.9 / CAR 3.792
                                                                         Yes ☐ No ☐ N/A ☐
2. Airworthiness Certificate in aircraft dated and signed   CFR 91.203(a) & 21.175
                                                                         Yes ☐ No ☐ N/A ☐
3. Annual Inspection Total time_____ Description of work accomplished _____Date completed__
    and A&P/IA Signature ___   CFR 43.11 & 91.417   Yes ☐ No ☐ N/A ☐
4. All AD's, recorded in maintenance records and check recurring AD's
    a. Airframe   CFR 39 & 91.417   Yes ☐ No ☐ N/A ☐
    b. Engine   CFR 39 & 91.417   Yes ☐ No ☐ N/A ☐
    c. Propeller   CFR 39 & 91.417   Yes ☐ No ☐ N/A ☐
    d. Appliances Check for a list of items CFR 39 & 91.417   Yes ☐ No ☐ N/A ☐
5. Reduce Vertical Separation Minimums **(RVSM)** with Letter of Authorization (LOA)
                                         CFR 91.706   Yes ☐ No ☐ N/A ☐
6. Last **Annual** inspection completed: date _____   CFR 43.11 & 91.417
    a. CFR 65.91 IA Name _____ Certification No._____ Yes ☐ No ☐ N/A ☐
    b. 145 Repair station sign off date Repair Station number _____ Yes ☐ No ☐ N/A ☐
7. Last **Progressive** Inspection phase signed of date CFR 91.409(d) Yes ☐ No ☐ N/A ☐
    a. Phase inspection dated and signed by A&P/IA CFR 91.409(d)(1) Yes ☐ No ☐ N/A ☐
    b. 145 Repair station number _____CFR 145.5/107/201/204 Yes ☐ No ☐ N/A ☐
8. Last **100-hour** inspection date _____ Total time _____ CFR 91.405(b)
    a. 145 Repair station number _____CFR 145.5/107/201/204 Yes ☐ No ☐ N/A ☐
    b. A&P sign off date Certification No, ____CFR 43.15, 65.85, 91.409 Yes ☐ No ☐ N/A ☐
    c. A&P/IA Signature _____CFR 43.11 & 91.417 Yes ☐ No ☐ N/A ☐
9. Equipment list current and in aircraft CAR-3.73 and CFR 23.29 & 91.9 Yes ☐ No ☐ N/A ☐
10. Equipment list up-dated to match conformity of aircraft   CAR 3.777 CFR 91.9
                                                                         Yes ☐ No ☐ N/A ☐
11. Status of Life Limited parts **Effective 04—15-2002**   CFR 43.10   Yes ☐ No ☐ N/A ☐

12. Current approved flight manual **after 03-1-1979** in aircraft CFR 21.5/23.1581, 91.9

Yes ☐ No ☐ N/A ☐

13. Current flight manual POH **before 03-1-1979** in aircraft Yes ☐ No ☐ Revision number/date _____ Limitations and placards CAR 3.778 CFR 21.5, 21.1559, 23.1581, 91.9

Yes ☐ No ☐ N/A ☐

14. Current weight & balance report dated & signed CAR 3.71, **23.1519**, 23.1581, 91.9

Yes ☐ No ☐ N/A ☐

15. Identification data plate secured to aircraft fuselage exterior CFR 45.11   Yes ☐ No ☐ N/A ☐

16. If applicable, check the MEL to determine that: CFR 91.213   Yes ☐ No ☐ N/A ☐

    a. Issued by N-number and serial number to the aircraft operator   Yes ☐ No ☐ N/A ☐

    b. A Letter of Authorization (LOA) from a district office; check deferred items for placards and dates   Yes ☐ No ☐ N/A ☐

17. Maintenance Records for each Engine, Propeller, Airframe and Appliances in accordance with

CFR 91.417   Yes ☐ No ☐ N/A ☐

18. **ATC transponder** date ____ **24 calendar months** check. CFR 91.413 & 23.1301

Yes ☐ No ☐ N/A ☐

19. **ELT** TSO-C91a /TS0-C126 **every 12 months** check date 06/21/1985 CFR 91.207

Yes ☐ No ☐ N/A ☐

20. **Altimeter test every 24 months**.   CFR 91.411and CFR 43 Appendix E   Yes ☐ No ☐ N/A ☐

21. **Pitot static transponder test every 24 months**   CAR 3.665CFR 43 Appendix F

Yes ☐ No ☐ N/A ☐

22. Deferred items under Part 91.213 for Day VFR   CFR 91.213   Yes ☐ No ☐ N/A ☐

    a. Is the item placarded   Yes ☐ No ☐ N/A ☐

    b. Is there a maintenance record entry   Yes ☐ No ☐ N/A ☐

    c. Is the item disabled or removed   Yes ☐ No ☐ N/A ☐

Cockpit Inspection

1. **Placards** read correctly Instrument & placards are correctly located per POH/AFM & TCDS CFR 23.1541-1567/ CAR 3.755,   CFR 91.31   Yes ☐ No ☐ N/A ☐

2. INOP placards   CFR 91.213   Yes ☐ No ☐ N/A ☐

    a. INOP instruments disabled or removed by an A&P   CFR 91.213   Yes ☐ No ☐ N/A ☐

    b. Equipment list up-dated   CFR 91.213   Yes ☐ No ☐ N/A ☐

    c. Maintenance record entry   CFR 91.213   Yes ☐ No ☐ N/A ☐

    d. Weight and balance record updated   CFR 91.9   Yes ☐ No ☐ N/A ☐

    e. Minimum Equipment List (MEL) for aircraft   CFR 91.213(a)(1)   Yes ☐ No ☐ N/A ☐

3. Vacuum indicating system, **Life limited** pump   CFR 23.1301   Yes ☐ No ☐ N/A ☐

4. Compass card Yes ☐ No ☐ Readable CAR 3,385   CFR 23.1547 & 25.1547

Yes ☐ No ☐ N/A ☐

5. Additional instruments not on equipment list or Form 337 CAR 3.661CFR 21.113

Yes ☐ No ☐ N/A ☐

6. Type of clock installed original analog or digital working AC 20-94   Yes ☐ No ☐ N/A ☐

7. Nav Radio P/N 1 _____, P/N 2 _____ matches equipment list   Yes ☐ No ☐ N/A ☐

8. Conforms to Type Certificate (TC) per POH/AFM see item (5,6)   Yes ☐ No ☐ N/A ☐

9. Cockpit fuel smell   CAR 3.440 / CFR 23.863   Yes ☐ No ☐ N/A ☐

10. Data plate information matches registration   CFR 45.11/13 & 47.3   Yes ☐ No ☐ N/A ☐

11. Intercom jack, how many any extra ____ and required Form 337   Yes ☐ No ☐ N/A ☐

12. Fire extinguisher gage Green ☐ Red ☐   CFR 23.1199   Yes ☐ No ☐ N/A ☐

13. Fire Extinguishing Agent **commuter category** installed   CFR 23.1197   Yes ☐ No ☐ N/A ☐

14. Fire extinguisher easy access to pilot   CFR 23.851   Yes ☐ No ☐ N/A ☐

15. Oxygen equipment and supply lines condition   CFR 23.1441thru1453   Yes ☐ No ☐ N/A ☐

16. Oxygen bottle if required Green ☐ Red ☐   CFR 23.1441   Yes ☐ No ☐ N/A ☐

     Hydro AA 5 years HT 3 year retire at 24 years AC 43.13-1b para 9-51   Yes ☐ No ☐ N/A ☐

17. Instrument filter covers installed   Yes ☐ No ☐ N/A ☐

18. Yoke chain safety wired, loose or corrosion present   CFR 43.13   Yes ☐ No ☐ N/A ☐

19. Cockpit control knob shape correct type CAR 3.384   CFR 23.781   Yes ☐ No ☐ N/A ☐

20. Flap, gear, knobs installed CAR 3.384   CFR 23.781   Yes ☐ No ☐ N/A ☐

21. Electrical wiring more **than ½ inch slack** AC 43.13-1B para 11-118   Yes ☐ No ☐ N/A ☐

22. Electrical wiring clamps/marking as required   AC 43.13-1B sec. 11   Yes ☐ No ☐ N/A ☐

23. Tie-wraps items of mass in the cabin   CFR 23.561   Yes ☐ No ☐ N/A ☐

24. Loose wires under dash not clamped   CFR 23.1351   Yes ☐ No ☐ N/A ☐

25. Fuel selector moves to all positions & placarded CAR 3.364 CFR 23.951   Yes ☐ No ☐ N/A ☐

26. Brake master cylinder leaking R/H ☐ L/H ☐   CRF 43.13   Yes ☐ No ☐ N/A ☐

27. Thoroughly clean the aircraft and aircraft engine   CFR 43App D   Yes ☐ No ☐ N/A ☐

28. Cargo tie downs or nets if installed   CFR 91.525   Yes ☐ No ☐ N/A ☐

29. General, uncleanness and loose equipment that might foul the controls, apparent and obvious defects and insecurity of attachment.   CFR 43App D   Yes ☐ No ☐ N/A ☐

30. Stall warning system horn works   CAR 3.120 CFR 23.1323   Yes ☐ No ☐ N/A ☐

31. Windshield STC for one piece   CFR 43 Appendix A   Yes ☐ No ☐ N/A ☐

32. Windows tinted TCDS/Equipment list   Yes ☐ No ☐ N/A ☐

33. Sun visor installation or STC with form 337   CFR 43.13   Yes ☐ No ☐ N/A ☐

34. Windshield and windows conditions   CAR 3.382 CFR 23.775   Yes ☐ No ☐ N/A ☐

35. Windscreen clear ☐ scratches ☐ cracks ☐ crazing ☐
         Reference CFR23.775 AC 43.13-1b and MIL-P-5425   Yes ☐ No ☐ N/A ☐

36. Windows stopped drilled, cracked, or crazed CAR 3.382 CFR 23.775, and AC 43.13-1B Chapter 3 paragraph 318 (a)(2), and MIL-P-5425   Yes ☐ No ☐ N/A ☐

Instruments   CFR 91.205

Flight Instruments minimum required

1. An Airspeed indicator   CAR 3.655CFR 23.1303   Yes ☐ No ☐ N/A ☐

2. An Altimeter indicator   CAR 3.655 CFR 23.1303   Yes ☐ No ☐ N/A ☐

3. Direction indicator   CAR-3.666 CFR 23.1303   Yes ☐ No ☐ N/A ☐

Minimum Instruments Required Visual-flight rules (day)

1. Air speed indicator   CAR 3.655 CFR 91.205(b) Yes ☐ No ☐ N/A ☐

2. Altimeter   CAR 3.655 CFR 91.205(b) Yes ☐ No ☐ N/A ☐

3. Magnetic direction indicator   CAR 3.655 CFR 91.205(b) Yes ☐ No ☐ N/A ☐

4. Tachometer for each engine   CAR 3.655 CFR 91.205(b) Yes ☐ No ☐ N/A ☐

5. Oil pressure gauge for each engine using pressure system CAR 3.655 CFR 91.205(b)

                                                           Yes ☐ No ☐ N/A ☐

6. Manifold pressure gauge for each altitude engine   CAR 3.672 CFR 91.205(b) Yes ☐ No ☐ N/A ☐

7. Fuel gauge indicating the quantity of fuel in each tank   CFR 91.205(b)   Yes ☐ No ☐ N/A ☐

8. Landing gear position indicator, if retractable   CFR 91.205(b)   Yes ☐ No ☐ N/A ☐

Minimum Instrument for Instrument flight rules

1. Two-way radio communications & navigation equipment   CFR 91.205(c)   Yes ☐ No ☐ N/A ☐

2. Gyroscopic rate-of-turn indicator   CAR 3.668 CFR 91.205(c) Yes ☐ No ☐ N/A ☐

3. Slip-skid indicator — CFR 91.205(c) — Yes ☐ No ☐ N/A ☐
4. Sensitive altimeter adjustable for barometric pressure — CFR 91.205(c) — Yes ☐ No ☐ N/A ☐
5. Clock displaying hours, minutes, and seconds with sweeping second hand pointer or digital presentation — CFR 91.205(c) — Yes ☐ No ☐ N/A ☐
6. Generator or alternator of adequate capacity — CFR 91.205(c) — Yes ☐ No ☐ N/A ☐
7. Gyroscopic pitch and bank indicator (artificial horizon) — CFR 91.205(c) — Yes ☐ No ☐ N/A ☐
8. Gyroscopic direction indicator (directional gyro) — CFR 91.205(c) — Yes ☐ No ☐ N/A ☐

Powerplant Instrument (all aircraft) CAR-3 Subpart F and Part 23
1. Fuel quantity indicator per tank — CAR 3.672 CFR 23.1305(a) — Yes ☐ No ☐ N/A ☐
2. Oil pressure indicator for each engine — CAR 3.674 CFR 23.1305(a) — Yes ☐ No ☐ N/A ☐
3. Oil temperature indicator for each engine — CFR 23.1305(a) — Yes ☐ No ☐ N/A ☐
4. Oil quantity measuring device for each engine — CAR 3.674 CFR 23.1305(a) — Yes ☐ No ☐ N/A ☐
5. Fire warning indicator if required by — CFR 23.1205 — Yes ☐ No ☐ N/A ☐
6. Tachometer indicator for each engine — CFR 23.1305(b) — Yes ☐ No ☐ N/A ☐
7. Cylinder head indicator for each engine — CFR 23.1305(b) — Yes ☐ No ☐ N/A ☐
    a. Cowl flaps installed CAR 3.675 CFR 23.1305(b) Yes ☐ No ☐ N/A ☐
    b. Commuter category aircraft CFR 23.1305(b) Yes ☐ No ☐ N/A ☐
8. Manifold pressure indicator for each engine and for each engine with an controllable pitch propeller — CFR 23.1305(b) — Yes ☐ No ☐ N/A ☐

Instrument Arrangement   CAR 3.661   CFR 23.1321
1. Attitude indicator on panel top center position — CFR 23.1321 — Yes ☐ No ☐ N/A ☐
2. Airspeed indicator adjacent to and directly to left of the instrument in the top center position. — CFR 23.1321 — Yes ☐ No ☐ N/A ☐
3. Altitude indicator adjacent to and directly to right of the instrument in the top center position. — CFR 23.1321 — Yes ☐ No ☐ N/A ☐
4. Magnetic direction indicator placard must state whether the calibration was made with radio receivers **on or off** — CFR 23.1547 — Yes ☐ No ☐ N/A ☐
5. Magnetic direction indicator more than **10 degrees** off — CFR 23.1547 — Yes ☐ No ☐ N/A ☐

Instrument Markings   CAR 3.755   CFR 23.1543
1. Marking on cover glass must be in alignment with face — CFR 23.1543 — Yes ☐ No ☐ N/A ☐
2. Each arc and line must be clearly visible to pilot — CFR 23.1543 — Yes ☐ No ☐ N/A ☐
3. All related instruments must be calibrated in compatible units — CFR 23.1543 — Yes ☐ No ☐ N/A ☐

Electrical System   CAR 3.694   CFR 23.1367
1. Switches
    a. Able to carry rated current — CAR 3.682 CFR 23.1367 — Yes ☐ No ☐ N/A ☐
    b. Enough distance or insulating material between current carrying parts and the housing so that vibration will not cause shorting — CAR 3.681 CFR 23.1367 — Yes ☐ No ☐ N/A ☐
    c. Labeled as to operation and circuit controlled — CFR 23.1367 — Yes ☐ No ☐ N/A ☐
2. Circuit Breakers/Fuses
    a. Circuit protection — CAR 3.690 CFR 23.1357 — Yes ☐ No ☐ N/A ☐
    b. Each resettable circuit trip free cannot be overridden — CFR 23.1357 — Yes ☐ No ☐ N/A ☐
    c. Fuses readily available and spare — CAR 3.692 CFR 23.1357 — Yes ☐ No ☐ N/A ☐
    d. Breakers labeled and rating — CAR 3.691 CFR 23.1357 — Yes ☐ No ☐ N/A ☐

3. Master Switch
   a. Wired to disconnect each electrical power source from the distribution systems
      CAR 3.688 CFR 23.1361   Yes ☐ No ☐ N/A ☐
   b. Switch is easily discernible and accessible to crew CAR 3.695 CFR 23.1361 Yes ☐ No ☐ N/A ☐
4. Wiring inspection   CAR 3.681 CFR 23.1351 and AC43.13 chapter 11
   a. Chafed or frayed wires   Yes ☐ No ☐ N/A ☐
   b. Insulation penetration   Yes ☐ No ☐ N/A ☐
   c. Outer insulation cracking   Yes ☐ No ☐ N/A ☐
   d. Damage or exposed wires   Yes ☐ No ☐ N/A ☐
   e. Evidence of over heating   Yes ☐ No ☐ N/A ☐
   f. Evidence of arcing   Yes ☐ No ☐ N/A ☐
   g. Evidence of chemical contamination   Yes ☐ No ☐ N/A ☐
5. Wire Marking   CFR 23.1351 and AC43.13 chapter 11
   a. Gage, circuit, and gage size   Yes ☐ No ☐ N/A ☐
   b. Marked 15 inched maximum intervals   Yes ☐ No ☐ N/A ☐
6. Grounding Points   CFR 23.1351 AC 43.13 chapter 11, AC 25-16 and AC 25-10
   a. Tightness of nuts (torque)   Yes ☐ No ☐ N/A ☐
   b. Cleanliness of attach points   Yes ☐ No ☐ N/A ☐
   c. Corrosion   Yes ☐ No ☐ N/A ☐
7. Sleeving and Conduits   CFR 23.1351 AC 43.13 chapter 11, AC 25-16 and AC 25-10
   a. Damages outer surfaces (kinks, holes, flats spots, etc.)   Yes ☐ No ☐ N/A ☐
   b. Wear   Yes ☐ No ☐ N/A ☐
   c. Adequate drain holes   Yes ☐ No ☐ N/A ☐
8. Clamping Points   CFR 23.1351 AC 43.13 chapter 11, AC 25-16 and AC 25-10
   a. Improper installation   Yes ☐ No ☐ N/A ☐
   b. Clamp/wire damage   Yes ☐ No ☐ N/A ☐
   c. Clamp cushion migration   Yes ☐ No ☐ N/A ☐
   d. Loose wires   Yes ☐ No ☐ N/A ☐

Equipment / Furnishings

1. Equipment installed functions properly   CAR 3.622 CFR 23.1301(d)   Yes ☐ No ☐ N/A ☐
2. Flight manual correct for aircraft TCDS   Yes ☐ No ☐ N/A ☐
3. Trim tab indicator readable and functions properly CFR 43.13   Yes ☐ No ☐ N/A ☐
4. Emergency brake handle installed   CFR 21.31   Yes ☐ No ☐ N/A ☐
5. Batteries proper installation, & charging   CAR 3.683 CFR 23.1353 Yes ☐ No ☐ N/A ☐
6. Battery vented overboard CAR 3.683 CFR 23.1353 & AC 43.13-1B PARA 11-22
                                                                           Yes ☐ No ☐ N/A ☐
7. Battery NiCad gage for thermal run away   CFR 23.1353   Yes ☐ No ☐ N/A ☐
8. Thermal/Noise insulation   CFR 23.853   Yes ☐ No ☐ N/A ☐
9. Relief tube, corrosion areas   CFR 43.13   Yes ☐ No ☐ N/A ☐
10. New interior material Certs.   CAR-3.388 and CFR 23.853/25.853 Yes ☐ No ☐ N/A ☐
11. Interior replaced Yes ☐ No ☐ New ☐ Have Burn Certifications   Yes ☐ No ☐ N/A ☐
12. Seat covers, sheep skin material Certs.   CAR-3.388 and CFR 23.853   Yes ☐ No ☐ N/A ☐
13. Seat covers (automotive) require burn certification   CFR 23.853   Yes ☐ No ☐ N/A ☐
14. Worn seat material CFR 25.853 for a CAR-3.388 aircraft Part 91 & 23.853, AC 43.13-1B Para 9-61
                                                                           Yes ☐ No ☐ N/A ☐
15. Has interior been altered or material substituted   CFR 21.303/43.11 Yes ☐ No ☐ N/A ☐
16. Seat back locks broke   CAR 3.390 CFR 23.785   Yes ☐ No ☐ N/A ☐

17. Seat rails holes elongated Yes ☐ No ☐ Check AD.   CFR 39   Yes ☐ No ☐ N/A ☐
18. Seating configuration, how many seats allowed TCDS   Yes ☐ No ☐ N/A ☐
19. Head rest missing and not on equipment list   CFR 91.9   Yes ☐ No ☐ N/A ☐
20. Seat belts for stitching, cuts, or frayed   CFR 91.107 & 23.785   Yes ☐ No ☐ N/A ☐
21. Seat belts proper storage and marking   CAR 3.715TSO-22 & 23.785   Yes ☐ No ☐ N/A ☐
22. Seat Belts Plastic locking ring missing, FWD ☐ AFT ☐   CFR 45.14   Yes ☐ No ☐ N/A ☐
23. Seat belt secured when not is use   CFR 23.785(d)   Yes ☐ No ☐ N/A ☐
24. TSO C-22 marking on seat belts   CAR 3.390/715 CFR 45.15 CFR 91.205(b)(13,14)

       Yes ☐ No ☐ N/A ☐

25. **Shoulder harness required after July 18, 1978**   CFR 23.785(g)(1)   Yes ☐ No ☐ N/A ☐
26. **Shoulder harness required after Sept. 16, 1992 (PAX) helicopter**   Yes ☐ No ☐ N/A ☐
27. Cabin divider(s) / Curtains / Door(s)   CFR 23.853   Yes ☐ No ☐ N/A ☐
28. Heating system / AD's / decay test   CAR 3.388 CFR 23.859   Yes ☐ No ☐ N/A ☐
29. Cabin cooling (air conditioning), Ck /   CAR 3.393 CFR 23.831   Yes ☐ No ☐ N/A ☐
30. Outflow / Safety / Dump valve(s)condition   CAR 3.394 CFR 23.843   Yes ☐ No ☐ N/A ☐
31. Pressurization seals /boots /gaskets condition   CAR 3.396 CFR 23.831   Yes ☐ No ☐ N/A ☐
32. Glare shield painted flat black   CFR 23.773   Yes ☐ No ☐ N/A ☐
33. Door latches lock   CFR 23.783   Yes ☐ No ☐ N/A ☐
    a.   Door sprung   CAR 3.389 CFR 23.783   Yes ☐ No ☐ N/A ☐
    b.   Door Seals worn   CAR 3.387 CFR 23.783   Yes ☐ No ☐ N/A ☐
    c.   Door slide track lock broken   CAR 3.387 CFR 23.783   Yes ☐ No ☐ N/A ☐

Misc. Fuselage

1. Cabin pressure controller service compressor 24 months   CAR 3.395 CFR 23.843   Yes ☐ No ☐ N/A ☐
2. Pressurization seals /boots /gaskets, voids, and cracks   CFR 23.843   Yes ☐ No ☐ N/A ☐
3. Antenna installation doubles per   AC43.13 2A, CFR 23.571/572   Yes ☐ No ☐ N/A ☐
4. Corrosion on antenna's   CAR 3.395 CFR 23.609   Yes ☐ No ☐ N/A ☐
5. Fabric covered aircraft condition good ☐ poor ☐   AC 43.13-1B Ch 2   Yes ☐ No ☐ N/A ☐
6. Emergency exit placards   CAR 3.768 CFR 23.1557(d)   Yes ☐ No ☐ N/A ☐
7. Any addition mirrors installed on wings requires Form 337 CFR 43Appen.A

       Yes ☐ No ☐ N/A ☐

8. Condition of paint, is corrosion present **NOT** allowed   CAR 3.295 CFR 23.609

       Yes ☐ No ☐ N/A ☐

Aircraft exterior inspection

1. Wash and clean all oil, grease and dirt from aircraft   CFR 43 Appendix D   Yes ☐ No ☐ N/A ☐
2. Nationality and registration marks per CFR 45.29 Check 3 inch marking per date **Jan. 1, 1983** and repaint. Over 30 years 2 or12 inch   CFR 45.22(b)   Yes ☐ No ☐ N/A ☐
3. Rotating beacon installation proper doubler **Required after 08-11-71**   CFR 23.1401

       Yes ☐ No ☐ N/A ☐

4. Anti collision light system installed CAR 3.705 CFR 91.209(b) / CFR 23.1401 Yes ☐ No ☐ N/A ☐
5. Anti collision light installed after 03/11/1996 Red or white CFR 91.206(b)(11)

       Yes ☐ No ☐ N/A ☐

6. AFT nav light proper color **white**   CAR 3.702 CFR 23.1385-1399   Yes ☐ No ☐ N/A ☐
7. Panel seams miss match, extra paint in front of static port   CFR 23.1325   Yes ☐ No ☐ N/A ☐
8. Static ports paint in hole or other things L/H ☐ R/H ☐   CAR 3.665 CFR 23.1325

       Yes ☐ No ☐ N/A ☐

9. Static vent painted over L/H ☐ R/H ☐   CAR 3.665 CFR 23.1325   Yes ☐ No ☐ N/A ☐
10. Pitot heat indicator amber light   CFR 23.1326   Yes ☐ No ☐ N/A ☐
11. Pitot heat element operational   CFR 23.1326   Yes ☐ No ☐ N/A ☐
12. Pitot tube worn around hole Yes ☐ No ☐ Not plugged   Yes ☐ No ☐ N/A ☐
    a. Air Speed Last inspection date _____   CFR 23.1325   Yes ☐ No ☐ N/A ☐
13. Static wicks missing
    a. Right wing   CFR 23.867   Yes ☐ No ☐ N/A ☐
    b. Left wing   CFR 23.867   Yes ☐ No ☐ N/A ☐
    c. Right elevator   CFR 23.867   Yes ☐ No ☐ N/A ☐
    d. Left elevator   CFR 23.867   Yes ☐ No ☐ N/A ☐
    e. Rudder   CFR 23.867   Yes ☐ No ☐ N/A ☐

Landing Gear CAR-3 and Part 23

1. Correct tire and wheel for the aircraft   CAR 3.362 CFR 23.733   Yes ☐ No ☐ N/A ☐
2. Tire service Main _____ R ☐ L ☐ Nose Tire ☐ CAR 3.362 CFR 23.733   Yes ☐ No ☐ N/A ☐
3. Tires condition wear, cuts, or weather cracking L/H ☐ R/H ☐ NLG ☐   AC 43.13 para 9-14
                                                                              Yes ☐ No ☐ N/A ☐
4. Landing Gear struts leaking L/H ☐ R/H ☐ NLG AC 43.13 par 9-2/4   Yes ☐ No ☐ N/A ☐
5. Landing gear struts extension L/H _____ R/H _____ AC43.13 para 9-2/4
                                                                              Yes ☐ No ☐ N/A ☐
6. Landing gear fairing condition L/H ___ R/H ___ Nose ___ CFR 23.607, CFR 23.1193
                                                                              Yes ☐ No ☐ N/A ☐
7. Fairing cracked, Hardware missing.   CFR 23.607/1193   Yes ☐ No ☐ N/A ☐
8. Landing gear fairings missing, check equipment list and W&B   CFR 21.29   Yes ☐ No ☐ N/A ☐
9. Steering shimmy dampener leaking, won't track CFR 23.745   Yes ☐ No ☐ N/A ☐
10. Brake pads worn. L/H ☐ R/H ☐ **0.100 in-thickness min.**   CAR 3.363 CFR23.735
                                                                              Yes ☐ No ☐ N/A ☐
11. Brake lines condition, frayed, corrosion on fittings L/H ☐ R/H☐   CFR 23.735
                                                                              Yes ☐ No ☐ N/A ☐
12. Brake rotor corrosion, warped, or under size L/H ☐ RH ☐ CFR 23.735   Yes ☐ No ☐ N/A ☐
13. MLG strut / axle / torque links L/H condition   CFR 23.721   Yes ☐ No ☐ N/A ☐
14. MLG strut / axle / torque links R/H condition   CFR 23.721   Yes ☐ No ☐ N/A ☐
15. NLG strut / axle / torque links L/H condition   CFR 23.721   Yes ☐ No ☐ N/A ☐
16. MLG L/H door actuating system / Hoses condition   CFR 23.1435   Yes ☐ No ☐ N/A ☐
17. MLG R/H door actuating system / Hoses condition   CFR 23.1435   Yes ☐ No ☐ N/A ☐
18. NLG door actuating system / Hoses condition   CFR 23.1435   Yes ☐ No ☐ N/A ☐
19. MLG L/H Landing gear actuator switch(s) condition   CFR 23.729   Yes ☐ No ☐ N/A ☐
20. MLG R/H Landing gear actuator switch(s) condition   CFR 23.729   Yes ☐ No ☐ N/A ☐
21. Repack wheel bearing   CRR 43 Appendix D   Yes ☐ No ☐ N/A ☐
22. Wheel nut cotter pin proper length and installed correctly AC 43.13-1-B   Yes ☐ No ☐ N/A ☐
23. NLG Landing gear actuator switch(s) condition   CFR 23.729   Yes ☐ No ☐ N/A ☐
24. Land gear strut chrome damaged—reference manufacture maintenance manual
                                                                              Yes ☐ No ☐ N/A ☐
25. Landing light covers cracked, missing hardware L/H ☐ R/H ☐ CFR 23.729 Yes ☐ No ☐ N/A ☐
26. Position / Warning / Safety squat switch or (WOW) switch   CFR 23.729 Yes ☐ No ☐ N/A ☐
27. Emergency extension / blow down   CAR 3.358 CFR 23.729   Yes ☐ No ☐ N/A ☐
28. Gear Emergency operation does it work   CAR 3.357 CFR 23.729   Yes ☐ No ☐ N/A ☐
29. Landing Gear Retract/Extension System   CAR 3.356 CFR 23.729   Yes ☐ No ☐ N/A ☐

30. Main landing gear locking mechanism for operation CRR 43 Appendix D   Yes ☐ No ☐ N/A ☐
31. Main gear trunnion strut bushings for wear L/H ☐ R/H ☐   CFR 43.13   Yes ☐ No ☐ N/A ☐
32. Main gear bungee cord condition L/H ☐ R/H ☐ Manufacture manual   Yes ☐ No ☐ N/A ☐
33. Main landing & nose gear lubrication while on jacks L/H ☐ R/H ☐ CFR 43.13 Yes ☐ No ☐ N/A ☐
34. Lube type of grease used per manufacture _____   CFR 43.16   Yes ☐ No ☐ N/A ☐
35. Floats and skis for security and defects CRR 43 Appendix D   Yes ☐ No ☐ N/A ☐

Landing Gear	**Specification**	**Actual**
Actuator cushion	Up ____ Down ____	Up ____ Down ____
Down lock over center	N ___ L ____ R ____	N ___ L ____ R ____
Down Lock clearance	N ___ L ____ R ____	N ___ L ____ R ____
Up lock clearance	N ___ L ____ R ____	N ___ L ____ R ____
Up lock cable tension	N ___ L ____ R ____	N ___ L ____ R ____

Hydraulic System

1. Hydraulic distribution hoses condition/life limit   CAR 3.726 CFR 23.1435   Yes ☐ No ☐ N/A ☐
2. Hydraulic pressure relief valve   CFR 23.1435   Yes ☐ No ☐ N/A ☐
3. Hydraulic accumulator charge   CAR 3.728 CFR 23.1435   Yes ☐ No ☐ N/A ☐
4. Hydraulic reservoir / venting   CFR 23.1435   Yes ☐ No ☐ N/A ☐
5. Hydraulic filter change life limit   CFR 23.1435   Yes ☐ No ☐ N/A ☐
6. Hydraulic electric motor brushes and condition   CFR 23.1351   Yes ☐ No ☐ N/A ☐

Flight Control/Wing

1. Wing attach fittings for cracks, elongated bolt holes L/H CAR 3.317 CFR 23.572
   Yes ☐ No ☐ N/A ☐
2. Wing attach fittings for cracks, elongated bolt holes R/H CAR 3.317 CFR 23.572
   Yes ☐ No ☐ N/A ☐
3. **Wing L/H** dents, cracks, Loose rivets, Corrosion, nav light **RED** CFR 23.603/1385
   Yes ☐ No ☐ N/A ☐
4. L/H wing Fuel vent direction **check AD's** FWD ☐ AFT ☐ CFR 23.975   Yes ☐ No ☐ N/A ☐
5. **Wing R/H** dents, cracks, Loose rivets, Corrosion, nav light **GREEN** CAR 3.295 CFR 23.603/1385
   Yes ☐ No ☐ N/A ☐
6. R/H Fuel vent direction FWD ☐ AFT ☐ CFR 23.975   Yes ☐ No ☐ N/A ☐
7. **Flaps L/H** cracks _____, loose hardware _____, Properly installed _____. Stop drill cracks
   CAR 3.339 CFR 23.655/697   Yes ☐ No ☐ N/A ☐
8. **Flaps R/H** cracks _____, loose hardware _____, Properly installed _____. Stop drill cracks
   CAR 3.339 CFR 23.655/697   Yes ☐ No ☐ N/A ☐
9. **Aileron R/H** cracks ___, Loose hardware ___, Properly installed   Yes ☐ No ☐ N/A ☐
10. Cable rigging loose Annual/100 hour inspection CAR 3.337 CFR 23.655/685/689
   Yes ☐ No ☐ N/A ☐
11. **Aileron L/H** cracks Loose hardware, Properly installed   CAR 3.294   Yes ☐ No ☐ N/A ☐
12. Cable rigging loose Annual/100 hour inspection CAR 3.337 CFR 23.655/685/689
   Yes ☐ No ☐ N/A ☐
13. Deicer boots condition worn, holes, debonded, type CAR .7127 CFR 23.1416/1419
   Yes ☐ No ☐ N/A ☐

14. **Rudder** moves up & down, bearing loose, cracks, repairs CAR 3.332 CFR 23.685

Yes ☐ No ☐ N/A ☐

15. Rudder / trim tab attach fittings condition, loose CAR 3.337 CFR 23.685   Yes ☐ No ☐ N/A ☐

16. **Lubrication**, systems lube per manufactures recommendations   CFR 43.13
Yes ☐ No ☐ N/A ☐

17. Electrical bonding straps broken or frayed CAR 3.337-1 CFR 23.867   Yes ☐ No ☐ N/A ☐

18. **Horizontal Stab L/H** cracks ☐, Loose rivets ☐, Hardware installation and safetied ☐, Stop drill cracks CFR 23.572 Stops ☐   CFR 23.675   Yes ☐ No ☐ N/A ☐

19. **Horizontal Stab R/H** cracks ☐ Loose rivets ☐ Hardware installation and safetied ☐ Stop drill cracks CFR 23.572, Stops ☐___   CFR 23.675   Yes ☐ No ☐ N/A ☐

20. Stopped drilled holes in elevator without doublers R/H ☐ CFR 23.572   Yes ☐ No ☐ N/A ☐

21. Stopped drilled holes in elevator without doublers L/H ☐ CFR 23.572   Yes ☐ No ☐ N/A ☐

22. Elevator trim control system rigging   CAR 3.337 CFR 23.659   Yes ☐ No ☐ N/A ☐

23. Elevator trim indicator control works   CAR 3.337 CFR 23.677(a)   Yes ☐ No ☐ N/A ☐

24. Elevator / trim tab attach fittings L/H   CAR 3.337 CFR 23.572   Yes ☐ No ☐ N/A ☐

25. Elevator / trim tab attach fittings R/H   CAR 3.337 CFR 23.572   Yes ☐ No ☐ N/A ☐

26. Elevator trim / servo tab structure L/H   CAR 3.337 CFR 23.572   Yes ☐ No ☐ N/A ☐

27. Elevator trim / servo tab structure R/H   CAR 3.337 CFR 23.572   Yes ☐ No ☐ N/A ☐

28. Control surface attach fittings condition   CAR 3.328 CFR 23.572   Yes ☐ No ☐ N/A ☐

29. Control surface balancing all primary controls after repair or paint CAR 3.159 CFR 23.659

Yes ☐ No ☐ N/A ☐

30. STOL devices / control system condition   CFR 23.572   Yes ☐ No ☐ N/A ☐

31. Boundary layer control / vortex generators, cracks and condition CFR 23.572 Yes ☐ No ☐ N/A ☐

32. Flight Control Surface Travels / Cable Tension CAR 3.345 CFR 23.143   Yes ☐ No ☐ N/A ☐

33. Gust lock, condition, worn holes   CAR 3.341 CFR 23.572   Yes ☐ No ☐ N/A ☐

34. Autopilot trim indicator annual/100 hour check rigging CAR 3.343 CFR 23.143

Yes ☐ No ☐ N/A ☐

35. Autopilot system condition   CFR 23.143   Yes ☐ No ☐ N/A ☐

36. Yaw damper condition   CAR 3.347 CFR 23.143   Yes ☐ No ☐ N/A ☐

37. Electric trim rigging and condition   CAR 3.343 CFR 23.143   Yes ☐ No ☐ N/A ☐

38. Flight control pulleys worn, broken, or frozen up CAR 3.345 CFR 23.689   Yes ☐ No ☐ N/A ☐

39. Flight control cables broken strands/rust Reference AC43.13CFR 23.689   Yes ☐ No ☐ N/A ☐

40. Flight control Surface Travel/Cable Tension CAR 3.345 CFR 23.391 to 23.459

Yes ☐ No ☐ N/A ☐

Travel Spec Actual	Tension	Spec	Actual
Control Column	_____	_____	_____
Aileron	_____	_____	_____
Aileron Trim Tab(s)	_____	_____	_____
Rudder	_____	_____	_____
Rudder Trim Tab	_____	_____	_____
Elevator/Stabilator	_____	_____	_____
Elev / Stab Tab(s)	_____	_____	_____
Flap	_____	_____	_____
Moveable Stabilizer	_____	_____	_____
Rudder Pedals	_____	_____	_____

Engine Inspection

Engine Type Certificate Number T/C _____ Rev. _____

Engine Part Number _____ S/N _____

Reference CAR Subpart E, CFR 23 Subpart E Powerplant, and 43 Appendix D

1. Thoroughly clean the engine — CFR 43 App. D — Yes ☐ No ☐ N/A ☐
2. Perform engine static run — CFR 33.26/43.15 — Yes ☐ No ☐ N/A ☐
3. Perform engine idle run R.P.M. check — CFR 33.26/43.15 — Yes ☐ No ☐ N/A ☐
4. Perform magneto drop check — CFR 33.37 — Yes ☐ No ☐ N/A ☐
5. Mag "P" lead wires not cracked or broken — CFR 33.28 — Yes ☐ No ☐ N/A ☐
6. Shut down engine and check for engine oil and fuel leaks   CFR 33.25 — Yes ☐ No ☐ N/A ☐
7. Engine Data plate installed — CAR 3.670 CFR 45.13 — Yes ☐ No ☐ N/A ☐
8. L/H engine Make Model/Series matches TCDS   CFR 45.13 — Yes ☐ No ☐ N/A ☐
9. R/H engine Make Model/Series matches TCDS   CFR 45.13 — Yes ☐ No ☐ N/A ☐
10. Certification basic of components installed 337's   CFR 45.15 — Yes ☐ No ☐ N/A ☐
11. Instruments CFR 23.1305 instruments — Yes ☐ No ☐ N/A ☐
     a. Cylinder head temperature limitations placard CFR 43.15 — Yes ☐ No ☐ N/A ☐
     b. Oil temperature check limitations placard — CFR 43.15 — Yes ☐ No ☐ N/A ☐
     c. Engine — CFR 23.1301 — Yes ☐ No ☐ N/A ☐
     d. Accessories — CFR 23.1301 — Yes ☐ No ☐ N/A ☐
12. Engine cowl loose/missing hardware Location — CAR 3.625 CFR 23.1193 — Yes ☐ No ☐ N/A ☐
13. Firewall bent, cracked, or missing fasteners — CAR 3.623 CFR 23.1191 — Yes ☐ No ☐ N/A ☐
14. Firewall wire and hose grommets condition — CAR 3.623 CFR 23.1191(c) Yes ☐ No ☐ N/A ☐
15. Firewall has corrosion — CAR 3.624 CFR 23.1191(e) Yes ☐ No ☐ N/A ☐
16. Engine mount structure for cracks, dents, etc. — CFR 23.23 — Yes ☐ No ☐ N/A ☐
17. **Retorque** cylinder base nuts and case half per manufacture recommendations Yes ☐ No ☐ N/A ☐
18. Engine shock mount cracks, worn, hardware condition — CFR 33.33 — Yes ☐ No ☐ N/A ☐
19. Flex tubing condition weather cracking, worn, etc.   CAR 3.638 CFR 23.1183 Yes ☐ No ☐ N/A ☐
20. Engine oil leaking Location _____ — CAR 3.638 CFR 23.1183 — Yes ☐ No ☐ N/A ☐
21. STC for Bracket air filter if installed & Form 337 CFR 21.111/1091 — Yes ☐ No ☐ N/A ☐
22. Air Filter dirty/foreign particles CAR 3.605 — CFR 23.1107 — Yes ☐ No ☐ N/A ☐
23. Condition of baffle seals and installation Good ☐ Poor ☐ Substituted type of baffle material ☐
          CAR 3.625 CFR 33.15/17/21& CFR 23.1043 — Yes ☐ No ☐ N/A ☐
24. Wire chafing, fuel lines, no wires clamped under them   CAR 3.681 AC 43.13-1B
          Yes ☐ No ☐ N/A ☐
25. Electrical wire Slack between supports **Max 1/2 inch** AC 43.13-1B fig.11.9 — Yes ☐ No ☐ N/A ☐
26. Engine/Electric fuel pump condition wires, mounting Good/worn CFR 23 — Yes ☐ No ☐ N/A ☐
27. Ignition harness condition Good _____ Worn _____ — CFR 23 — Yes ☐ No ☐ N/A ☐
28. Clean and gap spark plugs per engine manufactures recommendations — Yes ☐ No ☐ N/A ☐
29. Rotate spark plugs per manufacture recommendation (1 gasket required) — Yes ☐ No ☐ N/A ☐
30. Starter ring broken teeth — CFR 23 — Yes ☐ No ☐ N/A ☐
31. Alternator/generator drive belts condition worn, cracked, broke — CFR 23 — Yes ☐ No ☐ N/A ☐
32. Cylinders cracked fins, rocker cover leaking 1__ 2__ 3 __ 4__ 5__ 6__ — Yes ☐ No ☐ N/A ☐
33. Cylinders barrel cracked (Chrome) 1__ 2__ 3 __ 4__ 5__ 6__ — Yes ☐ No ☐ N/A ☐
34. Cylinders check records for times & certs 1__ 2__ 3 __ 4__ 5__ 6__ — Yes ☐ No ☐ N/A ☐
35. Exhaust stacks cracks, defects, installation 1__ 2 __ 3__ 4__ 5__ 6__
          CAR 3.615 CFR 23. 1121 and CFR 33.21 — Yes ☐ No ☐ N/A ☐
36. Muffler cracked, location ___, **Recurring AD's**   CAR 3.617 CFR 23.1121 — Yes ☐ No ☐ N/A ☐

37. Muffler leak test to 2 psi internal pressure AC 43.13-1b Para 8-49 (d) Yes ☐ No ☐ N/A ☐
38. Rocker cover or push rods leaking oil past seals Yes ☐ No ☐ N/A ☐
39. Valve inspection (freedom of valve rockers when valves are closed) manufacture recommendations
    Yes ☐ No ☐ N/A ☐
40. Preheater shroud condition cracks, vibration CAR 3.617 CFR 23.1101 Yes ☐ No ☐ N/A ☐
41. Carburetor heat box condition of holes CAR 3.617 CFR 23. Yes ☐ No ☐ N/A ☐
    a. Proper hardware screws and nuts CFR 23. Yes ☐ No ☐ N/A ☐
        a. Engine controls properly safetying ☐ travel ☐ AC 43.13-1B para 7-122 thru 12
    Yes ☐ No ☐ N/A ☐
42. Engine case nuts torqued and right side up CFR 43 Appendix D (d)(2) Yes ☐ No ☐ N/A ☐
43. Crankcase for cracks, leaks and security of seam bolts CFR 33. Yes ☐ No ☐ N/A ☐
44. Engine mounts for corrosion, cracks **NONE Allowed** CFR 23.363 Yes ☐ No ☐ N/A ☐
45. Cowl flap control and operational limitations CAR 3.625 CFR 23.1047 Yes ☐ No ☐ N/A ☐
46. Cowl flap check for cracks CFR 43.13 Yes ☐ No ☐ N/A ☐
47. Alternate/ Ram air / Carb heat CAR 3.606 CFR 23.1093 Yes ☐ No ☐ N/A ☐
48. Turbo Waste gate (Non automatic) CFR 23.1091 Yes ☐ No ☐ N/A ☐
49. Vacuum pump lines, clamps condition Good ☐ Worn ☐ CFR 2 Yes ☐ No ☐ N/A ☐
50. Supercharger overall condition Good ☐ Bad ☐ CFR 23.1109 Yes ☐ No ☐ N/A ☐
51. Electrical wiring cracked, burned, broken CAR 3.693 CRR 23.1163(b) Yes ☐ No ☐ N/A ☐
52. Oil filter opening placard CAR 3.767 CFR 23.1557(c)(2) Yes ☐ No ☐ N/A ☐
53. Drain oil CFR 43 Appendix D Yes ☐ No ☐ N/A ☐
54. Clean oil screen CFR 43 Appendix D Yes ☐ No ☐ N/A ☐
55. Replace oil filter CFR 43 Appendix D Yes ☐ No ☐ N/A ☐
56. Check filter for metal particles in accordance with manufacture CFR 43.15, 23.1019
    Yes ☐ No ☐ N/A ☐
57. Check for metal particles or foreign matter on screens and sump drain plugs CFR 43 Appendix D
    Yes ☐ No ☐ N/A ☐
58. Oil drain plug/valve condition and positive locking CAR 3.574 CFR 23.1021 Yes ☐ No ☐ N/A ☐
59. Oil radiator supporting structure for security CAR 3.572 CFR 23.1023 Yes ☐ No ☐ N/A ☐
60. Oil tanks condition and free of vibration CAR 3.563 CFR 23.1013 Yes ☐ No ☐ N/A ☐
61. Hose inspection/replacement manufacture limits CFR 43.10 Yes ☐ No ☐ N/A ☐
62. Mechanic has a master orifice for differential compression tester (MFG requirement)
    Yes ☐ No ☐ N/A ☐
63. Differential Compression Test, 80psi /60 psi cylinder CFR 43 Appendix D and AC 43.13-1B paragraph
    8-14 Yes ☐ No ☐ N/A ☐
64. 1 ____ 2 ____ 3 ____ 4 ___ 5 ___ 6 ___ If **25%** difference check cylinder for problems.
65. Turbocharger inspect all air ducting and connections Per Manufacture Manual Yes ☐ No ☐ N/A ☐
66. Exhaust pressure check system condition and leaks 5 p.s.i. CFR 43.16 Yes ☐ No ☐ N/A ☐
67. Engine Condition perform completed engine run-up. Yes ☐ No ☐

Fuel System CAR-3 Subpart E and Part 23

1. Remove cowling and clean engine of all oil & dirt CRR 43 Appendix D Yes ☐ No ☐ N/A ☐
2. Injection fuel lines **Recurring AD** if required every 100 hours CFR 39 Yes ☐ No ☐ N/A ☐
3. Fuel bowl leaking CAR 3.431 CFR 23.999 Yes ☐ No ☐ N/A ☐
4. Fuel quantity sensor / transmitter condition CFR 23.955 Yes ☐ No ☐ N/A ☐
5. Fuel boost / Aux. pump(s) bypass condition CAR 3.449 CFR 23.955 Yes ☐ No ☐ N/A ☐
6. Fuel lines vibration/clamped CAR 3.550 CFR 23.993 & AC 43.13-1B para 8-31
    Yes ☐ No ☐ N/A ☐

7. Carburetor security, throttle arm/bushing loose   CAR 3.551 CFR 23.994   Yes ☐ No ☐ N/A ☐
8. Mixture control linkage condition   CAR 3.630 CFR 23.1147   Yes ☐ No ☐ N/A ☐
9. Throttle control binding condition   CAR 3.628 CFR 23.1143   Yes ☐ No ☐ N/A ☐
10. Engine primer leaking   CAR 3.442 CFR 23.1141   Yes ☐ No ☐ N/A ☐
11. Remove and clean carburetor screen Manufacture Maintenance Manual   Yes ☐ No ☐ N/A ☐
12. Induction System Screens condition   CAR 3.448 CFR 23.1107   Yes ☐ No ☐ N/A ☐
13. Fuel pump condition and AD requirement   CFR 23.991   Yes ☐ No ☐ N/A ☐
14. Fuel system lines and fittings conditions   CAR 3.550 CFR 23.993   Yes ☐ No ☐ N/A ☐
15. Fuel system drains, lock shut and drains properly   CFR 23.999   Yes ☐ No ☐ N/A ☐
16. Clean and inspect fuel tank strainer condition   CFR 23.977   Yes ☐ No ☐ N/A ☐
17. Filler cap must have electrical bonding (chain on cap)   CFR 23.973   Yes ☐ No ☐ N/A ☐
18. Fuel placards **L/H wing** Yes ☐ No ☐ **R/H wing** CAR 3.761 CFR 23.1557(c)
     Yes ☐ No ☐ N/A ☐
19. Fuel tank caps seal condition, tight seal, flat, cracked CAR 3.445 CFR 23.973(c)
     Yes ☐ No ☐ N/A ☐
20. Fuel tank sump drained of water   CAR 3.444 CFR 23.971   Yes ☐ No ☐ N/A ☐
21. Fuel tank condition for cracks, vibration, leaks   CFR 23.963   Yes ☐ No ☐ N/A ☐
22. Fuel line and hose condition left/right side   CFR 23.993   Yes ☐ No ☐ N/A ☐
23. Fuel drain valve positive locking   CAR 3.551 CFR 23.999   Yes ☐ No ☐ N/A ☐
24. Fuel strainer or filter condition   CAR 3.448 CFR 23.997   Yes ☐ No ☐ N/A ☐
25. Blistering of sealant in a fuel cell caused by corrosion   CFR 23.963(c)   Yes ☐ No ☐ N/A ☐
26. Fuel nonmetallic liners leaks   CAR 3.442-1 CFR 23.965((d)   Yes ☐ No ☐ N/A ☐
27. Unusable fuel supply check reference (TCDS)   CAR 3.440 CFR 23.959   Yes ☐ No ☐ N/A ☐
28. Fuel gauge reads zero when fuel tank is empty   CAR 3.440 CFR 23.1337(b)
     Yes ☐ No ☐ N/A ☐
29. Lubricate all control rod ends and fuel system components MFG instructions Yes ☐ No ☐ N/A ☐

Propeller Inspection

Propeller Type Certificate Number T/C _____ Rev. _____

Propeller Part Number _____ S/N _____

1. Propeller Part number and serial number   CFR 45.11   Yes ☐ No ☐ N/A ☐
2. Is there a propeller maintenance record (log book)   CFR 43.2(a)   Yes ☐ No ☐ N/A ☐
3. If no propeller log book sign 100-hour off in airframe record   CFR 43.11   Yes ☐ No ☐ N/A ☐
4. Propeller seal leaking   CFR23.907   Yes ☐ No ☐ N/A ☐
5. Propeller for nicks, cracks, and damage AC 43.13-2B Para 8-73   Yes ☐ No ☐ N/A ☐
6. File marks after dressing propeller **NOT** allowed   CFR 43.13   Yes ☐ No ☐ N/A ☐
7. Mechanic record entry after dressing nicks   CFR 43.9   Yes ☐ No ☐ N/A ☐
8. Propeller spinner had doubler added to repair cracks **Not ALLOWED** CFR 23.907
     Yes ☐ No ☐ N/A ☐
9. Propeller spinner(s) cracks ___, **NO cracks allowed** nuts safety wired __ Missing screws from spinner
   None allowed _____ Reference Service Letters if cracked:
   a. Sensenich **See aircraft maintenance manuals**   Yes ☐ No ☐ N/A ☐
   b. McCauley 1992-14C—part **must be replaced**   Yes ☐ No ☐ N/A ☐
   c. Hartzell HC-SL-61-91 **Requires a Field Approval**   Yes ☐ No ☐ N/A ☐
10. Propeller grinding when rotating AC 43.13-1B para 8-2(c)(2)   Yes ☐ No ☐ N/A ☐
11. Corrosion pitting on blades or hub **None Allowed** CFR A35.3   Yes ☐ No ☐ N/A ☐
12. Paint on propeller blades, type per manufacture manual CAR 3.295 CFR 23.609
     Yes ☐ No ☐ N/A ☐

13. If repainted after rework type of paint applied lacquer base or polyurethane enamel and was it recorded in the propeller maintenance record — CFR 43.5 — Yes ☐ No ☐ N/A ☐

14. STC for different propeller than original per TCDS — CFR 21.111 — Yes ☐ No ☐ N/A ☐

15. STC propeller check engine gages for new limitations — CFR A35.4 — Yes ☐ No ☐ N/A ☐

16. Is the propeller the right diameter / width — CAR 3.416 CFR 23.45 — Yes ☐ No ☐ N/A ☐

17. Propeller ground clearance — CAR 3.422 CFR 23.925 — Yes ☐ No ☐ N/A ☐

18. Has the propeller tips been altered (rounded or square) — CFR 43 Append A — Yes ☐ No ☐ N/A ☐

19. Are their repairs in the propeller maintenance records — CFR 43.9 — Yes ☐ No ☐ N/A ☐

20. Has the shot peen been removed after reworked at hub — CFR 43.9 — Yes ☐ No ☐ N/A ☐

21. Has the hub seal been replaced (service life) — CFR 43.9 — Yes ☐ No ☐ N/A ☐

22. Prop Hub is oil/grease filled and/or leaking — CFR 35.3 — Yes ☐ No ☐ N/A ☐

23. When was the last hub overhaul — CFR 35.3 — Yes ☐ No ☐ N/A ☐

24. Pitting corrosion on Hub **NONE ALLOWED** — CFR 35.3 — Yes ☐ No ☐ N/A ☐

25. Hub, blade clamps, and pitch change mechanisms should be inspected for corrosion **NONE ALLOWED** — CFR A35.3 — Yes ☐ No ☐ N/A ☐

26. Were new propeller bolts installed — CFR A35.3 — Yes ☐ No ☐ N/A ☐

27. Were new nuts used on the propeller bolts — CFR A35.3 — Yes ☐ No ☐ N/A ☐

28. New cotter pins installed in retaining nuts per Manufacture — CFR A35.4 — Yes ☐ No ☐ N/A ☐

29. Is the spinner shimmed to the spinner bracket if required — CFR A35.3 — Yes ☐ No ☐ N/A ☐

30. Pitch change counterweights on blade clamps should be inspected for security, safety — CFR A35.3 — Yes ☐ No ☐ N/A ☐

31. Adequate counterweight clearance within the spinner — CFR 23.925 — Yes ☐ No ☐ N/A ☐

32. Are the propeller blades in track — CFR 23.925 — Yes ☐ No ☐ N/A ☐

33. De-icier boots for signs of deterioration and security — CFR 23.929 — Yes ☐ No ☐ N/A ☐

34. Propeller **total time** is recorded in propeller record — CFR 91.417(2) — Yes ☐ No ☐ N/A ☐

35. Propeller vibration rate — CAR 3.431 CFR 23.907 — Yes ☐ No ☐ N/A ☐

36. Propeller clearance to ground and gear — CAR 3.417 CFR 23.925 — Yes ☐ No ☐ N/A ☐

37. Check blade play and blade track. — CFR 43.13 — Yes ☐ No ☐ N/A ☐

38. Lubricate the propeller assembly. Refer to Hartzell Service Letter HC-SL-61-184 for procedure. (If you have a Hartzell) — CFR 43.13 — Yes ☐ No ☐ N/A ☐

39. Propeller backing plate made of composite check propeller hub for pitting corrosion — Yes ☐ No ☐ N/A ☐

Avionics Installed

Type of Avionics: List by part number and serial number. CAR 3.721

	Yes	No	N/A
ALTIMETERS	☐	☐	☐
ENCODING	☐	☐	☐
Mfg: ACK Model: ACK 30	☐	☐	☐
Type of Avionics: AUDIO PANEL	☐	☐	☐
Mfg: KING Model: KMA 20	☐	☐	☐
Type of Avionics: COLLISION AVOIDANCE SYSTEMS	☐	☐	☐
Mfg: RYAN INTERNATIONAL CORPORATION Model: ATS 7000	☐	☐	☐
Type of Avionics: GPS	☐	☐	☐
Mfg: KING Model: KLN 90	☐	☐	☐
Type of Avionics: RNAV	☐	☐	☐
Mfg: KING Model: KNS 80	☐	☐	☐
Type of Avionics: LOC	☐	☐	☐
Mfg: KING Model: KI 208	☐	☐	☐

Type of Avionics: NAV-COMM   Yes ☐ No ☐ N/A ☐
Mfg: KING Model: KX 170 B Channels: 720   Yes ☐ No ☐ N/A ☐
Type of Avionics: COMM   Yes ☐ No ☐ N/A ☐
Mfg: KING Model: KY 197 Channels: 720   Yes ☐ No ☐ N/A ☐
Type of Avionics: TRANSPONDERS   Yes ☐ No ☐ N/A ☐
Mfg: KING Model: KT 76A   Yes ☐ No ☐ N/A ☐
Type of Avionics: STORMSCOPE   Yes ☐ No ☐ N/A ☐
Mfg: 3 M Model: WX 1000+   Yes ☐ No ☐ N/A ☐
Type of Avionics: GS   Yes ☐ No ☐ N/A ☐
Mfg: KING Model: KI 201   Yes ☐ No ☐ N/A ☐
Type of Avionics: AUTOPILOTS   Yes ☐ No ☐ N/A ☐
Mfg: S-TEC Model: SYSTEM 60 PSS   Yes ☐ No ☐ N/A ☐
Mfg: CENTURY Model: CENTURY II B   Yes ☐ No ☐ N/A ☐

De-Icing Systems

1.	Known Ice System:	CFR 23.1416	Yes ☐ No ☐ N/A ☐
2.	Ice Lights work and condition	CFR 23.1416	Yes ☐ No ☐ N/A ☐
3.	Prop De-Ice condition	CFR 23.1416	Yes ☐ No ☐ N/A ☐
4.	De-Ice Type:	CFR 23.1416	Yes ☐ No ☐ N/A ☐
5.	Wing Tail Boots condition	CAR 3.712 CFR 23.1416	Yes ☐ No ☐ N/A ☐
6.	Boots Condition:	CAR 3.712 CFR 23.1416	Yes ☐ No ☐ N/A ☐
7.	Windshield De-Ice condition	CFR 23.1416	Yes ☐ No ☐ N/A ☐
8.	Windshield Wipers condition	CFR 23.1416	Yes ☐ No ☐ N/A ☐
9.	Jet Intake De-Ice condition	CFR 23.1416	Yes ☐ No ☐ N/A ☐
10.	Pitot Heat condition	CFR 23.1416	Yes ☐ No ☐ N/A ☐

Additional Equipment

1.	Dual Controls:	CFR 23.777	Yes ☐ No ☐ N/A ☐
2.	Type: Yoke.	CFR 23.777	Yes ☐ No ☐ N/A ☐
3.	Stall Warning System works	CFR 23.703	Yes ☐ No ☐ N/A ☐
4.	Stick Shaker works	CFR 23.672	Yes ☐ No ☐ N/A ☐
5.	Rotating Beacon works	CAR 3.703 CFR 23.1401	Yes ☐ No ☐ N/A ☐
6.	Strobe Light works	CFR 23.1401	Yes ☐ No ☐ N/A ☐
7.	Taxi Lights works	CAR 3.655 CFR 23.1383	Yes ☐ No ☐ N/A ☐
8.	Navigation Light works	CAR 3.661 CFR 23.1389	Yes ☐ No ☐ N/A ☐
9.	Long Range Fuel	CFR 23.959	Yes ☐ No ☐ N/A ☐
10.	Aux Fuel Qty works	CFR 23.955	Yes ☐ No ☐ N/A ☐
11.	Single Point Refuel condition	CFR 23.953	Yes ☐ No ☐ N/A ☐
12.	Lavatory condition	CFR 23.1561	Yes ☐ No ☐ N/A ☐
13.	Galley condition	CFR 23.1561	Yes ☐ No ☐ N/A ☐
14.	Cabinetry condition	CFR 23.1561	Yes ☐ No ☐ N/A ☐
15.	Other Equipment condition	CAR 3.725 CFR 23.1561	Yes ☐ No ☐ N/A ☐
16.	Intercom System works	CFR 23.1561	Yes ☐ No ☐ N/A ☐
17.	Entertainment equipment CD player check for alteration form CFR 43 App. A		Yes ☐ No ☐ N/A ☐
18.	Gap seal kit installed	CFR 43 App. A	Yes ☐ No ☐ N/A ☐
19.	Brackett Aero Filter STC installed	CFR 43 App. A	Yes ☐ No ☐ N/A ☐
20.	Air Filter replacement **date** Bracket air filter check hours CFR 43 App.		Yes ☐ No ☐ N/A ☐

Special Inspections

			Hours	Months	Years
1.	Airworthiness Directives AD's	CFR 39	☐	☐	☐
2.	Engine fuel and oil lines	Per Manufacture Manual	☐	☐	☐
3.	Brake lines	Per Manufacture Manual	☐	☐	☐
4.	Air filter engine	Per Manufacture Manual	☐	☐	☐
5.	Air filter instruments	Per Manufacture Manual	☐	☐	☐
6.	Wing structural areas	Per Manufacture Manual	☐	☐	☐
7.	Hard and over weight landings	Per Manufacture Manual	☐	☐	☐
8.	Lighting strike damage	Per Manufacture Manual	☐	☐	☐
9.	Hail damage	Per Manufacture Manual			
10.	Severe Turbulence Inspection	Per Manufacture Manual	☐	☐	☐
11.	Corrosion damage Inspection	Per Manufacture Manual	☐	☐	☐
12.	Radio Equipment	Per Manufacture Manual	☐	☐	☐
13.	Emergency Locater Transmitter (ELT)	CFR 91.207	☐	☐	☐
14.	Pitot Static	CFR 91.411	☐	☐	☐
15.	Transponder	CFR 91.411	☐	☐	☐
16.	Rigging checks	CFR 43 App. D	☐	☐	☐
17.	New Weight and balance aircraft for compensation / hire		☐	☐	☐
18.	Magneto 200, 500 and etc. coil, contacts, etc. Inspection		☐	☐	☐
19.	Rigging Inspection	Per Manufacture Manual	☐	☐	☐
20.	Oxygen bottles Inspection (Hydrostat) AC 43.13-1B Chapter 9 Section 3		☐	☐	☐
21.	Lubrication Inspection	Per Manufacture Manual	☐	☐	☐
22.	Hose Inspection Fuel and Hydraulic	Per Manufacture Manual	☐	☐	☐
23.	Compass magnetic direction (calibration)	CFR 23.1327	☐	☐	☐
24.	Airspeed indicator inspections	CFR 23.1323	☐	☐	☐
25.	Remove the rocker box covers and check for freedom of valve rockers (400-hour)		☐	☐	☐

Misc., Items Aircraft Inspection

Below are some of the reported items found on New and Low time aircraft, which should stress the importance of performing a thorough inspection:

1. Aileron control cable not over pulley;   Yes ☐ No ☐ N/A ☐
2. Aileron cable improperly installed in bellcrank/cable retaining pin was not installed;
                                                                                                     Yes ☐ No ☐ N/A ☐
3. Bolts loose on the vertical and horizontal stabilizer fin attachments   Yes ☐ No ☐ N/A ☐
4. Broken and cracked electrical terminals;   Yes ☐ No ☐ N/A ☐
5. Control cable turnbuckles not safetied;   Yes ☐ No ☐ N/A ☐
6. Flap follow-up cable chafing on brake line;   Yes ☐ No ☐ N/A ☐
7. Foreign items in fuel cells/tanks;   Yes ☐ No ☐ N/A ☐
8. Fuel lines twisted, bent, kinked, obstructing flow;   Yes ☐ No ☐ N/A ☐
9. Fuel lines chafing—inadequate clamping   Yes ☐ No ☐ N/A ☐
10. Incorrect propeller bolts installed;   Yes ☐ No ☐ N/A ☐
11. Jam nuts drilled but no safety wire installed;   Yes ☐ No ☐ N/A ☐
12. Lock clips missing from control cable turnbuckles;   Yes ☐ No ☐ N/A ☐
13. Loose rivets in horizontal stabilizer leading edge;   Yes ☐ No ☐ N/A ☐
14. Main wheel tires do not clear wheel bays;   Yes ☐ No ☐ N/A ☐

15. Numerous drill chuck marks in aft face of pressure bulkhead. Yes ☐ No ☐ N/A ☐
16. Oil lines leaking at connections; Yes ☐ No ☐ N/A ☐
17. Primer line "T" fitting not installed; Yes ☐ No ☐ N/A ☐
18. Propeller blade retention ferrules under torqued; Yes ☐ No ☐ N/A ☐
19. Elevator trim cable wrapped around primary rudder control cable; Yes ☐ No ☐ N/A ☐
20. Rivet holes drilled but rivets not installed, different areas; Yes ☐ No ☐ N/A ☐
21. Rudder cable bellcrank attach bolts loose; Yes ☐ No ☐ N/A ☐
22. Rudder cable bolts fitted upside down; and Yes ☐ No ☐ N/A ☐
23. Unreliable fuel quantity indications. Yes ☐ No ☐ N/A ☐

Sample AD Compliance List

AIRWORTHINESS DIRECTIVE COMPLIANCE RECORD

N-Number _____

Make _____ Model _____ S/N_____

AD Number	Subject	Date and Hour of Compliance	Method of Compliance	One Time	Recurring	Next due	Authorized Signature

Sample Logbook Unairworthy Maintenance Entry

September 30, 2012. Total time 853.00 hours Tach reading 420.80. I certify that this aircraft has been inspected in accordance with an annual inspection and a list of discrepancies and unairworthy in accordance with Part 43 Appendix D items dated (insert date) has been provided for the aircraft owner or leaser. George B. Jones IA272182

Sample Logbook Airworthy Maintenance Entry

September 30, 2012. Total aircraft time 853.00 hours. Tach reading 420.80 Replaced right main wheel bearing, P/N 19844, upper bushing in R&L landing gear frames, both brake hoses, P/N 34052, and bled brakes. I certify that this aircraft has been inspected in accordance with an annual inspection and was determined to be in airworthy condition in accordance with Part 43 Appendix D. or (Manufacture manual revision 123 date 04/01/2012

George B. Jones IA272182

FAA Web Site Links: (http://www.faa.gov)
- **Type Certificate Data Sheets (TCDS)**

http://www.airweb.faa.gov/Regulatory_and_Guidance_Library/rgMakeModel.nsf/MainFrame?OpenFrameSet
- **Regulations, AC's. and & Forms:** http://www.faa.gov/mechanics/regs_policy/
- Airworthiness Directives:

http://rgl.faa.gov/Regulatory_and_Guidance_Library/rgAD.nsf/MainFrame?OpenFrameSet

Life limits CFR 43.10

This checklist is not exhaustive and does not supersede Manufacture's publications and is up-dated periodically!

Calendar/ Hourly Life limited Items:	Years.	Hours.
Airframe		
Gyro air filters, central	5	500
Non-Teflon fuel, oil, and hydraulic hoses	15	3000
Teflon fuel, oil, and hydraulic hoses	20	4000
Seat belt / shoulder harness webbing	20	
Stabilizer attach bolts	25	6000
Wing bolts	25	6000
Engine		
Engine shock mounts	15	TBO
Non-Teflon fuel, oil, and hydraulic hoses	8	TBO
Teflon fuel, oil, and hydraulic hoses	15	TBO
Continental Engines	2000 SL	98-9

Special Inspection Items:	Years.	Hours.
Airframe		
Gyro air pump carbon vanes	6	500
Electric hydraulic pump motor	15	500-1500
Electro mechanical gear actuator	15	3000
Gear actuator motor brushes	2	250
Gear motor internal inspection / lubrication	15	3000
Flight control trim actuator(s)	15	4500
Electrical flap actuators/motors	20	4000
Stabilizer mounting bolts torque inspection	5	
Wing attach bolts torque inspection	5	
Propeller		
Fixed pitch propeller recondition	6	2000
Mounting hardware 20 2000		
Constant speed propeller overhaul	6	2400
Prop governor reseal	15	1500
Governor (Woodward)	5	2400
Accumulators	5	1800
Engine		
Alternator	500	
Gear drive alternator internal inspection	5	300
Belt driven alternator internal inspection	5	500
Internal magneto inspection	5	500
Valve inspection/dry lash clearance	15	TBO
Cam / cam follower inspection (TCM engines)	15	mid life
Bendix fuel injector servo overhaul	20	TBO
Pressure carburetor overhaul	20	TBO
Primer nozzles cleaned and spray pattern	5	
Continental unmetered fuel pressure check	2	400
Diaphragm fuel pumps overhaul	20	TBO
Internal starter inspection	5	mid-life

Turbocharger oil inlet check valve(s)	10	1000
Turbocharger oil scavenge check valves(s)	10	1000
Hydraulic wastegate actuator(s) resealing	10	1000

This is only a guide and should not be considered FAA approved data for life limits. Consult the manufacture recommendations, type certificate data sheets (TCDS), AD's, or the limitations section of FAA-approved airplane or rotorcraft flight manuals.

Reg # _____	Manufacturer	Model Number	Serial Number
Aircraft			
Engine #1			
Engine #2			
Engine #3			
Engine #4			
Propeller #1			
Propeller #2			
Propeller #3			
Propeller #4			

Category	Manufacturer	Part Number	Serial Number
Accumulators			
Air Conditioner			
Air Data Inertl Ref Unit			
Air Filter			
Airspeed Indicator			
Alternators			
Altimeter			
Angle of Attack sensor			
Attitude Hdg Reference Sy			
Auto-pilot			
Autopilot Servo			
Auxiliary Power Unit			
Ball/Swivel Quick Connctr			
Batteries			
Brake Assemblies			
Cabin Doors			
Cabin Superchargers			
Carburetors			
Circuit Breakers			
Cockpit Voice Record			
Coffee Makers			
Combustion Heaters			
Cylinder Assemblies			
Cylinder, Propane			
DME-Dist Measuring			
Dusting/Spraying Ops			
EFIS-Elec Flight Inst Sy			

ELT			
Emergency/Survival Equip.			
Emergency Pwr Supplies			
Engine Gage Units			
Fire Detectors			
Fire Ext Dischargers			
Fire Extinguishers			
Flight Data Recorder			
Flight Director Sys			
Flight Management Sy			
Floats			
Fuel Cells			
Fuel Flow Transmitter			
Fuel Injected System			
Fuel Pumps			
Fuel Selector Valve			
Fuel System			
GPWS(Gnd Prxmty Warn Sys)			
Gear Boxes			
Glass Fiber Fabrics			
Glider Tow Couplings			
Global Positioning System			
Governors			
Hardpoint Assemblies			
Hoists			
Horizontal Sit Ind-HSI			
Hoses			
Ignition Switches			
Instrument Filters			
Instrument Landing Sys			
Integr. Avionics Computer			
Intercom/System			
LORAN			
Landing Gear			
Lavatory Receptacles			
Lighting			
Magnetic Compass Sys			
Magnetos			

Navigation Systems			
Oil Coolers			
Oil Filters			
Oxygen Masks			
Oxygen System			
Parachutes			
Piston Pin			
Pistons			
Pitot Static Heater			
Protect Breathing Equip			
Push-pull Control			
Radio Magnetic Indicator			
Receiver(s)			
Refueling System			
Safety Belts			
Seat Track Fittings			
Seats			
Smoke Detectors			
Spark Plugs			
Speaker(s)			
Standby Vacuum Systems			
Starter			
Starting Vibrator			
TCAS Terr Collision Avoid			
Tires			
Traffic Advisory System			
Transducers			
Transponder			
Turbine Power Conversion			
Turbochargers			
Turn and Bank Indicator			
Unapproved Parts			
Vacuum Pumps			

Index

A

B

C

D

E

M

Magnetic, 89, 160, 161, 172, 178, 179

Magnetic compass, 89, 178

Maintenance, 1, 2, 7, 8, 11, 12, 13, 15, 22, 23, 24, 25, 26, 29, 30, 31, 32, 33, 34, 39, 40, 41, 42, 43, 44, 45, 46, 48, 52, 54, 55, 62, 64, 67, 70, 71, 72, 73, 76, 77, 84, 85, 86, 87, 89, 90, 94, 100, 101, 102, 103, 106, 107, 108, 112, 117, 122, 131

Maintenance Inspection, 39

Maintenance Contract, 109, 122

Maintenance Records, 29, 40, 42, 45, 63, 67, 72, 73, 76, 77, 87, 114, 115, 119, 158, 159, 170

Major Alteration, 3, 7, 14, 18, 29, 33, 34, 40, 45, 46, 47, 69, 70, 87, 89, 90, 98, 118, 119, 120, 121, 140, 156

Major Repair, 3, 7, 13, 14, 18, 29, 33, 34, 40, 44, 45, 46, 47, 48, 69, 70, 71, 72, 87, 89, 90, 107, 118, 119, 120, 121 140, 156, 157

Mechanic, 2, 3, 9, 11, 12, 14, 16, 17, 18, 26, 30, 31, 32, 33, 36, 39, 40, 42, 45, 52, 53, 57, 64, 70, 75, 76, 77, 80, 84, 85, 87, 89, 105, 106, 107, 108, 110, 120, 121 123, 130, 131, 132, 133, 139, 140, 141, 144, 155,156

Minimum Equipment List, 21, 83, 86, 87, 102, 104, 159

Minor Alteration, 7, 39, 45, 46, 70, 90

Minor Repair, 7, 33, 71

N

N-number, 21, 51, 92, 157, 159, 174

National Transportation Safety Board, 8

Navigation, 7, 49, 72, 143, 160, 179

Navigation Light, 171

Negligence, 37, 38, 39, 73, 74, 75, 107

Nuts, 57, 96, 162, 167, 168, 170

O

Oil, 11, 43, 49, 71, 77, 83, 98, 106, 160, 161, 163, 167, 168, 170, 172, 175

Oil Screen, 168

Oil tank, 168

Operate, 7, 30, 31, 44, 68, 70, 73, 74, 75, 83, 84, 85, 89, 93, 103, 104, 134, 146

O-rings, 25, 89

Original Equipment Manufacture (OEM), 34, 52

Overhaul, 1, 7, 9, 11, 14, 25, 31, 39, 40, 41, 46, 54, 63, 64, 70, 79, 91, 175

Oxygen, 160, 172, 179

Oxygen System, 179

P

Paint, 112, 163, 164, 166, 169, 170

Paperwork, 78, 133, 156

Parts, 1,6, 7,9, 11, 14, 23, 24, 25, 29, 31, 32, 34, 39, 40, 47, 48, 49, 54, 55, 56, 60, 61, 64, 68, 70, 71, 77, 79, 80, 81, 82, 90, 91, 93, 94, 96, 97, 100, 101, 107, 109, 117, 118, 135, 140, 158

Parts Manufacture Authorization (PMA), 1, 39, 47, 56, 80, 91, 93, 94, 95, 96, 97, 109

Pilot Operating Handbook (POH), 45, 68, 69, 70, 84, 159

Placards, 66, 68, 69, 70, 77, 107, 118, 159

Powerplant Rating, 3, 14, 123, 130, 131, 133, 139, 140, 141

Preventive maintenance, 7, 24, 26, 29, 32, 43, 44, 52, 55, 62, 64, 70, 108, 112

Progressive Inspection, 3, 14, 18, 31, 33, 34, 40, 86, 88, 105, 118, 120, 121, 140, 158

Propellers, 3, 5, 11, 14, 20, 24, 27, 54, 79, 89

Q

Quarter, 65

R

Radio, 49, 71, 78, 152, 159, 160, 172

Ratings, 76, 78, 89, 106, 130, 131, 132, 138, 139, 141

Reasonable, 36, 67, 73, 75, 134, 138

Rebuilt, 25, 33, 41, 44, 70

Repair, 1, 7, 9, 11, 12, 13, 14, 18, 22, 25, 29, 30, 31, 32, 33, 34, 38, 39, 40, 41, 42, 44, 45, 46, 47, 48, 52, 53, 54, 57, 59, 63, 64, 66, 68, 69, 70, 71, 72, 75, 77, 78, 80, 81, 84, 85, 86, 87, 88, 89, 90, 91, 92, 101, 106, 107, 109, 110, 113, 117, 118, 120, 122, 131, 140, 155, 156

Repairman, 130, 131

Rigging, 165, 166, 172

Rivets, 56, 60, 77, 89, 135, 165, 166

References

A brief history of the federal aviation administration and its predecessor agencies. FAA website. [Online]. Available: http://www.faa.gov/, http://bookstore.trafford.com/Products/SKU-000150319/Handbook-of-Aeronautical-Inspection-and-PrePurchase.aspx ISBN: 978-1-41205-065-4 By Denny Pollard, http://www.stacheair.com/, http://origin.www.faa.gov/ats/ato/150_docs/FAQ_Mx_10Aug04.doc
FAQ Mx 10Aug04.doc